Well, son, I'll tell you:
Life for me ain't been no crystal stair.

LANGSTON HUGHES

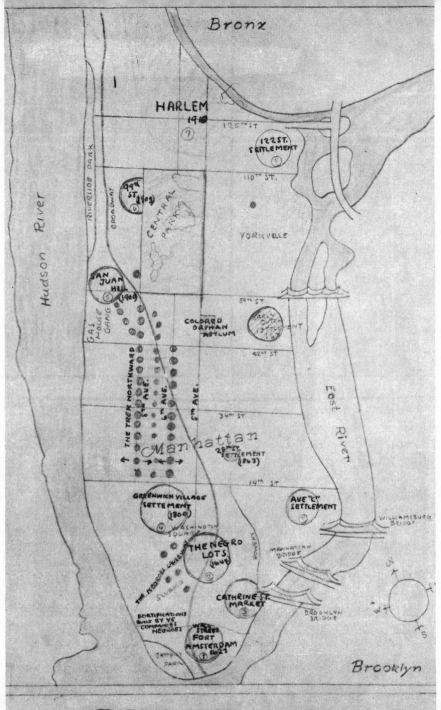

THE TREK NORTHWARD
Movement of the Negro population in N.Y.C.
by Everett Beanne, Fed. Wr. Pr., 5-11-39

THE NEGRO IN NEW YORK

AN INFORMAL SOCIAL HISTORY

1626 - 1940

ROI OTTLEY

&

WILLIAM J. WEATHERBY

Editors

PRAEGER PUBLISHERS
New York • Washington • London

This book is edited from manuscripts in the Schomburg Collection of Negro Literature and History, The New York Public Library. These manuscripts were originally prepared by the Federal Writers Project under the working title, "Harlem—The Negroes of New York (An Informal Social History)."

PRAEGER PUBLISHERS
111 Fourth Avenue, New York, N.Y. 10003, U.S.A.
5, Cromwell Place, London S.W.7, England

Published in the United States of America in 1969
by Praeger Publishers, Inc.

99140

Library of Congress Catalog Card Number: 72-98461

Printed in the United States of America

CONTENTS

BOOK THREE
(1865 - 1910)

BOOK FOUR
(1910 - 1940)

FOREWORD

"THE REALIZATION OF A DREAM" by Jean Blackwell Hutson, Curator, Schomburg Collection of Negro Literature and History

Several times during the years I have been Curator of the Schomburg Collection editors have expressed interest in publishing THE NEGRO IN NEW YORK. It is like the realization of a dream long deferred to have this publication finally appear. In fact, the history of THE NEGRO IN NEW YORK as related to me by Roi Ottley, who deposited this material in the Schomburg Collection, had been that of publication deferred and prevented because information contained in it was too startling for conservative taste. In the process of clearing out a storeroom of acquisitions I learned that Roi Ottley had brought to the Schomburg Collection many boxes of research papers assembled under the Writers Program of New York City. He brought them in order that the valuable contents should not be lost. Evidently he did this in 1940 at the termination of the project. It was perhaps ten years later that he related the story to me.

About that time two librarians, Miss Kathleen Hill, who was then cataloger of the Schomburg Collection, and I, spent about a week arranging these papers in thirty-five manuscript boxes. The boxes are composed of the basic research materials under specific subject headings in the form in which the research reports were submitted to the supervisors of the project. These subject divisions are listed and described in detail in the Dictionary Catalog of the Collection. We found three drafts representing attempts to synthesize the preliminary research memoranda in the numerous subject categories. The material published here is mainly that which was labelled "Complete manuscripts third and pre-final draft. Does not include final editing and corrections."

Presumably the editing was done by Roi Ottley, but other names appear as editors in the earlier records. The compilers and research assistants include many who developed professional excellence in various fields of writing. The list includes Everett Beanne, Waring Cuney, Ralph Ellison, Arthur Gary, Lawrence Gellert, Bella Gross, Abram Hill, Lawrence Jordan, Claude McKay, Carlton Moss, Richard Nugent, Carl Offord, Theodore Poston, Harry Robinson, J. A. Rogers, Floyd Snelson, Ellen Tarry, Simon Williamson, and Ted Yates.

Ottley's *New World A-Coming,* published in 1943, seemed to be based upon research done in connection with the Writers Program, THE NEGRO IN NEW YORK. Many books have been based at least partially in this research. Most recent of them were: Osofsky's *Harlem: the Making of a Ghetto* (1965) and an exciting school document, *Harlem: what teachers, parents and children should know about our community*. The latter work was prepared by a committee working with Miss Beryl Banfield, who was in 1965 assistant principal of P.S. 175 Manhattan.

EDITORS' FOREWORD

"THE UNDERTONES AS WELL AS THE OVERTONES"
by *the late Roi Ottley, Editor*

This book is an informal history which traces the growth of the
Negro population from the eleven who arrived in New Amsterdam
in 1626 to present-day Harlem. An attempt has been made to supplement the bare facts by recording the undertones as well as the
overtones of Negro life, and it is believed that the book conveys a
faithful impression of the very substance of that life. The picture
that is presented, much of it in intimate detail, also provides an
oblique view of the city as a whole. Into focus come such characters
as Booker T. Washington, Marcus Garvey, W.E.B. DuBois, A. Philip
Randolph, Father Divine, Jack Johnson, Bert Williams and Marian
Anderson, as well as a multitude of less eminent figures such as Pig
Foot Mary, Dusty Dustmoore, "Roll" Jordon and the Black Eagle.
Catharine Market, Fraunces' Tavern, Five Points, bloody San Juan
Hill are but a few of the more vividly revealed historic New York
spots; high-lighted also are many of the more important or atmos-
pheric places in contemporary Harlem.

Negro life in its genesis, its pattern of progress and its future is
of the greatest importance to the surrounding white community.
This book, then, is a comprehensive study of the past and the present;
reflects as well the Negro's faith in the basic ideal of Democracy.
In a measure it should result in a better understanding of urban
Black Belts throughout the nation.

THE NEGRO IN NEW YORK has been more than fifteen months in
preparation. During this period over twenty Negro and white
workers assisted in bringing the book to completion. In its final form
it is, however, chiefly the work of a single Negro. Numerous Negro
and white authorities were consulted during the writing of the book.
Especially helpful were the criticisms and corrections from the na-

tional WPA consultant, Sterling Brown; from Richard Wright, novelist; from Lawrence Reddick, curator of the Negro Division of The New York Public Library; and from Arthur Faucett, biographer of Sojourner Truth. Such Negro leaders as Walter White, executive secretary of the National Association for the Advancement of Colored People; Hubert T. Delany, Tax Commissioner of the City of New York; the Rev Adam C. Powell, Jr, Pastor of the Abyssinian Baptist Church, have also read the manuscript. Valuable suggestions were offered by V. F. Calverton, editor of the Anthology of American Negro Literature, and from Lester B. Granger, former director of the New York State Temporary Commission and now secretary of the Negro Welfare Committee of the City of New York.

His Honor the Mayor of New York City, Fiorello H. La Guardia, and City Council President Newbold Morris, as representatives of the City Government, are the official sponsors for the Writers' Project.

HOW THE HISTORY WAS ASSEMBLED: ONE WRITER'S MEMORIES by *Ellen Tarry*

(Work on the history rescued a group of professional journalists and writers from unemployment at the height of the Depression. But thirty years is a long time for a memory to remain fresh, and some of the team who are still alive and willing to be interviewed have more of an emotional recollection of the period than a detailed memory of their labors of research and writing. Most of them apparently worked on only one or two subjects—such as *Religion* or the *Underground Railroad*—and were not aware of the overall plan or where their work fitted into the whole project.

One of the writers, Henry Lee Moon, now Director of Public Relations for the National Association for the Advancement of Colored People, recalled in an interview (November 4, 1966) that the team was under the general direction from Washington of Sterling Brown, now Professor of English at Howard University, with a local supervisor, such as Claude McKay or later Roi Ottley, working directly with the writers. Another member of the team, Ellen Tarry, described (November 2, 1966) this writer-supervisor system from the point of view of the writer, how she came to join the team and how it worked. We give below the transcript of her remarks, corrected by Miss Tarry, to fill in a little of the background of how the history came to be written.—Ed.)

There was a writers' group in Harlem at that time—it's so long ago I can't remember the name—but somebody in this group introduced me to Claude McKay and he asked me to come down and work on the Federal Writers' Project. I was interviewed by a man named Kingman, who appeared to be one of the supervisors. They (the Federal Writers) were in a building on 42nd Street right across from the New York *News*. Later they moved down to King Street, I think it was.

At the time of my interview I showed Kingman clippings from my newspaper work in Alabama, and he said he'd be glad to have me on the team. What held my appointment up was the requirement that you had to have relief status. At first, when Claude McKay, Henry Lee Moon, Ted Poston and Billy Rowe and all that crowd were hired, you didn't need it. But by the time I got there, it was necessary. And so it was only after I'd proved I should be getting some kind of help that I could go to work on the Federal Writers' Project. It must have been about 1936. I remember it was about the time the sit-down strikes began. I can remember that just before or just after I began work I took candy bars and coffees to my friends who were locked in all night.

We all knew eventually that we were writing a history of the Negro in New York. But I do not remember that anyone showed us the overall plan or what anybody else was doing. We were just given assignments which we talked over with the supervisor. I remember Claude and Henry Lee Moon and Ted Poston were supervisors; I believe Roi Ottley was the last one. After discussing assignments with the supervisor, we went to the Schomburg Collection or the 42nd Street Library for research. I practically lived at those two places working on my assignments—Religion and the Underground Railroad. Long afterwards when my daughter filled out a job application for a library page, one question was *Has any member of your family ever worked here?* and she replied: "Yes." I was never on the staff there, but I guess I must have impressed on her I'd done an awful lot of work there!

The routine would be to go in each morning and I guess sign in and discuss our assignment and the progress we were making and then go back to the library. At least that was my routine. I think maybe some of the boys had a different one. A lot were newspapermen and I guess could get restless with research. My memory's not sharp there but I think we completed assignments in the form of an essay. I have the feeling that it was only the last year or so that we were working deliberately on a history of the Negro in New York. My journalism had been mainly feature writing and my work there tended to take that form. Even at the end of my work there, I was not aware of the overall plan. Though we were aware that much of the same background was later a part of Roi Ottley's book *New World Acoming* which was published later.

We were paid $27 and maybe some spare change. We used our own type-writers, pencils and paper. We bought these tools out of the $27. When we got the pink dismissal slips in 1939, half of my Alabama relatives were here visiting the 1939 World's Fair. And suddenly I found I no longer had a job. That's how I remember the date of termination.

We all split up then, none of the group stayed together. But I never cease to be grateful for the opportunity I had to retain my skills as a writer because if a writer gets rusty there's a possibility you die from the rust. That is why I'm always glad to acknowledge the debt I owe the Federal Government, the WPA and the Roosevelt Administration. If it hadn't been for them, I might have done nothing more. Now my ninth book is coming out in the spring.

HOW THE THIRD DRAFT WAS EDITED: THE VITALITY OF A WORK IN PROGRESS by *William J. Weatherby*

The pile of manuscript in the Schomburg Collection is the third *pre-final* draft, with some missing passages filled in with chapters from the second draft. This patchwork naturally caused some repetitions, and these were cut out by merging two chapters into one, a solution described in detail in a footnote at the appropriate place.

Except where the end of a chapter was missing altogether, a complete narrative then existed, but one which lacked the uniform style and polish of a final version. In preparing the manuscript for the printer, an editor could therefore do a final version himself or treat the manuscript as a document to be preserved and presented as it is.

For a manuscript as famous as this one, there was really no choice. To prepare a final draft would have required extensive rewriting and the inclusion of new material in order to maintain a uniform style and to meet the standards of later histories, which have made use of this one as well as having the benefit of new sources and our contemporary hindsight. Moreover, this method of editing the manuscript would also destroy what seems now, over a generation since the history was written, to be one of its main attractions: its value as a document of the period. The team's emphasis, its omissions, and even its marginal notes reflect an attitude as characteristic perhaps of Negro writers in the late thirties as James Baldwin's preface is eloquently characteristic of the middle sixties; the two attitudes together in the same book, in fact, show by their difference in tone, by the change between them, much of what has happened in the generation since the history was written.

The editor's approach has therefore been to do as little as possible to the narrative and to preserve even the laconic marginal comments. No rewriting has been done except where sentences were hopelessly muddled (and only a handful were so tidied up). Scrawled suggestions for the final editing have been included in footnotes along with the marginalia, although the history's own footnotes, erratically acknowledging some of its debts, have been checked and, in many cases, corrected and rewritten; indeed, the footnote researcher, Mrs. Mary Flad, could not always find the quotation in the source given, and this has been faithfully reported.

Thanks are due to Mrs Hutson and the staff of the Schomburg Collection and to Mr Wendell Wray for their help in turning the manuscript into a book and, one trusts, a permanent part of Negro literature and American history.

PREFACE

by

James Baldwin

THE NEGRO IN NEW YORK is an unavoidably sketchy and uneven document, compiled by the Writers' Program of New York City during that very brief period of the WPA when it was recognized that writers existed in our country and had to eat, and even had a certain utility—though, probably, no real value. The curator of the Schomburg Collection of Negro Literature and History, Jean Blackwell Hutson, points out that the material in this book has been sitting in the Collection since 1940, with "publication deferred and prevented because information contained in it was too startling for conservative taste." That the information in this book should be startling is an interesting comment on the conservative, that is to say, the prevailing, attitude toward American history. If so many people did not find the information in this book "startling," they might be less at the mercy of their ignorance, and our present situation would be healthier than it is.

The book can be startling only to the brainwashed, in which category, alas, nearly all Americans are presently to be found, and, of course, it would be very hard to use it as a basis for a rousing television series. It strips the Americans of their fig leaves, as it were, and proves that Eden, if it ever existed, certainly never existed here. It proves that anyone who contends that the Northern racial attitudes have not always been, essentially, indistinguishable from those of the South is either lying, or is deluded. Of course, one has become deluded when one has believed a lie too long.

It is impossible to read this book and not realize how disastrous has been the effect, in so many millions of lives, of the Industrial Revolution—that same revolution which has been hailed as being so liberating a force. Indeed, it liberated peasants from the land, to say nothing of their lives, small children from their parents, women from their safety, and men from their honor. The tremendous amount of labor needed to cultivate the New World, and the enormous profits to be carried back to Europe as a result of this cultivation, meant that human flesh, any human flesh, became a source of profit. And there is nothing in European, or subsequent American history to indicate that any consideration whatever deflected the new conquerors from this goal. Such uneasy consciences as we know to have been were as nothing compared to the heartening, yes, the virtuous sound, of money being made and of money making money. The Dutch, who ruled this city, and the Europeans who traded in this harbor, sought one freedom only, the freedom to make money, and in searching for this freedom they did not hesitate to use women and small children, as well as thieves and pirates and murderers. The poor Irish, God knows, fared no better at the hands of the industrialists than any captive African. The Irish situation began to change only after it was no longer necessary, or politic, to use the poor Irish laborer to cow the Negro laborer, or vice versa: no doubt, many Irishmen will find this information startling indeed. (But it is no more startling than the fact that, during the potato famine of 1845, their English masters allowed the Irish to starve, in order to protect British merchants. This unhappy circumstance has produced many a virtuous, self righteous Irish cop, as well as the winning folklore of, say, *The Bells of Saint Mary's*.)

The rise of Northern industry, and the consolidation of this power, caused the racial lines of the North to be drawn up very differently, but not less severely, than those in the South: where the poor white, until this hour, has yet to comprehend what his bosses have always understood very well—that any coalition of himself and the black will destroy the system which has kept both black and white in ignorance and peonage for so long. And a marvelous fore shadowing of the scapegoat role the black was to play in American life is contained in Peter Stuyvesant's explanation of his surrender to the British. The city could not withstand the British siege, he explained, because three hundred slaves, brought in just before the British arrived in the harbor, had eaten all the surplus food. Scarcely any American politician has since improved on this extraordinarily convincing way of explaining American reverses.

What the Negro did in New York, and how, is the subject of the book before you, and not the subject of this foreword. But: "(the British) regulated servitude with the thoroughness of modern business methods—every step necessary for its protection and preservation was taken. Blacks were therefore set apart from whites on the theory that to permit them to mingle freely with white people would endanger the chances of keeping them enslaved. This policy was carried out in every straining detail; so much so that a law was passed 'that no Negro shall be buried in Trinity church-yard'." Nor would some of our more conservative political leaders find the following proclamation, issued in 1706 by Governor Lord Cornbury, the cousin of Queen Anne, in the least startling:

"Requiring and commanding (all officers) to take all proper methods for the siezing and apprehending of all such Negroes as shall be found to be assembled—and if any of them refuse to submit, then fire upon them, kill or destroy them, if they cannot otherwise be taken—I am informed that several Negroes in Kings County (Brooklyn) have assembled themselves in a riotous manner, which if not prevented may prove of ill consequence."

Then, as now, Negroes were in the streets—and this is before the American War of Independence; then, as now, white people professed not to know the reason why; then, as now, it was the slave who was the wrongdoer and not the system which had made him a slave. And then, as now, the Negro's hopes were used with the utmost cynicism by those who could use these hopes to perpetuate their own dominance. Thus, the Declaration of Independence terrified the slave owners, and they would never have armed their slaves if the British had not done so first, promising freedom to any Negro who joined the British lines. Thereupon, the soon-to-be-Americans armed two regiments of blacks, promising freedom to all who served three years, or who were honorably discharged (two interesting stipulations). That this cynical and treacherous pattern has not altered from that day to this is scarcely worth mentioning: but it is worth observing that, whereas Americans profess not to know what the Negro wants, they always know what to promise him whenever they need his body.

And here, during the Depression, is a member of the New York City Realty Board: "I believe a logical section for Negro expansion in Manhattan is East Harlem. At present this district has reached such a point of deterioration that its ultimate residential pattern is most puzzling.—An influx of Negroes into East Harlem would not work a hardship on the present population of the area, because its present residents could move to any other section of New York without the attendant racial discrimination which the Negro would encounter if he endeavored to locate in other districts."

Well, we know how the "puzzling" residential pattern of East Harlem eventually resolved itself: into a pattern which changes not. And we will not even discuss the shameful and brutal role played in all this by the churches, by the labor unions, and by revered corporations and utilities. Nor will we—in order to avoid startling our readers—observe that the economic pattern to be discerned in the pages which follow is so brutal, so utterly blind and selfish, and so irresponsible that Russian roulette, by comparison, seems safer than playing jacks.

Here is what Mayor LaGuardia's commission had to say about the Harlem race riot of 1935: "as a population of low income, (it) suffered from conditions that affected low income groups of all races, but the causes that kept Negroes in this class did not apply with the same force to whites. These conditions were underscored by discrimination against Negroes in all walks of life. The rumor of the death of a boy which spread throughout the community had *awakened the deep-seated sense of wrongs and denials and even memories of injustices in the South.*" (Italics mine: the pot is calling the kettle black.) The riot's cause was "the smouldering resentments of the people of Harlem against racial discrimination and poverty in the midst of plenty." The riot was "a spontaneous and an incoherent protest by Harlem's population against a studied neglect of its critical problems."

At least, no one said that the riot was Communist inspired. And what was done? "The Board of Education promoted Mrs. Gertrude E. Ayer to the principal-ship of Public School No. 24, Manhattan, in 1936, and she became the first Negro woman to advance to such a position." (Also, as far as I know, and certainly until very lately, the last. That was my school, and my Principal, and I loved and feared the lady—for she really was a lady, and a great one—with that trembling passion only twelve year olds can feel). But let us continue this progress report: "That same year, the Department of Hospitals appointed Dr. John West...the director of the new Central Harlem Health Center which had been built at a cost of $250,000. At the same time, the Mayor reported that 435 buildings were torn down in the Harlem slum area. New schools, a housing project, a large recreational center, with a swimming pool, sports fields, tennis courts, and a band concert stadium known as the Colonial (!) Recreation Center, situated at 145th Street on Bradhurst Avenue, have been part of the city's acknowledgment of the needs of the Negro people... Throughout his long American history, the Negro's faith has been in the ultimate triumph of democracy. At no time has his goal been as visible as it is today."

The last words were written just before our entry into World War II. If—for those of you who are not too hopelessly startled— the show seems familiar, it is because the show has been running a very long time, and most of the actors have had no choice but to speak the lines and make the moves assigned to them. There is a rumor—striking terror and chaos in the heart of the box-office— that some people have become so weary of the spectacle that they have sent for a new show, which is presently on the road. But not until the wheels of those wagons are on our children's necks will we consider reading or revising or throwing away this script.

In the meantime, ladies and gentlemen, after a brief intermission—time out for one or two committee reports, time out for an anti-poverty pep talk, time out to make a Vietnamese child an orphan and then lovingly raise him to love all our works, time out for a White House conference, time out to brief and augment the police forces, time out to buy some Negroes, jail some, club some, and kill some—after a brief intermission, ladies and gentlemen, the show begins again in the auction room. And you will hear the same old piano, playing the blues.

BOOK ONE

(1626 – 1800)

CHAPTER I

WEARY NEW WORLD

New Amsterdam, 1626-1664.—Though historians tell of black men who were members of Henry Hudson's crew, this narrative is concerned with the Negro in New York, and his story begins with the establishment of a Dutch colony in 1626.

In 1623 a group of wealthy merchants in Holland had organized the Dutch West India Company and had sent thirty families with a shipload of 103 horses and cattle to colonize New Amsterdam, then a trading post. Three years later the colony was raised to the status of a province and a director-general sent over to rule it. He was given supreme authority, and like all succeeding officials, his duty, sufficiently single in purpose, was to watch with jealous eyes the interests of the Dutch West India Company. Cash returns were of prime importance, and on these his job hinged.

The early stages of colonization gave considerable impetus to the influx of vagabonds and adventurers from Europe, and of fugitive servants from the adjacent English colonies. The settlers were of Dutch, Huguenot, Walloon, English, and Jewish origin. The administration of the first Dutch governor, Peter Minuit (1626-1633), was characterized by governmental corruption, get-rich-quick schemes, and tolerance towards lapses from strict moral codes, although many of the colonists were religious refugees. This state of affairs held through an unbroken succession of officials intent upon making their fortunes. It was only under the rule of that magnificent dictator, Peter Stuyvesant, the last Dutch governor (1647-1664), that New Amsterdam embarked upon its golden age as the metropolis of New Netherland and attained its full stature as a city of fleshpots and burgher breweries.

1

On his arrival in 1626, the first official act of the director-general, Peter Minuit, was to drive the historic bargain in which he bought for beads and trinkets the island of Manhattan from the Indians of the Manhattes tribe. In the traditional Dutch manner, Minuit then proceeded to take part in a roistering drinking bout. After this bit of side business, and the naming of the little settlement New Amsterdam, he erected a fort situated near the present Battery, and a simple blockhouse with palisades. Trees were cleared for a warehouse where the Indians came to trade. A horsemill was built, and the loft above it was fitted out with rough benches for religious services. Rude houses sprang up, built according to each man's taste and direction.

PIONEERS BY PROXY

While the colonists were so arduously engaged, a ship belonging to the Dutch West India Company sailed into the harbor, bringing eleven black men, the first on record to set foot in what is now New York. No fragment remains to suggest what the dark strangers thought of their first meeting with these white settlers of alien tongue; nor what they felt in the wilderness of an alien land. What is certain, however, is that they were a welcome aid to the weary pioneers who needed reinforcements for the task of building a new world community.

The beginning of servitude in New York was marked when, immediately after their arrival, they were put to work as the "Company's Negroes," building roads, cutting timber, clearing land, and erecting dwellings and forts. At other times, the directors of the company had private use of them as domestics and farm hands. Only four names appear in the company's books: Paul d'Angola, Simon Congo, Anthony Portugese and John Francisco, names which may well be clues to their places of origin.

The importation of Negroes was not limited to ships belonging to the Dutch, for all privateers who sailed under the French flag regarded New Netherland as a neutral port and came here occasionally to dispose of the cargo they had captured. There are two such instances on record: one in 1642, when the French privateer, La Grace, brought in a few Negroes, and another in 1652 when forty-four were seized in a raid of the St Anthoni, a Spanish vessel enroute from Jamaica to Cuba. Up to this time the only women in the colony were "white-squaws" and a few Indian drudges. But two years after the arrival of the first black men, the directors thoughtfully imported three Negro women, the first of their sex to be sold into slavery in this part of the new country. They were spoken of as "Angola slaves, thievish, lazy and useless trash."

Only a scattered few were added to the colony's black population, until vigor was given to the slave traffic by the patroonships, a form of feudalism introduced by the Dutch West India Company in 1629.[1] This plan, which coaxingly offered gifts of land in return for its coloniaztion, appears to have been attractive for in 1629 Kiliaen van Rensselaer, among others, began to send agents to the colony to choose sites He secured land "stretching two days into the interior" along the east side of the Hudson River. In the fashion of the day, he remained at Amsterdam, managing his affairs in the colony through an agent. From 1629 to the end of Dutch rule (1664), the merchants in Holland continued to send out bands of settlers, known as indentured or bond servants, and established in New Netherland patroonships that proved to be the foundations of great American fortunes.

There was a shortage of white indentured servants in the colony, and it was not long after the beginning of these feudal estates that the patroons introduced Negroes to work their land. Government aid was given these private investors when the States-General in Holland granted special "freedoms privileges and exemptions" to the lords of New Netherland in 1634. It decreed, among other things, that when Dutch privateers captured trading vessels "each Patroon would be allotted twelve black men and women out of the prize in which Negroes shall be found."

Black men were not content to remain slaves while many of the burghers comfortably quaffed beer, smoked pipes, visited tavern mistresses, and generally lived a life of ease. In the "Black Winter" of

---

[1] The company's directors in Holland, seeking to encourage colonization, publicly promised to any "master" who risked the cost of sending fifty adult settlers from Europe to the colony as much land as he could cultivate. Within his domain he was to be a semi-independent "patroon" or "lord," with civil and criminal jurisdiction and the power to appoint magistrates. The settlers sent out by a patroon were to bind themselves to serve terms ranging from one to six years. During this period they were known as indentured servants, and pledged themselves not to leave his land or his control.

1644, eighteen years after the arrival of the first Negroes, eleven of them petitioned the director and the council of New Netherland for their freedom.[2] It is not unlikely that they had seized a time when the poor white colonists, desperate on a meagre dole of food and clothing, had boldly sought reforms in the corrupt provincial government. In a daring letter to the States-General in Holland, the white settlers had accused Kieft, then governor (1637-1647), of responsibility for their suffering and demanded his removal as a "miserable despot."

AFTER LONG SERVICE . . .

In February 1644, an act was passed manumitting the eleven blacks and their wives because of their "long and faithful services." To enable them to provide for their own support, they were given land; but as the price of their freedom, they were required to pay yearly for "the term of their natural lives," 22½ bushels of corn, wheat, peas or beans, and one fat hog valued at eight dollars. Failing this, they were to be returned to servitude.[2] The land grants were located far out from the edge of the settlement on a tangled swamp known today as Greenwich Village and Washington Square, a section that was destined to remain essentially a Negro neighborhood for more than two centuries.

Emancipation of the parents did not include their offspring. This act shocked the more pious element of the citizenry, who protested that it was a violation of divine law. How anyone born of a free Christian mother could be a slave and be obliged to remain such was beyond their chaste comprehension! Their worried leader, Dominie Johannes Megapolensis, in despair after three years of moral persuasion, placed the grievance before the States-General of the United Netherlands. In reply the West India Company declared that "the Company's Negroes, taken from the Spaniards, being all slaves, were on account of their long service, manumitted on condition that their children serve the Company whenever it pleased," and appeasingly added, "No more than three are in service, vis., one which Stuyvesant has with him on the Company's bouwerie; one at the Hope House; one wench with Martin Cregier, who hath reared her from a little child at his own expense." This answer apparently

[2] New York Colony. Statutes, *Laws and Ordinances of New Netherland, 1638-1674* ed E.B. O'Callaghan (Albany, Weed, Parsons 1868) 36-37.

closed the matter as no further protest is recorded. But it was not the last to be heard of that "wench," Lysbet Antonis, the child hired out to Cregier by the Company: she was accused of setting his house afire some years later.

LABOR SHORTAGE

Even before the first blacks were freed, the West India Company had already been successful in reducing the number of independent traders in the Dutch African colonies, in a plan to obtain company control of the slave trade there and launch a more determined slave traffic to the New World. The company, in a lengthy report of its affairs in January 1648, observed that the colony was "the most fruitful" within the jurisdiction of the Dutch government and the best adapted to the raising of all sorts of produce if it "were suitably peopled and cultivated," and stated that "the slave trade," which "hath long lain dormant to the great damage of the Company," was the solution.[3]

The first New York slaver on record was the *Tamendare,* a company ship built in New Netherland, which arrived in the summer of 1646 with a cargo of Negroes who were sold for "'pork and peas." The record says this vessel touched Barbados. Most of the Negroes were, however, brought from Curacao, where a Dutch colony had been established. The *Wittenpaert* and the *Gideon* are the only ships recorded as employed in importing Negroes directly from Guinea. The directors, zealously concerned with every detail for successful voyages, supplied the skipper of the *Gideon* "with some wrist and ankle shackles to restrain therewith the refractory Negroes on board."[4]

In a land where agriculture was the chief means of livelihood, hard work was a prime necessity, but the motley rabble which soon began to arrive in New Amsterdam expected a life of indolent ease, with no more labor than was required to snatch furs from the backs of tame animals. Most of them flatly refused to perform the labor necessary to clear the forests and bring the rich land under cultivation. Instead they spent their time in carousing, fighting, and

---

[3] *Documents Relative to the Colonial History of the State of New York* ed E. B. O'Callaghan, 11 vols (Albany, Weed, Parsons 1858) I 246.
[4] *Documents Illustrative of the History of the Slave Trade to America* ed Elizabeth Donnan, 4 vols (Washington D.C., Carnegie Institution 1932) III 424.

attempting to steal sufficient food to live upon. Besides, since every free white man had some opportunity to become a small merchant or farmer, few ambitious men sold their labor. Added to these difficulties was the fact that the lucrative fur trade proved irresistible to the indentured servants and many "daily ran away from their masters" to adjacent territories under English rule leaving "the corn and tobacco to rot in the field and the harvest at a standstill."

The officials attempted to solve this problem in two ways: first, by bringing in more slaves, because of the shortage of farm hands and the great expense of obtaining such workers from Holland, the supply there being by no means equal to the demand; and second, by an ordinance enacted in 1640, forbidding all inhabitants of New Netherland to harbor or feed "fugitive servants" under the penalty of fifty guilders, "for the benefit one-third for the informer, one-third for the new Church, and one-third for Fiscal." [5] Similar regulations, some more stringent, were passed in later years. Their application extended to Negro runaways as well as white bond servants, for one set of laws and ordinances were held sufficient to cover all forms of servitude in the colony.

In 1656 the tireless "Lord Majors" at Amsterdam demanded "a list of the blacks" in the colony, in order that they might "attach the Negroes . . . in the hands of their masters, so that the said Negroes may not be alienated or sold out of New Netherland." Still the number of slaves brought into the colony failed to show the increase desired. In an effort to swell their numbers, the "Lord Majors" sent five Negroes to Governor Peter Stuyvesant the following year. The "bill of lading" noted that they were "all dry and well conditioned." A frantic note was added to the quest for laborers in 1655 and again in 1659, when white boys and girls, snatched from Holland's orphan homes and almshouses, arrived in New Amsterdam to be sold as indentured servants at thirty guilders apiece.

JACK-OF-ALL-TRADES

Most of the slaves in New Amsterdam were owned by the West India Company, whose "Keeper of Negroes" used them in any capacity decreed by the company. The shortage of labor caused

---

[5] New York Colony. Statutes, *Laws and Ordinances*, O'Callaghan 24.

them to be assigned to many varied occupations. Accordingly, when an old Swiss, Claes Cornelissen, was murdered in 1641, and it was reported to have been the act of a "savage," meaning an Indian, a number of the stronger and more active slaves were each armed with a small axe and half pike and dispatched in a vengeful hunt of the red man. In the spring of the same year, the Schout (sheriff) Tonnenman was instructed "to send the City's [Manhattan's] Negroes" under order "to collect and bury" dead hogs which lay "here and there on the street . . . to prevent the stench, which proceeds therefrom." When the palisades were erected as a defense against an expected attack by the English in 1653, Stuyvesant was found "contributing the Company's Negroes to help build the city's fortifications." This wall, extending more than two thousand feet across the island, paralleled a lane which is known today as Wall Street.

The need for skilled workers became particularly acute as the colony expanded, and in the spring of 1657 Stuyvesant appealed to the directors at Amsterdam for some ship carpenters. The Holland officials replied that it was too expensive to employ such people and therefore "trades as carpenters, bricklaying, blacksmithing and others ought to be taught to the Negroes as it was formerly done in Brazil," adding that "this race has sufficient fitness for it." Deeds of the period in which Negro caulkers, blacksmiths, and carpenters are mentioned suggest that these instructions were carried out. So desperate did the shortage of labor become that a force consisting of only five boys and one man was detailed on one occasion to defend the colony. Dominie Michiels was even found "lending his boy-servant to the farmers who were short of hands."

The sharp need of laborers is best illustrated by an incident which took place in the early part of 1641, during Governor Kieft's administration. One of the six "Company's slaves," while working at the fort, killed one of his "fellow-Negroes." There appears to have been no evidence against any specific slave; and so torture, the common expedient of those days, was threatened to wring self-accusation from all six men. To escape this ordeal the Negroes declared they had jointly committed the deed. The court was in a dilemma; laborers were scarce and six were too many to lose. The old Dutch magistrates turned to the ancient solution; they ordered that lots be drawn to determine which one of the Negroes should be executed. It fell, "by God's direction," on a stalwart fellow named Manuel de Gerritt, called "the Giant," and he was sentenced to be hanged. The whole community turned out to witness the execution. Pieter, the city's Negro hangman, placed Manuel on a ladder in the fort with two strong halters about his neck. When the signal was given, Pieter pulled the ladder from under him, but both ropes broke, and the fellow tumbled to the ground. The bystanders clamored so loudly for his pardon that Kieft spared his life on the pledge of future good conduct. Manuel was one of the eleven slaves who were manumitted in 1644.

"QUALITY OR CONDITION"

The life of the black man in New Amsterdam seems to have had many parallels with that of the white indentured servant, who had few rights and privileges during his period of service. Restrictive ordinances were enacted that were as severe on the whites as they were on the blacks. Laws were passed as early as 1638 which affected all persons in the service of the West India Company, "be their state Quality or Condition," regulating hours of work, social relationships and general movement about the community.[6] The loose life of the inhabitants was the reason offered for enacting the repressive measures. The worried city fathers forbade, in particular, "adulterous intercourse with heathens, blacks or other persons" to end the debauchery that was going on in the brothels, taverns and "low groggeries"; nothing was said in the edict concerning marriage with such people, however.[7] Beyond these futile gestures, the authorities made no attempt to halt the march of harlots and fugitive servants from the neighboring English colonies into the settlement, the need for labor being what it was. In time a considerable section of the colony became a veritable mess of sin, and thus a lucrative field of graft for corrupt officials.

The morals of the Negroes were always a concern of the Dutch, however. It was as a result of gentle urging from a pious dominie that the first recorded marriage between Negroes took place in the Dutch church on May 5, 1641, when Anthony van Angola took the vows with Lucie d'Angola. Twenty years afterward, the earliest

---

[6] New York Colony. Statutes, *Laws and Ordinances,* O'Callaghan 10-12.

[7] New York Colony. Statutes, *Laws and Ordinances,* O'Callaghan 10-12.

adoption among free Negroes in the city was registered when the city court granted the petition of Emanuel Pietersen and his wife, Dorothy Angola, who came before it "praying that a certificate of freedom may be granted for a lad named Anthony Angola, whom they adopted when an infant and have since reared and educated." On that occasion Pietersen paid the West India Company three hundred guilders for the freedom of the boy.

DUTCH DAWDLING

The courts were one of the prime influences in shaping the lives of the early settlers. Magistrates, with little precedent to follow, codified the law by rule of thumb as they went along. Court records of this period are replete with amusing squabbles over slaves, swine, cattle, breaking into enclosures, and the stealing of affections. The verdicts were as uproariously funny as the complaints.

The most frequent cases heard were over brawls and slander induced by "kleyn beer," the manufacture of which was a major industry. A favorite beverage and the customary seal to all business transactions, it was sold and consumed in great quantities. It was considered in good form to drink several large jugs at a sitting; no social sanctions held, nor was repentence required of those who became slightly tipsy. It was also customary for the magistrates to have their drinks brought in while they sat on the bench, and to charge them to the public expense. The brew was drunk freely at the ordination of elders and deacons and at funeral solemnities. When mellowed by kleyn beer, some of the old burghers and farmers cut many capers and not a few twisters in their occasional lapses from righteous living; even the watchful eye which usually kept a sharp lookout for the coming of a hostile Indian sometimes became dimmed.

Holidays provided the most solid excuses for sprees; Christmas and the beloved *Pinkster* (Pentecost) were the principal ones. On these days there would be dancing in the streets in which the blacks participated, and at which they were "exquisite performers on three-stringed fiddles." Above the noisy play of the white colonists were always heard the "peals of broad-mouthed laughter of the Dutch Negroes," who were, no doubt, also warmed by the suds as well as the holiday spirit.

Festival days seldom failed to attract large crowds from the rural districts. Burghers and farmers, accompanied by their slaves, traveled forty and fifty miles to the city, where they witnessed African dances performed by Negroes. The most popular musical instrument was described as a sheepskin-covered eel-pot, on which a black musician pounded out rhythms with his bare hands. A Negro named Charley, who was said to be 125 years old, "did most of the beating," to the strains of strange African songs. He also led the dance, when young and old, black and white, "would put in the double-shuffle heel-and-toe break-down." Some years after the fall of New Amsterdam, an Englishman, a Captain Graydon who had been a prisoner in the Dutch colony, was heard to remark: "Their blacks, when they had them, were very free and familiar; sometimes sauntering about among the whites at meal time, with hat on head, and freely joining occasionally in conversation, as if they were one and all of the same household." [8]

Blacks were, indeed, an integral part of the Dutch family and community life. Beyond the requirements of their labor and beyond their talent in dancing and singing, they gained reputations for their predictions of the weather, a value which the farming hazards of that day made appreciable. In a lively account, Washington Irving describes much of this phase of their life in his satiric Knickerbocker portraits, which, though drawn with strokes of exaggerated humor, contain much truth:

> These Negroes, like the monks of the Dark Ages, engross all the Knowledge of the place, and being infinitely more adventurous and more knowing than their masters, carry on all the foreign trade; making frequent voyages in canoes, loaded with oysters, buttermilk, and cabbages. They are great astrologers, predicting the different changes of weather almost as accurately as an almanac. In whistling they almost toast the far-famed powers of Orpheus' lyre, for not a horse or an ox in the place, when at the plough or before the wagon, will budge a foot until he hears the well-known whistle of his black driver and companion. And from their skill at casting up accounts upon their fingers, they are regarded with as much veneration as were the disciples of Pythagoras.

---

[8] John Fanning Watson, *Annals and Occurrences of New York City and State in the Olden Time* (Philadelphia, Henry F. Anners 1846) 171.

MIXED CONGREGATIONS

The church was perhaps as important an institution as the court and played even a larger part in shaping the social customs of New Amsterdam. At no time did the Dutch bar blacks from receiving the Word of God in their six churches. At one time forty Negroes helped to compose the Calvinist congregation of Stuyvesant's Bouwerie Chapel; and it is said that the blacks grieved as much as the whites when their pastor, Dominie Drisius, returned to Holland in 1664. Not all the Negroes of the colony were regular churchgoers. Perhaps some were just plain backsliders for on March 16, 1660, a white saloon-keeper called Jochemsen lost his license for a year and six weeks for selling beer to Negroes while Sabbath services were in progress.

Schooling, a function of the church, was also freely given to the blacks; how much they received is left to speculation. But a petition of Dominie Bogardus in 1638, requesting "a schoolmaster to teach and train the youth of both Dutch and blacks in the knowledge of Jesus Christ," is a clue. Such instructions probably included the rudiments of reading, writing, and ciphering with the accent on divine worship and catechism. And it is said that the black and the white children tumbled about the schoolhouse door in perfect equality.

Sincere piety might have been one of the reasons the Dutch were not allowed to whip their slaves without official authority, for in 1659 one Peter Cornelius Vander Veen asked for and received permission from the court to flog his female slave. No apparent violence was done to their sense of justice, however, when freed Negroes were made to pay the debts of their deceased ex-masters. In 1645, a year after his manumission, Paul d'Angola and his two children, and Clara Crioole, a free Negro, and her mulatto child, were hailed before the provincial secretary in a litigation which was brought against the estate of their deceased ex-master, Captain Jan de Vries. Simon Joosten, a Hollander, claimed that de Vries had borrowed six hundred guilders from him and had not repaid him. His demand was only satisfied when the Negroes were ordered to convey parcels of their land to him as a guarantee that they would meet this debt.[9]

---

[9] I.N. Phelps Stokes, compiler, *The Iconography of Manhattan Island* (New York, Robert H. Dodd 1922) 184-192.

Some attempt to establish public welfare that directly benefited Negroes was made by the Dutch. When surgeon Jacob Hendricksen Varrevanger petitioned the provincial council in 1658 that a hospital for "sick soldiers and Negroes" be established, he was instructed to look for a "suitable location, a steward and a nurse." Two years later two buildings were erected, no doubt the first hospital structures ever to be built on Manhattan Island. In all probability Lucas Santomee, a free Negro and son of an ex-slave, Peter Santomee, practiced there, as he was "well-known in the colony as a physician."

INDIAN WARS

Negroes also aided in the conquest of the land. Stuyvesant wrote to Curacao in February 1660 for "clever and strong" Negroes to "pursue the Indians," adding that it is "evident that in order to possess this country in peace and revenge affronts and murders we shall be forced into a lawful offensive war against them [the Indians]." This letter was followed by another, two months later, in which Stuyvesant pleaded for the return to New Amsterdam of some Esopus Indian captives he had sent to Curacao in order to "pacify" the Esopus nation. He had made the mistake of shipping numbers of their tribesmen to the Dutch African colony to be sold into slavery, and the Indians had demanded their return with the threat of reprisal. Whether he was successful in avoiding war with the red man on this occasion is not known, but it is likely that the difficulties and dangers caused by similar incidents did much to halt the broad enslavement of the Indians.

FREE NEGROES

All of the Negroes did not begin their careers in New Amsterdam as slaves, as so commonly supposed. The records seem to indicate that free Negroes were living in the Dutch colony even prior to the first manumissions. Domingo Antony, who owned parcels of land in 1643, appears as the earliest Negro landowner in the province. As early as 1634, in the minutes of the directors in Holland, reference is made to Negroes in the employ of the company seeking wages:

> There was read a petition from five Negroes arrived from New Netherland, claiming to have earned eight guilders a month, requesting settlement. Referred to the Commission for New Netherland.

TROJAN HORSE

For half a century the merchants of the colony enjoyed a measure of prosperity. New Amsterdam, with its fifteen hundred whites
and several hundred blacks, was by 1663 regarded as the metropolis of New Netherland; building and farming were rapidly ad-
vancing. The city owned shares in a slave ship and was investing
money in similar ventures. Restrictive laws continued to be passed,
one in particular against "Vagabonds, Quakers and Fugitives."
Meanwhile the Dutch were carrying on by water and by land
illicit but lucrative trade in slaves, liquor, and tobacco with the
English colonists in different parts of North America. Long jealous
of the growing commerce of Holland and irritated by the loss of
revenue from direct trade between the Dutch and the English
colonists, the English lords decided to wage war on the Dutch and
seize their colonial prize, New Netherland.

In 1664 the English fleet boldly descended on New Amsterdam, and at the sight of the menacing British frigates, men and
women and children flocked to Stuyvesant, beseeching him to surrender. His only answer was "I would rather be carried out dead,"
and in a fit of passion he seized the letter of the invading commander, Nicolls, outlining the terms of surrender, and tore it up.
The burgomasters, dissatisfied with the Dutch administration of the
colony, had other ideas. Fragments of the torn letter were collected
and a copy was handed to the burgomasters, who in turn broad-
cast its contents to the anxious populace. The people refused to
rally to the defense of the colony, though the invading soldiers
were on their doorstep and were heard talking of "where booty is
to be found, and where the young women live who wear gold
chains." Such was the state of affairs when Stuyvesant at last
surrendered.

In Stuyvesant's explanation to the Holland directors, he declared
that the principal cause of his surrender was the lack of food. Three
hundred slaves who had been brought in just before the arrival of
the British had eaten all the surplus food, he said, making it impossible for the city to stand siege.[10]

---

[10] Answer of the Hon Peter Stuyvesant to the observation of the West India
Company on his report on the surrender of New Netherland (1666). In *Documents
Relative to the Colonial History of the State of New York*, O'Callaghan II 430.

CHAPTER II

THE SLAVES REBEL

NEW YORK, 1664-1741.—The Dutch Metropolis must have presented a sorry sight to the European eye of Nicolls, the first English governor. Its earthen fort enclosed a windmill and a high flagstaff. There were also a prison and a governor's house; a double-roofed church above which loomed a square tower; a gallows and whipping post at the river's side, and a row of shabby houses which hugged the citadel for protection. Yet Nicolls described the place as "the best of all His Majesty's towns in America," which, with proper management, should produce boundless wealth. To the blacks it was certainly no paradise. A forecast of life under English rule was provided when, shortly after the British flag had been hoisted over New Amsterdam, the victors plundered the out-posts and sent the white soldiers of the vanquished Dutch to Virginia to be sold as slaves.

ENSLAVING TECHNIQUES

One of the first official acts of Governor Nicolls was to issue on the complaint of Peter Stuyvesant, the ousted governor, a warrant for the arrest of four Negro slaves who, timing their dash almost to the hour of occupation, had fled in the manner of the day, "carrying their passport under the soles of their shoes." To halt the sudden epidemic of runaways, a provision of the "Duke's Laws," [1] which were enacted the same year (1664), provided that "no Christian shall be kept in Bond-Slavery, except such who shall be judged thereto by Authority, or such as willingly have sold or shall sell themselves." [2]

---

[1] Duke's Laws were established for the governing of the English colony of New York. This code of laws was given to Governor Nicolls by the Duke of York and the colony was accordingly named after him.—*Documents Relative to Colonial History of the State of New York.*

[2] Edwin Vernon Morgan, *Slavery in New York* (New York, G. P. Putnam's Sons 1898) 8.

The slave owners protested against this law, declaring that Negroes would demand their freedom if they were baptized. They
also opposed legal marriage of slaves, which the Dutch had encouraged, on the grounds that it would have a manumitting effect.
In an attempt to secure popular support, it was even said that
Negroes had no souls but perished like beasts and therefore were
incapable of embracing Christianity. After ten years of agitation,
a law was passed (1674) that "no Negro slave who becomes a
Christian after he had been bought shall be set at liberty." This
act marked the beginning of chattel slavery in New York. But the
drastic nature of servitude under the English did not become fully
evident until 1706, when to appease an uneasy public conscience,
a law was passed to encourage the baptism of Negro, Indian, and
mulatto slaves. But to safeguard the slaveholders' investments, a
provision was subtly inserted which provided that children of such
persons must follow the state and condition of the mother.[3]

The task of imparting religion to the slaves was first under-
taken in 1704 by an English missionary group known as the Society for the Propagation of the Gospel in Foreign Parts. Mr Elias
Neau, a French Huguenot, was appointed director of a night
school established by the society in the latter part of the same
year. Prior to its erection, Neau had zealously taught the slaves the
first rudiments of schooling in his home. This work had not been
accomplished without considerable opposition from the slave owners, who declared that education would "render the slaves insolent
and difficult to control." The Negro insurrection in 1712 interrupted the work of Neau, but when it was discovered that only
one of his pupils had been involved in the plot and that one "un-
baptized," his work gained in appreciation.

DISCRIMINATION AFTER DEATH

It soon became apparent that Dutch dawdling in matters of
slavery was absent in the English, for the latter regulated servitude
with the thoroughness of modern business methods. Slavery was
considered a serious enterprise and every step necessary for its protection and preservation was taken. Blacks were therefore set apart

[3] A. Judd Northrup, *Slavery in New York* [State Library Bulletin: History No 4,
May 1900] (Albany, University of the State of New York) 256-267.

from whites, economically and socially, on the theory that to permit them to mingle freely with white people would endanger the chances of keeping them enslaved. This policy was carried out in every straining detail; so much so that a law was passed that "no Negro shall be buried in Trinity Churchyard." Accordingly, a "Negroes' burying ground" was parceled off, as if, to paraphrase the words of a modern Negro poet, even in heaven black cherubs do the celestial chores. The business of enslaving the blacks was legally clinched, June 25, 1710, when a slave named Will brought suit against his master, Joris Elsworth, to recover wages he claimed he had earned. This assault upon the slavery system was tried before a jury in the supreme court of the province and a verdict was returned against the slave.[4] Similar pleas by other slaves were rejected on this legal precedent.

NEGRO SLAVEHOLDERS

The effect of all this upon the free black population was not immediately apparent, for the change in the Negro's status was gradual, timed to the changing social pattern. On the surface life seemed to go on as before. Among other things, free Negroes continued to receive land grants. In 1674 Judith Stuyvesant, widow of the last Dutch governor, gave considerable land to a free Negro, Francisco Bastiaenz, on condition that "Francisco is bound, with his neighbors, to keep in repair the fence of said land." (In all probability she referred to the Negroes who had been given land under Dutch rule, and who were apparently still in possession of it.) But Negroes soon began to have trouble inheriting property, as many whites in the colony came to believe blacks had no rights they were bound to respect. This notion became especially prevalent among a number of poor whites, who themselves enjoyed very little more than the luxury of being white.

In 1717, a Negro butcher, who had inherited a slave along with other property, complained in a petition that the executor of his deceased master's estate, "Ebenezer Wilson, detains money and a Negro willed to him by said Morton [his master] yet requires the

---

[4] Edwin Vernon Morgan, *Slavery in New York: The Status of the Slave under the English Colonial government* [Reprinted from American Historical Association papers] (New York 1891) 6.

petitioner to clothe and support him [the inherited slave] in sickness." There is no record of what disposition was made in this case, but a similar incident occurred two years later, when the executors of the estate of Jacob and Elizabeth Regnier charged a freed Negro named Fortune with disposing of three Negro slaves he had inherited from his deceased master. Fortune, who was apparently a man of some affluence, was defended by an attorney and in a jury trial won a verdict in his favor, thus establishing the right of black men to own slaves.[5]

PIRATES AND PRIVATEERS

The English began to increase the slave population in wholesale numbers, after the ownership and the restriction of slaves had been legally established. Privateers and pirates were again active in this port. The pirates, hearing that the new governor, Benjamin Fletcher (1692-1698), was a man of easy ways, immediately headed for New York to dispose of captured blacks. Swaggering pirate captains soon became familiar figures in the streets of the city. A description remains of one named Tew, a typical member of that bizarre lot who arrived in this port:

> A slight dark man of forty, garbed in a blue cap with a band of cloth of silver, loose trunks of white linen and curiously worked stockings; while a chain of Arabian gold hung from his neck, and through the meshes of a knit belt gleamed a dagger, its hilt set with the rarest stones.

At one time more than nine pirate ships were idling in the harbor, while roistering crews of cutthroats frequented the blazing taverns at night. Their howls of joy and rage mingled with the screams of duped harlots and made honest folk shudder in their beds. Without the lure of the fleshpots, it is doubtful that these sea robbers would have lingered in the city after unloading their loot. The local merchants, leaning heavily on corrupt officials for privilege, were inclined to wink at the scandalous revelry of the water front, and accepted this debauchery as an inevitable by-product of the whole business of slave trading. In fact, the mer-

---

[5] Original minutes of the Mayor's Court, "Negro Defendant Wins Verdict," (April 14, 1719). In vol dated May 6, 1718, to June 14, 1720, at the Hall of Records of the City of New York.

chants of the town made good use of pirates like Captain Kidd, profiting from their illicit merchandise, both human and otherwise. New York ship owners like John Van Cortlandt [6] and Gabriel Ludlow were among the most conspicuous of this group of merchants.

WALL STREET

Slave trading grew so rapidly under English rule that by the beginning of the eighteenth century there were more than two thousand Negroes in the province, a little over thirteen per cent of the total population. But white labor was still wanted. Complaints were heard that no more than a hundred white laboring men were to be had for the high wage of three shillings a day, and so most of the work had to be done by blacks. The demand for slave labor kept pace with the rapid growth of the colony, especially since small shopkeepers, artisans, and tradespeople sought to emulate the land-owning class and to have slaves of their own. The slave traders showed shrewd business sense for they never flooded the market. But they made available a supply barely sufficient for the growing demand, and disposed of the surplus in the ready South. Poor members of the community who could not afford to buy slaves hired them from their masters whom they paid for the slave's services. To satisfy this class an order was issued by the Common Council in 1711 that slaves to be let out for hire within the city were "to take up their standing in order to be hired at the market house at the Wall Street Slip." [7]

For years this market had been a favorite meeting place of Dutch burghers and farmers who came from the various outposts to do business in New Amsterdam. However, a slave market was not established there until 1711. Afterwards it became known as the "Meal or Wall Street Market," the "place where Negroes and Indians could be bought, sold, or hired." White persons were also put on the auction block at the Wall Street Market and sold as indentured servants. The New York *Gazette* of September 4, 1732, carried an advertisement offering for sale, "Englishmen, Cheshire

---

[6] Samuel McKee, Jr., *Labor in Colonial New York 1664-1776* [Studies in History, Economics and Public Law, ed Faculty of Political Science No 410] (New York, Columbia University Press 1935) 117-119.

[7] McKee, *Labor in Colonial New York* 129.

cheese, Negro men, a Negro girl, and a few Welshmen." In later years newspapers carried many advertisements of slaves being offered for sale here. Typical notices appeared in the New York *Gazette-Post Boy:*

TO BE SOLD

A Negro Indian Man Slave, about forty years of age, well known in Town, being a Fidler. He will understand all kinds of Farmer's work, and is a very good Brick-Maker. Inquire of Capt. Nicholas Fletcher, near Spring Garden.

. . .

A likely healthy Negro wench about 25 years of age, has had the smallpox, understands House work, and is sold for no fault but being a breeder; she has a child at the Breast which is to be sold with her. Inquire at the Printing Office in Beaver St.

BLACK MAN'S BURDEN

Negro slaves hired out at the Wall Street Market engaged in a variety of occupations, and in time developed skill in sundry types of work. Early in the English period Negro coopers, blacksmiths, tinners, and carpenters were to be found, many of whom had learned their trades under Dutch rule. Frequently they became the sole support of owners who had grown old, a custom that had hearty public approval. Any contrary behavior on a slave's part was more than likely to arouse indignation. The *Gazette,* in writing of a runaway, said, "We hear that a valuable Negro Slave, belonging to a poor blind Man in Town, whose chief support he was, stole a canoe, and went on board the *Republic. . . .*" A similar attitude is exhibited in a petition recorded in 1693, when Richard Elliot, a cooper, pleaded in court for the pardon of his two Negro slaves because he would be left penniless without them.[8] Again, in 1719, Hannams Burghe, a blacksmith, "being old and poor, prays that the sentence of death passed on his Negro may be commuted, he being his only support." Not in every instance were blacks compelled to care for their old masters; sometimes the act was motivated, not by the formal master-slave relationship, but by a sincere friendship which has been painted too frequently and too romantically as one of the more common aspects of slavery. Late in

---

[8] A law provided compensation amounting to the full market value to be paid to the master of executed slaves.

the century a freed Negro named Derry, who was the sole support of his ex-master's widow, won a lottery prize of ten thousand dollars. When informed of his good fortune, he said, according to the New York *Journal* of April 19, 1796, "Well, now I will be able to maintain my old mistress genteely."

It is not recorded whether the courts were moved by the many petitions made by masters for the continued services of offending slaves and servants, but in those cases where the owner did not intervene it is apparent that justice was administered with a heavy hand. About this time two Negro women were sentenced to be tied to a cart and given forty lashes on their naked backs. The order specified that the cart make a tour of the city and lashes be given the women at each street corner. A few months later two white women were similarly treated; they were stripped to the waist and publicly whipped for stealing cloth. Whenever slaves and indentured servants appeared in court, traditional English justice usually gave way to the needs of the slave-owners. In cases of theft the value of which did not exceed five pounds, the master who desired to retain the services of the convicted had to make good the amount, in which case the offender would be sentenced to a whipping. After this he resumed his duties with hardly an interruption in his service. Slaves were not permitted to testify against a freeman in any case, civil or criminal .

REFUGE WITH RED MEN

News of the inhuman treatment of slaves and servants reached the ears of Queen Anne, soon after her ascent to the throne. In 1703 she decreed that "the willful killing of Indians and Negroes" by their masters "may be punished with death." The previous year a local enactment had given the master the right to punish his slave, and it might have been the application of this law which inspired Her Majesty's decree. But the Queen made the error of appointing as governor, her cousin, Lord Cornbury (1702-1708), a man of vicious private life who promptly proceeded to line his pockets at the expense of the public. Unscrupulous and obnoxious, Cornbury had the habit of dressing himself and parading about in women's apparel, and giving drunken parties that lasted into the morning. Three years later (1706), contrary to the Queen's commands, Cornbury issued a scathing proclamation against the blacks:

> . . . Requiring and commanding [all officers] to take all proper methods for the seizing and apprehending [of] all such Negroes as shall be found to be assembled . . . . and if any of them refuse to submit, then fire upon them, kill or destroy them, if they otherwise cannot be taken. . . . I am informed that several Negroes in Kings County [Brooklyn] have assembled themselves in a riotous manner, which if not prevented may prove of ill consequence.

The enforcement of these restrictive measures met with surly resistance, and sometimes with rebellion. As early as 1683 it had been found necessary to pass an ordinance forbidding slaves above the number of four to meet together. This order proved insufficient restriction against the slaves, who were daily growing more desperate, and in 1702, the number permitted to "congregate" was reduced to three. At the same time they were forbidden to carry weapons on penalty of receiving ten lashes. To prevent runaway Negroes making alliances with the Indian tribes, a law was passed in 1705 prohibiting slaves from traveling beyond forty miles north of Saratoga, then Indian country. Blacks were also forbidden to ride horses, under the penalty of forty lashes. Prior to this time, slaves had often fled to Canada and to the neighboring Indians. To prevent blacks from taking asylum with the red men, a treaty was made with the Six Nations in which the Indians agreed to surrender any slave who sought refuge with them. The braves seem to have ignored this treaty; at least there appears to be no record of its observance. With the increase of the Negro population the large mass of unhappy blacks became more menacing to the colonists. In 1708, when "An Act Preventing the Conspiracy of Slaves" was enacted, there were more than three thousand of them in the colony.

MAIDEN LANE INCIDENT

Certain of the blacks, in anger at the many harsh measures enacted against them, struck back blindly. Court records of 1696 speak of a Negro slave named Prince who was stripped to the waist, tied to a cart and drawn through the city, eleven lashes being given him at every corner. From the testimony it seems that Mayor Merritt had ordered a group of "noisy Negroes" to disperse, and Prince had angrily "assaulted him on the face." Another incident with a tragic ending was the killing of the entire Hallett family in 1708 by an Indian man and a Negro woman, both slaves of this white family. Capital punishment was inflicted. The woman was burned to death and the man hanged.

Individual attempts by the blacks at retaliation became more and more frequent, but they were usually suppressed quickly. Negroes soon learned the bitter lesson that blind reprisal had taught, for in 1712 a large band of slaves met in a Maiden Lane orchard, and planned and carried out a revolt. In a masterpiece of understatement, Governor Hunter's report to the Lords of Trade in England described the affair as an attempt by the blacks "to revenge themselves for some hard usage . . . from their Masters."

On the night of April sixth, an alarm was sounded of a fire in the center of the town. In those days there was only one cry more dreaded—the warning that hostile Indians were coming. But this fire was to prove even more terrible than red men on the warpath! While the white inhabitants were engaged in putting out the flames some thirty Negroes descended upon them and started shooting. Slashing and hacking with crude knives and hatchets, the infuriated blacks killed nine whites and wounded six others. The piercing screams of the victims aroused the townspeople, and the booming of the fort's cannon brought the militia to the bloody scene. Outnumbered, the rebels fled to the woods. The next morning the militia was dispatched to "drive the island" in search of them. When discovered in their forest hiding place, six committed suicide, one man killing his wife and himself. The rest were captured and tried. Twenty-one were executed, including two Indians. The ringleaders, Clause, Robin, and Kuako, were tortured to death. Clause was broken on the wheel, Robin was hanged in chains to die slowly, and Kuako was burned alive. Governor Hunter regarded this as "'the most exemplary punishment inflicted that could be thought of."

The repercussions of this incident in the neighboring colonies is hardly a part of this story. But it should be observed that some of them passed laws, to end slave "conspiracies" after the insurrection. William Southeby petitioned the Pennsylvania Assembly in

1712 for the total abolition of slavery. A citizens' petition, which noted that "divers (Negro) Plots and Insurrections have frequently happened, not only in the Island but on the Main Land of America," caused the passage of an "Act to prevent the Importation of Negroes and Indians." [9]

In New York a new set of oppressive laws was enacted after the uprising. One law in particular was designed to impoverish the entire colored population: it ordered that "no Negro, Indian, or Mulatto made free hereafter was to enjoy, hold or possess any house, lands, tenements, or hereditaments within this colony." This law remained in effect for more than a century. To discourage the freeing of slaves, a master who manumitted a slave was required to pay the then enormous amount of two hundred pounds a year to the freed man during his lifetime. [10]

AS DOMESTICS

"Although there were instances of unruly slaves," wrote a chronicler of the times, some of the Negroes were "much attached to the families in which they were owned. The only separation that was known was when some of the younger members of the family would marry and leave the homestead . . . and take some of the younger slaves with them." In instances "where an old Negro wench had acted as the dry nurse of her young master or mistress, she would insist upon accompanying them, which was almost invariably consented to." The nurse often acted as a sort of family historian, whose seeming agelessness linked one generation to another. From the kitchen chimney corner, perched on "a seat appropriated for her use," she would delight all the members of the household, both white and black, with an assortment of weird stories during the long winter evenings. Such households had large staffs of domestic servants, some of whom were dressed in elaborate livery and carefully trained in their duties. The black women rivaled the genteel ladies of these homes as they went about their chores, trailing gracefully in their wide hooped skirts through lofty rooms filled with dignified Chippendale. The black male house-

---

[9] W.E.B. DuBois, *The Suppression of the African Slave Trade to the United States of America 1638-1870* (New York, Longmans, Green 1904) 22.
[10] *The Colonial Laws of New York (1664-1776)* (Albany, James B. Lyon, State Printer 1894) I 764-765.

servants, like the gentlemen of the period, wore powdered wigs and embroidered waistcoats, and were properly immaculate in their white embroidered ruffles.

CATHARINE MARKET

Blacks did manage to escape at infrequent intervals from the cold formality of the colonial household and from the solid drudgery of field labor. Time taken from routine duties was the time for play. The "country slaves" (Long Island and New Jersey) and the "city slaves" (Manhattan) would meet at the Catharine Market on their "holidays," of which Dutch *Pinkster* remained their principal one. Often they gathered on time stolen from their masters. At other times, when consent could be wheedled from their masters, they would journey to the market with loads of cracked eggs, roots, berries, herbs, fish, clams, and oysters, to sell for pocket change. Peddling these wares in baskets which they balanced on their heads, these Negroes became familiar figures in the city's markets. The Long Islanders, with their hair tied in queues with dried eelskin, and the Jersey slaves, with their plaited forelocks tied fashionably with lead from packages of tea, added a picturesque touch.[11]

Forerunners of a long line of talented entertainers, these blacks first introduced Negro dancing and singing in this city at the Catharine Market. Blacks had danced in the streets with the whites during the Dutch spring festivals; but under English rule, with its many restrictions against the mingling of slaves and freemen, the dancing of Negroes took on a definite racial character. In time Catharine Market became famous as a meeting place not for dancers and singers alone, but also for jockeys and boxers.

After the country slaves had disposed of their masters' produce at the various markets about the town, they would "shin it" for the Catharine Market to enter the list with the city Negroes. They were always ready with their sayings and doings to earn a few shillings. Sometimes bystanders hired them to do a "jig of breakdown," paying them in collections taken up and from amused tradespeople who had stopped to watch. The dancers brought along boards, called shingles, upon which they performed. These wooden

[11] Thomas F. Devoe, *The Market Book* 2 vols (New York, printed for the author 1862) I 344-345.

planks were usually about five or six feet long and equally wide, and were kept in place during the dancing by four of their companions. Rarely in their deft "turning and shying off" did they step from the boards. Music was usually provided by one of their party, who beat a rhythm with his hands on the sides of his legs. Tom-toms were also used in their music making.

The rivalry stimulated by these contests served to produce some excellent dancers, and even "raised a sort of strife for the highest honors." The city Negroes appear to have been more accomplished than their Long Island and Jersey friends. "They [the city performers] were for many years placed 'up head' in this nimble art," remarked an eyewitness. The most famous dancers were Ned (Francis), "a little wiry Negro slave"; Bob Rawley, who called himself "Bobolink Bob"; and a chap named Jack, who was referred to as "smart and faithful." The talent displayed by these dancers made one awed observer exclaim that the blacks danced as though they "scarcely knew they were in bondage."

Not a part of the main stream of the town's social life, Negroes found needed fellowship in these gatherings. In defiance of the law, they managed to meet and form clubs, some of which were known as the *Geneva Club* ("after a liquor they were fond of"), the *Smith Fly Boys,* the *Free Masons,* and the *Long Bridge Boys.* It may well be supposed that when the slaves met they exchanged, like servants the world over, the latest gossip about their friends and their masters. The laws enacted against them could hardly have escaped mention, because at this very time (1731), one particular measure hampered their meetings; it provided a penalty of forty lashes for a slave seen on the streets after nightfall without a lighted lantern or candle.

The slave gatherings became "so grievous to their masters" that a law was passed in 1740 that "after tht ringing of three bells and the proclamation made for silence," Negroes, Indians and Mulatto slaves found selling fruits and other produce were to be publicly whipped. It was complained that the "pernicious practice is not only detrimental to the masters . . . but the slaves absent themselves from their [master's] service . . . and cause distempers and disease in the inhabitants." The notion that colored people were disease-carriers had been prevalent for some time; so much so that considerable alarm was caused by the epidemic of smallpox in the fall of 1731, when more than a hundred blacks and some three hundred whites were "bury'd in a fortnight." But a more unhappy situation was in store for the colonists.

REVOLT OF 1741 [12]

For some time the colonists had been apprehensive about another slave revolt. They had not forgotten the bloody incident of 1712, and ever since had kept a close watch on the blacks. In 1741, when a slave "Plot to Burn New York and Murder Its Inhabitants" [13] was discovered, panic spread throughout the city. The business people closed their shops and mothers kept their children from school. Worried preachers prayed for deliverance, while brave souls trembled at a nightmare becoming a reality. Few troubled to ascertain the facts, flimsy as they were. Nor did many bother their heads about why the blacks were eternally unhappy!

The house of Robert Hogg, a merchant, was robbed of linen, silver coins and other goods valued at sixty pounds, on the night of February 28, 1741. A Negro named Caesar was arrested at John Hughson's tavern the following day, charged with having plotted the theft with a certain Wilson, who was a ship's boy on the man-o-war *Flamborough*. Suspicion also fell on the tavernkeeper—he was believed to have received the stolen articles—and his place was searched. A white woman, Mary Burton by name, who was an indentured servant to Hughson and lived at the tavern, when questioned said that she knew something about the robbery, but feared to tell lest she be "murdered or poisoned by Hughson and the Negroes." She was immediately lodged in the City Hall for safety.

At a preliminary hearing she testified that Caesar came to her room on the morning of the theft, and gave her a gift of money and some linen, saying he had robbed Hogg's house. Questioning of Hughson revealed that he also had received linen and silver, but he refused to sign a confession, whereupon he and his wife were released on bail. While the three-day investigation of this affair

---

[12] Some historians regard it in some ways as the most important single event in the history of the Negro in the Colonial Period.

[13] Daniel Horsmanden, *The New York Conspiracy, or a History of the Negro Plot* (New York, Southwick and Pelsue 1810) 385 p.

was in progress, a series of fires broke out. At first they were believed to be accidental, but were later attributed to Negroes. Suspicion fell on the entire black population, numbers of whom were rounded up and herded before the magistrates. While court was in session other fires broke out, one in Fort George, near the Battery, and others in dwellings of prominent citizens. A Negro was seen running from one of the burning houses. Immediately an alarm was raised that the blacks were rising in revolt. Judge Horsmanden, who wrote voluminously on this alleged plot, says "many people had such terrible apprehensions upon this occasion, and indeed there were cause sufficient, that several Negroes, who were met in the streets, after the alarm of their rising, were hurried away to Gaol." The fear of the officials became so great that Lieutenant-Governor Clarke ordered the militia to stand guard day and night.

Large rewards were offered for information leading to the arrest of the guilty persons. A furious hunt began, rivaled only by Salem's witch hysteria. A typical incident was the case of two Negroes who were arrested for "having things thought improper for, and unbecoming the condition of slaves." Many people, in their eagerness to earn the rewards, concocted stories involving innocent persons. Every man's neighbor became a suspect. Catholics, then an ostracized group, were dragged into the affair. The "Negro Plot" developed into a "Popish Plot" involving one John Ury, a Catholic priest who was "seen lurking about town, pretending to teach Greek and Latin." He was promptly taken into custody, and since he was unable to satisfy the authorities about his activities he was thrown into jail.

A BLACK-AND-TAN TAVERN

Mary Burton, called to testify before the grand jury, confessed to knowledge of a conspiracy on the part of Caeser and two Negroes known as Cuffee and Prince. Together with some thirty other Negroes who met frequently at Hughson's tavern, they had, according to her, plotted to burn the town and kill all the white inhabitants when they came out to extinguish the flames. (It had been grumbled among the blacks that "some people have too much and others too little, but the time is coming when master will have less and Cuff more!") Her testimony also implicated Hughson, his wife, Sarah, and another white woman named Margaret Sorubiero, a woman of many aliases, but commonly known as "Peggy Kerry, the Irish beauty." Accounts of the trial describe her as the mistress of Caesar, for whom she bore a child and to whom she was indebted for her keep at Hughson's tavern.

The notorious reputation of Hughson's place, with its free mingling of blacks and whites, did much to prejudice the cases of the accused. It was a resort conducted in defiance of the law, and was frequented by servants and slaves, who "played dice and frolicked there." Horsmanden, the chief justice in the trials, afterwards wrote that a witness told him "he saw a great many of them [Negroes] in a room dancing to a fiddle, and Hughson's wife and daughter along with them."

The plot was also believed to involve the country slaves, who in their daily visits to the city "became acquainted with this contemplated conspiracy." The Long Island slaves had formed themselves into a military company and under pretense of play, had "mustered and trained with borrowed arms and accouterments of their masters." In Hackensack, N.J., "eight miles from this city," the inhabitants were alarmed by "a most melancholy and affrighting scene," when seven barns went up in flames. Two Negroes were immediately suspected of being guilty. What occurred is quaintly recorded:

> Having been seen coming out of one of the barns with a gun laden, [the Negro] pretended, on being discovered, that he saw the person who had fired the barns, upon which his master ordered him to fire at him; and the Negro thereupon discharged his piece; but no blood was drawn from any mortal, that could be discovered.

The two Negroes were convicted and burned at the stake. In New York, meanwhile, Mary Burton's fantastic confessions caused such alarm that more than a hundred and fifty blacks and twenty-five whites were arrested and tried. As the trial progressed, the excitement grew. In a decidedly heated atmosphere a guilty verdict was reached. Eighteen Negroes were hanged; fourteen were burned alive; and more than seventy were deported to Africa. Of the whites, John Hughson and his wife, Caesar's mistress, Peggy Kerry, and the Catholic priest, John Ury, were all executed.

THANKSGIVING DAY

With the slave revolt suppressed the council decreed August 31, 1741, as a day of thanksgiving for deliverance from the "wicked and dangerous conspiracy." A few months later Mary Burton, the state's star witness, was declared "entitled to reward for her information leading to the conviction of the conspirators in the Negro plot." But still Governor Clarke fumed that "the insolence of the Negroes is as great, if not greater, than ever." In a letter to the council he called upon it "to see the Laws against Negroes duly and punctually executed." He may have been aroused by bold statements similar to that of a Negro slave named Tom, who was caught setting fire to a house and had "confessed that with the Negroes who were to come from Brooklyn and Long Island they would fire the whole town." Tom was burned alive on Gallows Hill. With great dispatch, new and restrictive measures against blacks were accordingly enacted which were even more repressive.

CHAPTER III

DEMOCRACY, A SLOGAN

NEW YORK, 1741-1785.—An event which probably eased the harshness of slave life under English rule was the beginning of the French and Indian War in 1754. The consequent excitement diverted the slaveholders' interests and started them haggling over the more important issue of who should bear the expense of fighting the French—the colonies or the mother country, England. As the war progressed, the recruiting of black men into the army as soldiers and laborers increased. During this time several Negro companies were part of General Braddock's ill-fated expedition against Fort Duquesne, site of the present city of Pittsburgh.[1] In 1758 a number of Negro militiamen served at Fort Williams, a stockade on the road to Oswego, New York.

SLAVERY DECLINES

The growth of industry and commerce in New York had made slavery increasingly unprofitable, and it gradually assumed a patriarchal form. The climate was cold for newly imported slaves, and the soil was best suited to crops, the cultivation of which by slave labor did not produce sufficient returns. New York had become a community of traders and farmers; therefore, the importation of slaves merely supplied a moderate demand for household servants. The number of slaves owned by a New York family rarely exceeded a dozen.

Slavery had become a domestic institution. There were no "field Negroes," no collections of cabins remote from the master's house

---

[1] Laura E. Wilkes, *Missing Pages in American History* (Washington DC, published by the Author 1919) 20.

known as the "Negro quarters." Instead, slaves lived under the same roof and ate the same food as the rest of the family. Many were "scrupulously" baptised and received religious instructions along with the children of the family. In the absence of special laws regulating slave trading within the city, the sale of slaves seems to have been largely controlled by sentiment. Sometimes a master would seek a slave-mother's consent before selling her child; even then she would often exercise her own caprice in designating the future master.[2]

The manner in which this benevolent attitude affected individuals is revealed by the career of a slave named Billy who belonged to Thomas Browne. Billy, the only child of a slave couple, when old enough to work, was sold to a Long Island farmer who, according to the custom of those days, worked with his servant in the field. From daily contact a friendship developed between master and slave. On his thirty-first birthday Billy told his master of his love for a girl named Jenny, whom he had met on his frequent errands to a near-by farm, and whom he wished to marry. His master readily gave consent to the match and they were married. In the manner of that day, the couple continued to live separately at the homes of their respective owners. Some years later Jenny's master purchased a farm in Westchester county and prepared to remove there with his family. At the imminent separation Billy and his wife anxiously took their problem to their respective masters; and it was settled by an exchange of two other slaves, bringing the couple under the same roof for the first time in their married life.

UNPROFITABLE SLAVERY

As early as 1705, enterprising New England saw that slavery was becoming unprofitable. That year the Boston *News Letter,* according to De Voe's *Market Book,* pointed out editorially that white servants were more profitable than black slaves. Though this paper did not touch the kernel of the situation, it did, however, sound the note that eventually led to the death knell of slavery in New York, and in the North generally:

---

[2] Watson, *Annals and Occurrences* 222-223.

A man then might buy a white man-servant, we suppose, for 10 pounds, to serve six, eight or ten years. If a white servant dies, the loss exceeds not 10 pounds, but if a Negro dies 'tis a very great loss to the husbandman; three years' interest of the price of the Negro will near upon, if not altogether, purchase a white man-servant . . . . (the) importing of Negroes into this or neighboring provinces is not beneficial either to the crown or country as white servants would be . . .

Many people brought forward personal panaceas for solving the slave problem, and an abundance of literature was written reflecting the various shades of opinion. A typical attitude is shown in the following advertisement which appeared for more than twenty years in every edition of the New York *Gazette:*

AN ESSAY ON SLAVERY
By

T. Allen, Francis Childs, & Co. and J. Fellows, at their respective bookstores.

Designed to exhibit in a new point of view, its effect on morals, industry, and the peace of society. Some of the acts and calculations are offered to prove the labor of freemen to be much more productive than of slaves; that countries are rich, powerful and happy in proportion as the laboring people enjoy the fruits of their own labor; and hence the necessary conclusion, that slavery is impolitic as well as unjust.

BOYCOTT OF SLAVE-MADE GOODS

The first organized opposition to slavery in New York was religious in form. In 1767 the Society of Friends (Quakers), at its annual meeting at Purchase, New York, elected a committee to visit slave-holding members and urge them to free their slaves. Nine years later the society decided to refuse all contributions from those members who had failed to comply. By 1787 there remained but one Quaker slave owner in the city and he, too, manumitted his slaves three years later.

One of their leaders, Elias Hicks, of Long Island, was especially active in demanding the abolition of slavery throughout the state. An early advocate of the boycott as an economic weapon, Hicks urged all citizens not to buy the products of slave labor.[3] The

---

[3] Alice Dana Adams, *The Neglected Period of Anti-Slavery in America 1808-1831* (Boston and London, Ginn and Co. 1908) 65.

Quakers were particularly active in this form of protest against the institution.

Many public-spirited citizens were drawn into the budding anti-slavery movement. In a public letter (April 9, 1777), John Jay, who later became Chief Justice of the United States, urged that a clause providing for the abolition of slavery in New York be embodied in the first State constitution. He was strongly supported by Gouverneur Morris, who wistfully pleaded that this should be done "so that in future generations every human being who breathes the air of the State might enjoy the privileges of a freeman."[4]

JUPITER HAMMON

Meanwhile a conciliatory attitude toward slavery was expressed by a Negro poet, Jupiter Hammon, whose first work appeared in 1760. When it was published he was "upwards of seventy years old" and a slave of a wealthy Lloyd family of Long Island. The privileges which that family granted him may largely account for his attitude, for Hammon praised liberty but said of his own condition in his *Address to Negroes in the State of New York:*

> Now I acknowledge that liberty is a great thing, and worth seeking for, if we can get it honestly; and by our good conduct prevail on our masters to set us free; though for my own part I do not wish to be free; for many of us who are grown up slaves have always had masters to take care of themselves; and it may be for our own comfort to remain as we are.

Little is known of Hammon's life, for he was almost completely neglected by historians of the last century. The earliest document referring to Hammon is a letter written by one Muirson, dated May 19, 1730, prescribing treatment for Jupiter, who suffered with "pains in his Leggs, knees, and thighs." It is evident that the Lloyd family gave him opportunity for instruction, beyond the most elementary training in reading and writing, and permitted him to attend church regularly. The name of America's first Negro poet, disregarded by the early Negro leaders, dropped into oblivion soon after his death and remained there for more than a century.[5]

---

[4] John Jay, *The Correspondence and Public Papers of John Jay,* ed by Henry P. Johnston, 4 vols (New York, G. P. Putnam's 1890) I 136.

[5] Vernon Loggins, *The Negro Author: His Development in America* (New York, Columbia University Press 1931) 9-16.

OPPRESSORS RESENT OPPRESSION

A new tide of public opinion swept over the colonists and caused interest in slavery to pale for a time. George III, who had ascended the throne of England, deplored the heavy debt he had inherited from the French and Indian War, and was determined to sweat its payment out of the colonists. His first attempt to make them "dance to the tune of obedience" was the enactment of the Stamp Act in 1765. At the same time he hastened to remind them that the merchants' tables in America groaned under the weight of rich viands and rare wines.

Indignation greeted the news; the cries were especially loud in New York and New England, where the act affected the commercial people; Jefferson's Virginia joined the protest. It was fortunate for the liberties of America that newspapers were also subject to a heavy stamp duty, for they fairly howled against the act. Threats filled the air as the people resolved not one stamp should be used. In the face of such determined opposition, the British Parliament repealed the act almost immediately, but the opposition which led to its repeal became the principal force behind the American Revolution.

RIGHTS OF MAN

When the Declaration of Independence reached the populace in 1776, a beginning toward democracy had been made. Its astonishing premise that all men are created free and equal brought a new liberal voice to the corridors of history. Thomas Paine's *Common Sense,* which was published early in that year, and which is regarded as one of the most effective appeals that ever "went to the bosom of a nation," completed the preparation of the public mind for the great step.

The doctrines of liberty, equality and the rights of man, so well advertised by the Declaration of Independence, were hailed by the black population, which in them saw visions of its own freedom. The very status of Negroes under the existing order being the lowest, they were, if anything, more ready than the whites for a change. But when numbers of blacks began to give literal meaning to these slogans of freedom, considerable apprehension was aroused among the slave owners. Aware that the fondest hope of their slaves was freedom, the masters were reluctant to arm them. As early as August 1776, the year of the Declaration of Independence, the colonists prepared for a Negro revolt. A Militia Act was passed by the Provincial Congress of New York, providing for a detachment to be left "to guard against the insurrection of slaves," who now menacingly numbered more than twelve thousand.[6] But the problem did not become acute until runaway slaves from Virginia were discovered in the British ranks, a circumstance which had a marked effect upon the enslaved blacks in New York. That the British intended to enroll escaped slaves as regular soldiers became apparent on July 3, 1779, when Sir Henry Clinton, commander of the King's forces occupying New York, issued a proclamation which appeared in the New York *Royal Gazette:*

> I do most strictly forbid any *Person* to sell or claim *Right* over any Negro, the property of a Rebel, who may take refuge in any part of this *Army*: And I do promise to every Negro who shall desert the *Rebel Standard,* full security to follow within these *lines,* any Occupation which he shall think proper.

Its effect upon Negroes was immediate. They fled in great numbers from their American masters to the British. Hoping to stall this movement, the colonists countered with an act of March 20, 1781, which provided for the enlistment of Negroes into the Continental Army and promised freedom to all who served three years, or who were honorably discharged. Two regiments of blacks were soon organized and sent against the British. This was not the first instance of Negro regiments being mobilized for the Revolutionary War. As early as 1778 Rhode Island recruited one which was placed under the command of Colonel Christopher Greene. This troop of ex-slaves, best known of the Negro units in the War of Independence, was wiped out at Point Bridge in Westchester County, New York, in a surprise attack (May 14, 1781) by De Lancey's Tories.

FRAUNCES' TAVERN

None gave more notable service to the cause of the colonists than "Black Sam" Fraunces, a West Indian Negro who had migrated to New York, and who in 1762 purchased the "elegant" De

---

[6] *History of the State of New York,* ed Alexander C. Flick, 10 vols (New York, Columbia University Press 1933) IV 15-17.

Lancey mansion on the corner of Broad and Pearl Streets, where he opened a tavern that was to become famous. Fraunces was both a noted patriot and the leading restaurateur of his day. The earliest record of Fraunces appears in an advertisement carried in the New York *Post Boy*, February 5, 1761, in which he introduced himself as a "caterer" who sold delicacies at the sign of the *Masons Arms*, near Bowling Green. He was, it said, supported by the reputation acquired as an "innkeeper in New York since 1755." But it was at *Fraunces' Tavern*, then called the *Queen's Head*, that Fraunces acquired his fame. His inn became the city's social, cultural, and revolutionary center; a rendezvous of rebels, so to speak. The Stamp Act was discussed and attacked there, and there also in 1774 the Sons of Liberty planned and successfully carried out a Tea Party, an affair similar to the Boston incident.

When the Revolutionary War started, Samuel Fraunces left the tavern to the care of his wife and enlisted as a private in Washington's own division. Despite the paucity of records of that time concerning Negroes, it is evident that he performed his duties with distinction, for in July 1782, he received a vote of thanks from Congress and a gratuity of two hundred pounds "in consequence of his generous advances and kindness to American prisoners and secret services." When Washington made his Farewell Address to his officers, December 4, 1783, he chose *Fraunces' Tavern* for the occasion. That same year Washington wrote to Fraunces: "You have invariably through the most trying times maintained a constant friendship and attention to the cause of our Country and its Independence and Freedom." In 1789, when Washington was inaugurated in New York as the first President of the United States, he made Fraunces steward of his household.

PRETTY PHOEBE

Bright as Samuel Fraunces' career was in Revolutionary annals, his daughter, young and pretty Phoebe, eclipsed his service to the country. A dramatic deed has won her the place of a heroine in American history. It was she who saved George Washington from an attack upon his life, which, had it been successful, would have been a "fatal stroke to this country." Dr Solomon Drowne, who was a surgeon in the Continental Army then stationed at the General

Hospital at Chambers Street, wrote a detailed account of this affair to his sister in Providence, R.I., June 24, 1776.

Phoebe, as Drowne relates, was Washington's housekeeper. At the outbreak of the Revolution she was in charge of the Mortier House on Richmond Hill, then a suburb of New York City. The mansion had been converted into a temporary headquarters for the commander-in-chief. There Phoebe learned of the plan to assassinate Washington from Thomas Hickey who had been chosen to commit the act. Posing as a British deserter, Hickey had managed to become a member of Washington's bodyguard, but made the mistake of falling in love with Phoebe and confiding the details of the plot to her. The royalist Governor Tryon of New York, who had fled and sought refuge aboard the English warship *Asia,* then anchored in the harbor, had instigated the plot in which, with the aid of friends on shore, he planned to murder Washington, General Putnam, and several other high officers. While Hickey was carrying out his part, the city was to be set afire, the cannons spiked, troops from warships landed in the city, and the British soldiers in the outlying sections were to attack the bewildered colonists.

Hickey made his first moves in accordance with this plan. Feeling that he had won Phoebe's love, he gave her a dish of poisoned peas to serve to Washington. Phoebe, in placing the plate before the general, whispered to him the nature of its contents. Washington threw the peas through the window, where chickens feeding in the yard below picked them up and fell dead. Hickey confessed and was hanged on June 28, 1776, at the corner of Grand and Christie Streets, in the presence of twenty thousand people. "For this measureless service," the American Scenic and Historical Society, in its *Retrospect* to the New York Chamber of Commerce in 1901, asked belatedly, "Should not true Phoebe some day have a tablet on the wall of her father's tavern?" Although *Fraunces' Tavern* remains the oldest historic landmark in the City of New York, there still is no tablet to Phoebe on its rough walls.

WASHINGTON'S EX-SLAVE

Something of the affection that George Washington inspired in Negroes is suggested by De Voe in his *Market Book.* He met a tradesman, Eliphalet Wheeler, who had a place of business on Broadway near Chambers Street, and who had told him about "a most remarkable colored woman," Mary Simpson, who, after having been freed by her master, Washington, was generally known as Mary Washington. Upon receiving her freedom she had supported herself by taking in washing, supplementing this income by the proceeds from a tiny basement store where, along with her own pastries and sweetmeats, she sold butter, eggs, and milk. Ever devoted to her beloved hero and ex-master she faithfully celebrated his birthday every year. She prepared an enormous "Washington cake," a great quantity of punch, and large pots of hot coffee. Then gracing the head of the table with a small leather trunk initialed "G.W." with brass-headed nails, and a large portrait of Washington, both of which he had given her, she played hostess to a continuous flow of patriotic visitors. She did this every year until her death, often explaining that she "was fearful that if she did not keep up the day with her display, Washington would soon be forgotten."

BLACK REFUGEE

During the Revolutionary War there were many colonists in New York who either attempted to refrain from participating, or who openly took the royalist side in the conflict. They clung to the "mother country," refusing to ally themselves with their fellow colonists in revolt. When the war was over they found themselves in a hopeless minority subject to humiliations at the hands of the victorious republicans. Rather than live under these conditions many returned to England or migrated to Canada. More than twelve thousand left New York at this time; some three thousand Negroes, both slaves and freedmen, were included in this exodus.[7] Many of them were taken to Nova Scotia and were settled there in a colony known as *Black Town,* at Port Roseway, Canada. Numbers of Negroes, slaves to Americans, escaped with the refugees despite the terms agreed upon by Washington and the English, that "any Negroes or other property of the American inhabitants" would not be permitted to leave with the British.[8] But according to eyewitnesses the blacks fairly swarmed on board the departing ships and could

---

[7] *History of the State of New York,* Flick IV 264-267.
[8] *Writings of George Washington,* ed Worthington Chauncey Ford, 14 vols (New York, G. P. Putnam's Sons 1891) X 244-247.

not be distinguished from the black servants of the British and refugee families.

How these blacks fared after they left New York few historians have bothered to investigate. But one of the Negroes who departed with the English later acquired a reputation as a skilled boxer and instructor in London. He was Bill Richmond, the world's first noted Negro pugilist. When the American Revolution broke out he had been a slave to the Duke of Northumberland who, at the time, lived on Staten Island. Richmond left the city with his master, and was placed in an English school where he received a "tolerably good education." He entered the prize ring at the age of forty-two and thrashed every opponent who stood up to him in his march to fame, finally earning a match with the greatest bare-knuckle fighter of all time, Tom Cribb. He met the Englishman, October 2, 1805, at Hailsham, in Sussex, where he lost after an hour and thirty minutes of bruising battle. Despite his defeat, Richmond's reputation as a gentleman and as a skilled boxer was such that he was able to conduct a successful inn, known as the *Horse and Dolphin,* and a boxing academy at the Royal Tennis Court for the nobility and gentry, where one of his patrons was the poet, Lord Byron. The "Black Terror," as Richmond was dubbed in the ring, died December 28, 1829, without ever having fought a battle in his native land.

JACKSON WHITES

The evacuation brought into prominence one of the most infamous aspects of the British occupation of New York, an aspect which spelled a curious destiny for an unwanted and despised group of blacks and whites left behind by the defeated army. Before the close of the war, some three thousand white women were brought from England to New York for the use of the British soldiers and the Hessian mercenaries stationed here. One Jackson, an agent for the British government in this traffic, had snatched these women from the brothels of Liverpool and other English seaport cities. Respectable working girls and housewives were also among those shanghaied and brought to New York in a number of ships, one of which was lost in a hurricane. Jackson, loath to lose the money these additional women would have brought and fearing that his contract might be canceled, sent a ship to the nearest English colony in the West Indies, and brought back a shipload of Negro women. On their arrival they were domiciled—with the white women—in Lispenard Meadows, a collection of miserable huts surrounded by a rudely built stockade.[9]

The "Meadows" became one of the largest, if inelegant, brothels on the North American continent. Americans were helpless as the floodgates of vice were opened. Low resorts reared their fantastic structures and swarmed with drunken soldiers. The lanes to and from the "Meadows" were shunned by republicans who dared not risk the insults and frenzy of the revelers. Harlots flourished brazenly as these dives prospered. The presence of these women in the "Meadows" was noted in the New York *Royal Gazette,* when several references were made to "Jackson's whites" and to "Jackson's Blacks" to indicate which group of inmates were visited by the soldiery.

Before the British left New York they ordered the women of the "Meadows" freed, but no attempts were made to send them back to their native lands. More than a thousand of these women were driven out of New York City together with an unknown number of stranded Hessians and British deserters. They were driven from town to town, stoned, cursed at, attacked by dogs, until finally they fled to the Ramapo Mountains, where they found a haven among peaceful Indians and runaway slaves.[10]

Years earlier, slaves who had escaped from their Dutch masters and later from their English owners had founded a settlement in these mountains with Indians who had fled the tribal wars. For more than a hundred and fifty years the descendants of these people have lived in this section, intermarried, and remained apart from American life. Today, scattered through the fertile valleys of the Ramapo Mountains of northern New Jersey and lower New York, less than an hour's ride from New York City, they still go their quiet way in a community of more than a thousand inhabitants known as the Jackson Whites.

[9] J. C. Storms, *The Origin of the Jackson—Whites of the Ramapo Mountains* (Park Ridge, N.J., reproduced from typewritten copy 1936) 9-11.
[10] Vineland Training School. Research Department, *The Jackson—Whites (MS): A Study of Racial Degeneracy* (Vineland, N.J. 1911).

The point at which they are mostly concentrated is Ringwood, New Jersey, across the state line from Hillburn, New York, a company town until recently, unconnected with any other place by either railroad or bus line. They live mostly in tar-paper shacks, use kerosene lamps and ancient outhouses, owned by the Ringwood Company. The shacks rent for six dollars a month to those who are working, and one cent to the unemployed. Until 1931 most of them worked in the now abandoned local iron-ore mine owned by the company. They were paid in credits good at the general store, and as in all such towns were hopelessly in debt to the company.

There is little agriculture; some of the women make sewing baskets of maple saplings, and some with the aid of forged adzes make wooden scoops, which they sell to tourists on the State highways. An unlicensed midwife practices in Ringwood; the infant mortality rate is 130 per 1,000. The New York *Telegram* reports: "One in ten has a radio—the old battery sets because there's no electricity. One of fifty has been to a motion picture. None has ever owned a new dress or suit or pair of shoes." In their unique world, during the past century, they had no need for restrictive laws; so marriage became a matter of will. Albert Payson Terhune, himself a resident of the Jackson White area, describes them in his novel, *Treasure* (1926), as "white trash," "degenerate mountaineers," and "blue-eyed niggers." The origin of the Jackson Whites has countless parallels in the United States. The "Brass Ankles," of the southern Atlantic coast, provide the closest resemblance.

These people form a neglected part of America's heritage.

CHAPTER IV

ECHOES OF HAITIAN THUNDER

NEW YORK, 1785-1800.—For several years after the Revolutionary War, this city was the scene of demonstrations celebrating American Independence.[1] Great crowds gathered at Fraunces', Tontines', and at many other taverns, drinking toasts to freedom and to the struggles for liberty in France and Poland. The rejoicing populace paraded about the city, wearing revolutionary cockades of red, white, and blue. French sailors on leave from their ships were greeted by Americans shouting *Vive la Republique!* and singing *Allons, enfants de la patrie*. . . . An eyewitness testified that "people were maddened by impulses of feeling," so moved were they by the successful conclusion of the war.

But in all the festivities Negroes were absent from the banquet tables, although eight in every hundred New Yorkers were black. Many, it is true, had been freed during the war, and others were manumitted by benevolent masters, but they had not secured that measure of freedom for which they had fought side by side with the colonists. A callousness toward blacks generally prevailed which was noticed as late as 1822 when a local paper, referring to a horse race that was to be run at Washington, said: "The bets are immensely heavy. We have heard of one tendered on Sir Charles of 800 Negroes, valued at $300 each!"

Full accounts of the celebrations for the achievement of liberty and for the establishment of the rights of man are to be found

---

[1] John Corre's catering bill for the official celebration of the 10th anniversary of July 4, 1786, rendered to the corporation of the City of New York, was for 100 gallons of punch £75; 130 bottles of wine £32.10; cheese and crackers £20; and 10 pounds' worth of broken and missing wine glasses, tumblers, bowls, decanters, plates, bottles and pewter mugs.

alongside of advertisements offering rewards for runaway blacks in all New York newspapers of the period. Still more ironic was the "Revolution dinner" given by the friends of the French Revolution at the *Crown and Anchor Tavern* as reported by the New York *Advertiser* of September 13, 1791; while slaves hovered over the celebrants, tending their lusty wants, an impassioned plea was made to "unite in promoting freedom and happiness of mankind." Nowhere in this report was mention made of freedom being extended to the Negro.[2]

POLITICAL VAGRANTS

The explanation for this attitude toward black men seems to be found in the fact that the Revolutionary War was fought, primarily, to free the commercial interests who, after securing their own well-being, were not greatly concerned with pressing claims far beyond their own immediate interests. "It is a notorious fact that even in these democratic United States universal suffrage was not dreamed of by the [Founding] Fathers, and the Constitution was so framed as to guard against the untrustworthy vagaries of the vulgar."[3] Not only Negroes but a good many other elements of society as well were left out in the cold. Furthermore, the Revolution was a movement in which the landowners, merchants, and aristocracy, at least at the outset, furnished not only the leadership but the great bulk of the rank and file as well. Since this leadership was largely bourgeois in character, and the Negro was not a member of this class, it was assumed that he did not share in the country's traditions, and he was therefore regarded as falling outside of the white community. But the whole antislavery and humanitarian agitation indicates that there was a growing number of people who felt increasingly the inconsistency between the talk of universal equality and freedom of man and the glaring fact of slavery. "I would never have drawn my sword in the cause of

---

[2] Being white, though, was not always a privilege, for the indentured servants in New York fared almost as badly as the blacks for a time. A petition to free these whites in 1784 failed, though it was extensively circulated. Fifty years after the signing of the Declaration of Independence, Germans and Irishmen were still sold on the auction block in New York.

[3] A letter dated July 21, 1928, from Rupert Emerson, Professor of History, Harvard University, presumably to one of the writers although it is not included in their papers in the Schomburg Collection.—Ed.

America," so great a friend of the American people as Lafayette wrote, "if I could have conceived that thereby I was founding a land of slavery."

MANUMISSION SOCIETY

Nevertheless, the spirit of revolution had aroused a fresh wave of antislavery sentiment throughout the country. In New York, despite opposition, slavery was found to be a repugnant, unprofitable institution. Washington, Jefferson, Madison, and Patrick Henry joined the chorus against it, and made possible the marshaling of a considerable array of forces against slavery. In 1785, two years after the close of the war, the Society for Promoting the Manumission of Slaves and Such of Them as Have Been and May Be Liberated was organized. John Jay was elected president, and Alexander Hamilton, secretary. Defending the rights of blacks and giving them the elements of education were among the general purposes of the society and through its efforts the legislature of New York began to take steps to end slavery.

During the next ten years, the legislature passed a series of laws progressively restricting slavery in the state. In 1795 John Jay, the first president of the Manumission Society, as it was commonly called, became Governor of New York, and slavery was finally doomed. The paradox of slavery in the midst of a people who themselves were crying for *liberty* was best expressed by Jay. In a letter to the legislature he scored those who, while asserting their own right to liberty, considered it consistent to deny freedom to the Negro. "To contend for our own liberty and to deny that blessing to others," he wrote, "involves an inconsistency not to be excused." By 1799 a bill was passed and signed by Jay providing for the final abolition of slavery on July 4, 1827. The passage of this act did not silence the opposition to Negro freedom.

HAITIAN REVOLT

But a momentous event (1791) awakened the proslavery people to the great dream of liberty which persisted in the hearts of black men. In the midst of the Manumission Society's agitation for Negro emancipation and the joyous celebration of American Independence, came startling news from Santo Domingo—the blacks of Haiti were arming! There followed frequent dispatches, each more alarming. The insurgent slaves were setting afire and butchering all white people, according to the reports. Then followed frantic pleas for aid from the whites in Haiti. Furious debates raged in New York's coffee houses and taverns over the slave revolt. Its mighty echoes were heard in the halls of Congress, where hotheads demanded that the United States send an army to crush the revolting blacks. America did not enter the conflict, but ships belonging to private citizens sailed from New York with supplies for the besieged whites.

Few saw any parallel between the revolt in Haiti and the revolutions of Poland and France. Instead, there was little sympathy and much open hostility to the cause of the blacks. Thomas Jefferson, one of the dominant spirits in the making of the Constitution, and today justly regarded as the father of democracy, strongly criticized the Haitian revolt. Jefferson is, curiously, an example of the manner in which leading men permitted their biased attitude towards the blacks to run counter to their progressive principles; and while it is true that Jefferson opposed slavery and slavetrading, he nevertheless supported deportation of free, native-born Negroes, because, as he said, blacks were an inferior people who could not be incorporated into American life.[4] Hugh Brackenbridge, Joel Barlow, Philip Fréneau and other early antislavery writers denounced him for his view. Abbé Gregoire, writing in 1808, omitted his name from the list of antislavery leaders to whom he dedicated his famous book on the intellectual and moral faculties of Negroes.[2]

THE "NEGRO PROBLEM"

The revolutionary struggle in the West Indies forced reconsideration of the whole meaning of American democracy and renewed the battle for the rights of all men. The issue of the Negro's citizenship had to be faced and the future scanned for solutions of the inconsistencies arising from slavery. Bitter legal battles were

[4] *The Writings of Thomas Jefferson*, ed H. A. Washington, 9 vols (New York, Derby and Jackson 1859) I 48-49.

[5] Henri Gregoire, *An Inquiry Concerning the Intellectual and Moral Faculties and Literature of Negroes*, trans D. B. Warden (Brooklyn, N.Y., Thomas Kirk 1810) 44-46; quoted in William Frederick Poole, *Anti-Slavery opinions before the Year 1800* (Cincinnati, Robert Clarke and Co 1873) 31.

fought over the slave trade and slavery. In New York the pro-slavery faction immediately seized on the revolt's unhappy aspects as a pretext to stir up feeling against the emancipation of Negroes. Rutledge of South Carolina, a national figure, flayed the advocates of Negro freedom mercilessly. He drew lurid pictures of black domination and brutality and declared that "this new-fangled French philosophy of liberty and equality" would bring disaster to the country. Dana of Connecticut warned that "French metaphysics of liberty and equality would reproduce here the same scenes as at Santo Domingo."

The "Negro Problem" was catapulted into the public scene as a national issue. Supporters of Negro servitude declared that the American slave insurrections, occurring with increased frequency, were inspired by the West Indian Negroes. For more than thirty years afterward all slave revolts on these shores were attributed to the Haitian blacks. Jefferson, too, was alarmed and uttered this warning: "It is high time we should foresee the bloody scenes which our children certainly, and possibly ourselves . . . will have to wade through, and try to avert them. If something is not done, and soon done, we shall be murderers of our own children." But the ever-present fear of American slave uprisings caused many pro-slavery advocates in Congress to support bills for the prohibition of the American slave trade.

HAITIAN REFUGEES

The proslavery ranks in New York soon received vocal support from a new quarter. For "almost every vessel brought fugitives from the infuriated Negroes in Port-au-Prince, Cape Francois," and other ports of the island. Creole planters, declassé aristocrats, and white slave-owners, fleeing the wrath of their former slaves, arrived in New York City, bringing with them a fierce hostility and a bitter prejudice towards the Negro. The city thronged with people of all shades of color from the French colonies, and took on the appearance of a great cosmopolitan hotel. La mode française disrupted old ways of living; French boarding houses sprang up on every street; Creoles from Haiti proudly flounced through the streets clad richly in West Indian materials; "coal black Negresses," in flowing white dresses and colorful turbans made of muchoir de

madras, strolled with white or mixed Creoles, adding to the pictur-
esqueness of the scene. These people formed a lively contrast to
the dour native Americans and émigrés from old France. White
Creoles, identified by their "ease and elegance," mixed but little
socially with New Yorkers, yet influenced greatly the culture and
thought of the city.

In reality these apparently wealthy folk were a pinch-purse
band, for few had escaped with more than their lives. Their property was now in the hands of their revolted slaves. The number
of refugees who were given aid in the city was estimated at more
than three thousand. Collections were made for them from all
ranks of people. Tragic stories of their plight were told and the
hardest republican hearts were generously softened. The city and
state governments gave land, farms, free transportation, tools, and
provisions to the white refugees to start life anew.

These people, most of whom were royalists, met violent opposition from the revolutionary exiles from old France. Feeling against
them ran so high among the French radicals that when Genet, the
minister of the newly established French Republic, arrived in New
York, he tried to stop the assistance being given to them. Eventually
he had to bow to the popular American opinion. Nevertheless,
desperate clashes were common, for the refugee Creoles, aristocrats,
and former slaveowners were not above plotting against Genet and
the French Republic. They organized their forces into secret societies, planning a return to Santo Domingo to drive out the republicans and to restore slavery. On one occasion they boldly attacked
Hautrieve, the French consul in this city. Genet was also set upon
in the streets during their frequent forays. Americans were soon
drawn into these partisan battles; some, indeed, took an active part
in attacking a delegation of whites, mulattoes, and blacks, official
representatives from the Republic of Haiti en route to France.
With the assistance of local sympathizers, the refugees published
newspapers in which they attacked the antislavery leaders, the
French republicans and the bewildered American government. The
United States, with no official attitude toward the Haitian revolt,
tolerated these papers. For more than fifty years afterward this
country was still in a quandary about Haiti.

PROPAGANDA

Stories of the "horrors of St Domingo" spread by the refugees and their friends stirred up much hatred against Negroes in New York, especially against those who were free, and greatly hampered the abolition struggle and the fight of free Negroes for equal rights. The slaveowners saw their worst dreams realized when reports of the rebellious conduct of American slaves also appeared in the local papers. The New York *Journal and Patriotic Register* of October 16, 1793, contained a typical letter of a South Carolina planter:

> Negroes have become very insolent, in so much that the citizens are alarmed, and the militia keeps a constant guard. It is said that the Saint Domingo Negroes have sown those seeds of revolt, and that a magazine has been attempted to be broken open.

This state of affairs only served to make the life of the slave harsher and that of the free black more restricted. The free Negro had to be especially careful in his dealings with slaves lest he be accused of inciting them to revolt. Every incident of Negro assertion was magnified and became an exhibit for the anti-Negro faction, which used it as an example of "the utter viciousness of the Negro." The question was asked, and even seriously pondered, "Can ladies, nay, can women of any degree contemplate the horrors and degradation which must fall on their own sex . . . in case of a sudden emancipation or of a general rising of the blacks?" The attack was broadened to include advocates of Negro emancipation, and the great French liberals, Lafayette, Abbé Gregoire, and Brissot de Warville, were among those listed as public enemies of the white race, and of white womanhood in particular.

PREJUDICE CRYSTALLIZES

The anti-Negro campaign forced prejudice into the social stream and it spread like a cancer in the large body of New York whites, though slavery as an institution was declining. Prejudice against Negroes as it is known today crystallized at this time, although it had been forming in a somewhat haphazard manner since the English rule of the colonies. Prejudice against a black skin, even if the owner were free, and prejudice against a slave became one and the same thing, most whites looking on one with the same contempt as on the other. This attitude became so pronounced that it excited wonder in many foreign visitors so that hardly a volume was written by them which did not contain some mention of it. Many of the strangers were amused, while others were appalled at the "jealous separation which takes place on all occasions between whites and blacks." The height of paradox was, according to these people, the fact that anyone with the slightest tincture of Negro blood, or tinge of complexion, was not permitted to mingle with white men.

This form of prejudice was early symbolized in New York by installing "Negro pews" in the churches. An attempt to continue the Jim Crowism after death produced "Negro burying grounds." But now even the dead were not allowed to rest, their bodies being exhumed by hoodlums from time to time. Though experiments with human bodies were illegal at this time, the doctors, too, in their zeal to find subjects for experimentation, raided the Negroes' cemetery. In a petition to the city council in 1788, free Negroes complained against the "wanton sallies of excess" in which their deceased friends and relatives were dug up from their graves and "mangled" and "exposed to beasts and birds." The petitioners said they were "well aware of the necessity of physicians and surgeons consulting dead subjects for the benefits of mankind," but these exhumations were conducted without any regard for "decency and propriety." No effective action was taken until whites likewise became victims and an outburst of popular superstitious fear against the dissecting of corpses caused the "doctors' riots."

All contact with blacks on equal terms was considered degrading, and to be avoided under penalty of social ostracism, even violence. If a white person walked arm-in-arm with a Negro on the street he was subject to the roughest sort of treatment. An Englishman visiting New York in this period wrote that he saw a Frenchman showered with brickbats merely for speaking civilly to a Negro woman who worked in the house in which he was lodging. One vicious aspect of this prejudice was the manner in which it reached into the victim's pocket. A traveler, whose feelings were outraged by demonstrations of sheer evil at every turn, said: "A barber of New York, himself a colored man, told me that he dare not shave one of his own race, for fear of losing the custom of the whites." Even the juvenile offenders at the House of Refuge, when ordered to work with Negro boys, did so to their "great horror."

SUCCESS STORY

Not the least of the effects produced by the Haitian upheaval was the emotion which it aroused in New York Negroes. Though they had no press to disseminate information of special interest to themselves, they heard wondrous tales of the bravery and the courage of the black men of Haiti. The manner in which the events reached their ears was simple. Throughout the war many American ships were engaged in trade with the black Republic and its enemies on the Haitian coast. These vessels carried Negro sailors, deck hands, and cooks who must have been the first to bring the thrilling story to eager black listeners. As the war raged on, black survivors of the many punitive massacres found their way to this city by stowing away on these ships. They came bearing tales, like so many glittering gifts, of heroic Christophe, Dessalines, and Toussaint. The American slaves had talks with blacks who passed in and out of New York City with their masters, particularly with those slaves who had been forcibly brought to New York by the white refugees. Newspaper accounts of the conflict, though distorted by their proslavery bias, encouraged Negroes, who made their own interpretations of the barest facts. The important thing was that somewhere black men were fighting for liberty. They were not unmindful, too, of the laws passed by many states to keep the dreaded West Indian Negroes out of the country lest they inspire insurrections. In later years the abolitionist papers helped to keep these scenes constantly alive before them.

Long yearning for a Moses, Negroes found him at last in the distant but heroic figure of Toussaint L'Ouverture, leader of the West Indian revolt. They easily identified themselves with him, for when the ferment began he was merely a trusted fifty-year-old slave on the plantation of M. Bayou, and up to the eve of the revolution he worked, like blacks everywhere in America, at the menial tasks of hoeing cane and grooming horses. With a burning love for his race, Toussaint was shocked into action by the cruelties of the white slaveowners, and joined the ranks of his people. They soon learned that he was upright and wise, and rallied to his side. In spectacular leaps he attained leadership of the rebellion; and with a genius for organizing turned his ragged, roving hordes into an efficient army overnight.

Surrounded by the fleets of vulture nations, Toussaint saw clearly the interests which were at stake. With rare statesmanship he played one power against the other. A decadent Spain, from whom no pledge of freedom for the blacks could be expected, was attacking Haiti from the east. An ambitious England, hand-in-glove with the planters to re-establish slavery, was bringing in her formidable fleet in the west. In the north, a spent France, alone among the nations, proclaimed liberty for the blacks. Toussaint, seeing hope for his race only in resistance, proclaimed Haiti's independence and accepted France's protection at the same time. From that day he became Toussaint L'Ouverture—"The first of the Blacks." His leadership of the West Indian revolt brought supremacy and self-government to the Haitian blacks. Though Toussaint was treacherously arrested and sent to France where he died in a dungeon in 1803, the white slaveowners never regained power.

In American affairs Toussaint's inspired command of the successful Haitian revolt had many important effects. It indirectly forced Napoleon to sell the vast territory of Louisiana to the United States for a trifling sum and it furnished the antislavery movement, as W.E.B. DuBois has said, with an irresistible argument. It was a success story that fired the imagination of the sore-beset blacks and gave them encouragement. More important still, the Haitian revolt gave welcome birth to a race-consciousness among Negroes, who discovered suddenly a new kinship with blacks the world over. As James McCune Smith,[6] one of the outstanding Negro leaders of New York, said in the cold perspective of later years, it created a national Negro movement in the United States, started by Negroes in Pennsylvania and New York, and raised the whole issue to new political levels. Jefferson concurred with this view when he said: "The West Indies appears to have given considerable impulse to the minds of the slaves in . . . the United States."

---

6 James McCune Smith, *A Lecture on the Haytien Revolutions, with a Sketch of the Character of Toussaint L'Ouverture* (New York, published by the Managers of the Colored Orphan Asylum 1841) 28 p.

PASSAGE TO UTOPIA

Some thirteen thousand black Americans, fired by visions of this new and free country as a land of promise, migrated to Haiti. The immediate cause of their migration may have been the interesting fact that one of the articles of the Haitian constitution, while providing for the exclusion of former slaveholding whites, virtually invited "every African, Indian, or their descendants, born in the [American] colonies, or in the foreign countries," to become citizens of Haiti. Charles MacKenzie, the British consul who arrived in Haiti in 1826, reported to his government that American settlers had received land grants from the government. Haiti had become a place of refuge for the oppressed of all countries, he said, adding the "considerable number of emigrants from the United States were by no means deficient in intelligence," though "during the rage for emigration from America to Haiti . . . they came expecting to find a schoolboy's Utopia."

FIRST NEGRO CHURCH

A new assertiveness among the blacks in America was thus born. A most important evidence of this was the revolt in the Church. In Philadelphia, the free Negroes under the leadership of Richard Allen broke away from church control by whites and started a fight against the "Negro pew." In 1796 New York Negroes started an independent church movement—the undefined but important beginnings of a liberation movement which did much to build a foundation for Negro unity in the United States. The "be patient" philosophy, so well exemplified in the then popular *Sermons Addressed to Masters and Servants,* was thrown overboard. Altogether, the events leading up to the church split were to have a far-reaching effect on the blacks of this city.

PETER WILLIAMS

Sometimes the life of an individual is so closely interwoven with a movement that his biography is actually the story of that cause. Such a person was Peter Williams who, as much as any one person, was responsible for the founding of the first Negro church in the city of New York. That he was an unusual character is evident from the fact that a church historian, writing with purely "denominational interest," devoted no less than three chapters of his book to his activities.[7] The earliest record of Williams' life appears in the Old Book of the John Street Methodist Church, the first Methodist Episcopal church in this city, of which he was sexton for seven years. Williams joined the Methodists at a time when their newly-formed church was holding services in a loft on Horse-and-Cart Street. An entry in the church records, May 15, 1778, speaks of "cash paid Peter the sexton from class collections—3-10." Though sexton and later undertaker of this church, Williams was yet a slave belonging to John Aymar, a tobacco dealer. Apparently this did not prevent him from performing his church tasks.

His status remained unchanged until the close of the Revolutionary War, when his master, a known Tory, was obliged to leave the country. Williams, an ardent patriot, wished to remain. A most unusual transaction took place when his owner was disposing of his property. Trustees of the John Street Church, with whom the Negro had developed a warm personal relationship, purchased him upon his promise to repay the amount. The sale of Williams to the Methodist elders is recorded as follows: "1783, June 10. Paid Mr. Aymar for his Negro Peter. . . . 40."

In three years he repaid the money. Final payment appears in the church books. The anonymous elder who made the entry was apparently that long-sought soul of brevity: "By cash received of Peter Williams, in full of all demands, on the 4th of November, 1785. . . . 5." Though Williams had purchased his freedom, the formality of officially recording his manumission was not carried out until October 20, 1796, when he received a certificate of freedom. "And to the last year of his life," relates his son, Peter, "he always spoke of that day as one which gave double joy to his heart, by freeing him from domestic bondage and his native city from foreign enemies."

By this time Williams had left his post as sexton, and with the experience he had acquired working with his former master, the tobacconist, had gone into business on Liberty Street. He prospered and soon bought the house and lot where his business was conducted.

---

[7] Rev. T. B. Wakely, *Lost Chapters Recovered from the Early History of American Methodism* (New York, printed for the author 1858) 438-479.

Throughout this period Williams remained an active member of the John Street Church, which had early devoted itself to saving the souls of Williams' fellows, taking them into the fold with sanctimonious piety. That this fellowship was less than true brotherhood, and in fact condescension, became more and more apparent as the Negro membership grew in numbers as well as in education, spirit, and independence. The color line was drawn in the communion and the baptismal font, and in many lesser but more aggravating ways. To a people who had listened to the slogans of liberty and the doctrines of the rights of man, and who had fought for freedom in the Revolutionary War and believed firmly that equality was to be extended to all Americans, those affronts, coming at a time when blacks were stirred over the West Indian revolt, were not to be borne.

Open rift came in 1795, when a number of Negro members of the John Street Methodist Church, led by Peter Williams, decided to put an end to the many discriminations by holding separate meetings. The final break came three years later, when a lot was purchased on the corner of Church and Leonard Streets, where, in 1800, a building which became known as the African Methodist Episcopal Zion Church was erected. In 1801 the church procured a charter which bore the signatures of Peter Williams, Francis Jacobs, and James Varick who became its first bishop. Henceforth it stood firmly as an independent church.

The movement that caused the Negro membership to leave the John Street Church was not local nor was it confined to a single denomination. It was described as a "grand united Negro movement." Negro Baptists, although they had worshipped with their white brethren in apparent harmony, split from the fold in 1808. The following year the Abyssinian Baptist Church was started by eighteen members in a building on Anthony Street. In 1818 St Philip's Protestant Episcopal Church came into being. Two years later it was incorporated and Peter Williams, Junior, the first Negro to be ordained in the Episcopal Church, became its rector. The Negro Presbyterian Church had its beginning in the autumn of 1821 in a small building on Rose Street with the young Rev. Samuel E. Cornish officiating. Soon every white denomination had a counterpart in black. Though other sects sprang up, including black Jews, by 1845 the popularity of the Negro Methodist churches, of which New York had fifteen, and the Baptist churches, of which there were nine, was unrivaled.

To the Negro his church was more than sectarianism; more, indeed, than religion. It was the center and stronghold of his independent existence; it was a refuge and shelter for the runaway slaves; it furnished a meeting place and a platform for the anti-slavery struggle; it cared for the sick and gave food and shelter to the destitute. Above all, it developed strong and intelligent leaders through whom Negroes of New York learned to stand with confidence, united in a common understanding of their rights. From the day that Peter Williams led the first rebellion against the white churchmen, black church leaders were to influence the thought of Negroes profoundly. This development prepared the way for an organized struggle for the emancipation of the blacks throughout the country.

Inspirational drive was given this movement in 1800, when a Negro slave named Gabriel Prosser led a revolt in Virginia, involving more than a thousand slaves, the reverberations of which were heard in every corner of this city.

BOOK TWO

(1800 – 1865)

CHAPTER V[1]

FREEDOM, AFTER A FASHION

1800-1827.—At the beginning of the nineteenth century, people were absorbed in exploiting the vast resources of the land, in expanding industry and commerce. The newborn Republic had embarked on an era of prosperity. It had also launched a profitable but illegal[2] traffic in slaves, for, with New York slavery doomed,[3] many local masters tried to dispose of their slaves in the reliable markets of the South. To meet this problem the legislature passed a bill prohibiting the shipping of slaves outside the state. But the owners cunningly circumvented the law and the sale of slaves became a bootleg affair. The liberty of the free blacks hung at times by a thread as corrupt public officials aided in the kidnapping of Negroes by slave-trade merchants.[4]

Meanwhile the seizure and illegal enslavement of Negroes was especially protested by the Manumission Society. The American Convention of Abolition Societies, in one of its yearly reports, declared it had received complaints[5] from more than ninety black men who were illegally held in slavery in New York. State efforts to protect free blacks and alleged fugitive slaves were fought and often hamstrung[6] by the South. In 1807 an attempt was made to put an end to the sale of slaves out of the state by requiring resi-

---

[1] "2nd Draft" was written at the top of this chapter, which includes marginal notes and queries, presumably for the preparation of the missing third draft. At the top of the right-hand margin was written and then crossed out: "Check this for more authentic picture—war was just over." In the left-hand margin: "1-Picture of country. 2-Slavery doomed. 3-Selling to South of slaves. 4-Law prohibiting. 5-Bootleg traffic." The marginalia (M) appear in footnotes in the appropriate places.—Ed.

[2] M: "Didn't become illegal till after law was passed."

[3] M: "Why??"

[4] M: "See material on David Ruggles."

[5] M: "Might be wise to examine these complaints if there are any available."

[6] M: "Not clear?"

dents of New York who desired to leave the state, accompanied by their slaves, to prove that they had resided within its boundaries for ten years and had owned the slave for a similar period.

A year later, 1808, Congress enacted the law abolishing the slave trade into the United States.[7] The event was greeted with considerable joy by the black population of the city.[8] In a petition to the Common Council, Peter Williams, "Chairman of a Committee of Africans," declared that slavery was an "impetuous and remorseless monster" through whose "insatiate appetite incalculable numbers of our fellow men have been unhappy victims," and asked that a general day of thanksgiving be appointed. The petition was granted. That rioting was expected is apparent, for the petition also requested "the privilege of employing a sufficient number of officers for the preservation of peace."

FIRST NEGRO ORGANIZATION[9]

The same year (1808) an organization was formed by Peter Williams and others to improve the conditions of Negroes. To this end, it petitioned the legislature for a charter of incorporation. Two years later, March 23, 1810, a charter was granted to the New York African Society for Mutual Relief, whose object was "to raise a fund to be appropriated toward the relief of the widows and orphans of the deceased members." The society's success was reflected by its purchase of a lot on Orange Street (now 42 Baxter Street) and the construction of a building in August 1820 on the site of the society's meetings.[10] It later purchased the property at 27 Greenwich Avenue, the rental of which guaranteed the relief fund. The society soon became an important part of the Negro community and was taken as a model in the formation of other societies, such as the Clarkson Society, the Wilberforce Benevolent Society, the Union Society, and the Woolman Society of Brooklyn. This, the first Negro organization of New York City, is still active.

A check of its membership list reveals several striking facts: between the years 1850 to 1865 no new members were recorded

---

[7] M: "Explain how and why."
[8] M: "See Wilberforce Society."
[9] M: "Law prohibiting Negroes organizing repealed. Start off with why this was necessary."
[10] M: "What did the society do?"

on its books. What role the society played during this period is obscure, as its Negro historian, and a member of the society from 1839 and writing in 1892, John J. Zuille, an active member of the Underground Railroad,[11] skips it completely. What is apparent, however, is that the society, limited[12] to fifty-odd members in 1892, was still carrying on a relief program. More important still is the fact that a Negro business class had emerged as revealed in the society's records.[13]

POLITICAL PAWNS

In the meantime there were certain improvements in the legal and social status of the blacks. In 1809 freedmen were given the right to receive and hold estates. Marriages, past as well as future, between slaves in the state, were declared to be legally valid. The first State Constitution (1777) had already granted the franchise to those free blacks who could satisfy the residence and the property requirements, qualifications which also applied to white voters. At the same time ex-slaves who paid taxes, or owned a "freehold"[14] valued at twenty pounds, or rented a "tenement" at forty shillings a year were permitted to vote.

Though all the duties of citizenship were imposed on the Negro, he enjoyed few of its privileges. For with the growth of the free Negro population, the Jeffersonian Democrats,[15] fearing the existence of an independent Negro vote which would hold the balance of power in a closely contested election, made strenuous efforts to limit the number of Negro voters. They fought with greater zeal when they saw that Negroes favored their bitter rival, the Federalists, who had advocated the emancipation of the blacks; it had

---

[11] M: "Underground R.R." [Scrawled in the top margin-Ed]

[12] M: "Out" [Delete?-Ed]

[13] William Hamilton, the society's first president, was a house carpenter; Henry Sipkins, the first secretary, was a mechanic; Henry Byrnes, Richard Augustus, Alexander Elston, Vince Loveridge, Isaac Gosiah and William Brookes were bootmakers; George de Grasse and Thomas L. Jennings, dealers in real estate; Peter Williams, Sr., E. Vincent and E. Davis, dealers in feed; Henry Scott, a pickle manufacturer; Thomas Boggot, a soap chandler; Cato Alexander, an innkeeper; Philip A. Bell, an editor and publisher; and William Miller, James Varick, Christopher Rush, Peter Williams, Jr., Thomas Paul, Samuel E. Cornish, Theodore S. Wright, John T. Raymond, and Timothy Eato, were ministers and a few of them businessmen.

[14] M: "Footnote 'Freehold.'"

[15] M: "This should be made very clear."

been almost a straight Federalist vote which carried the Emancipation Act in the legislature in 1799.

The Federalists were not abolitionists in the sense that the later antislavery leaders proved to be, however. Almost all the leaders of the Federalist party, as Jay, Hamilton, Clinton, and Duane who were members and even leaders of the Manumission Society, were also owners of slaves. John Jay appears[16] to have spoken their collective mind when he said: "I purchase slaves and manumit them at proper ages and when their faithful services shall have afforded a reasonable retribution."

The Democrats, then called Democratic-Republicans, were a party of the small farmers, tradesmen, mechanics, artisans, and laborers, and regarded the aristocratic Federalists as a party of the wealthy whose interests conflicted with their own. They often clashed over the rights of the Negro and the subject of slavery. The Tammany Society was especially violent in denouncing the Negro as a tool of the aristocrats and as the cause of low wages and long hours, and resorted to terror and violence to drive the blacks away from the polls. General Root, a leading Tammany figure, saw the "dangerous importance of the Negro" and said "a few hundred Negroes of the city of New York, following the train of those who ride in their coaches, and whose shoes and boots they had so often blacked, shall go to the polls of the election and change the political condition of the whole State."

In the struggle to maintain political power, the Federalists found the Negro vote strategically important, while Tammany scoffed that "Federalists with blacks unite." "How important then," exclaimed a Negro orator addressing a Negro audience in 1809, "that we, my countrymen, should unite our efforts with those of our Federal friends."[17] In the elections of 1813 the votes of three hundred Negroes gave the balance of power to the Federalists. Returned to power in 1814, the Democrats continued their attempts to disfranchise Negroes, and in 1821 obtained a partial success. Whereas the first State Constitution in 1777 made no distinction between

---

16 M: "Authority for this."
17 Dixon Ryan Fox, "The Negro Vote in Old New York," *Political Science Quarterly* xxxii No. 2 (1917) 256.
18 M: "Check carefully."

blacks and whites in qualifications for suffrage,[18] the "person of colour" had now to meet a more rigid test as to residence and property holdings. In 1821 only 163 Negroes voted; and three years later the total dropped to fifteen. It was not until 1870, when two-thirds of the states ratified the Fifteenth Amendment, that this basic democratic right was extended equally to Negroes. New York was not, however, one of those states that ratified the amendment.

AFRICAN FREE SCHOOLS

Negroes[19] were determined not to give up the little gains they had made. With help from white friends, they earnestly fostered education which would aid them in their struggle. This served to increase their yearning for freedom. As early as 1704, Elias Neau had given instruction to the slaves,[20] but the first real effort at education for Negroes was made by the Manumission Society in 1786, when it opened African Free School No 1 at 245 William Street, a few doors from Peter Williams' store, with forty pupils of both sexes. The school offered free instruction not only in reading, writing, and the manual and the domestic arts, but also in navigation.

The wide belief that Negroes were incapable of being educated did not pass unchallenged. Many vigorous letters-to-the-editor appeared in the newspapers of the time. This correspondence began to appear as early as 1805, when visitors to the classes and to the commencement exercises of the African School marveled at the progress of the pupils, and its achievements brought it considerable support. When the school building was destroyed by fire in 1814, the City Corporation donated two lots on Williams Street for a new one. With funds contributed by white philanthropists, a brick building to accommodate two hundred pupils was erected and opened the following year. African Free School No 2 was opened in Mulberry Street in May 1820. The trustees of the Manumission Society discriminated between white and black teachers in the matter of pay, however. E.S. Abdy, an English visitor of the period, made special reference to this and spoke of the case of a Negro teacher who received five hundred dollars a year, while his white colleague,

---

[19] M: "Style' [in the right margin at the start of this paragraph—Ed.]
[20] M: "How learning, etc."

"acknowledged to be inferior," received six hundred dollars for identical duties.

When the Manumission Society found it necessary to affiliate the African Free Schools with others controlled by the philanthropic Public School Society in 1834, there were 1,400 registered pupils. The policy of the new administration apparently differed from that of the Manumission Society for most of the Negro teachers were soon discharged and all the Negro schools were reduced to primary grades. The attendance of Negro pupils fell off and it was found necessary to appoint a Negro agent at a salary of $150 a year to solicit pupils when the two "Upper Schools" were opened. John Peterson, who was to become one of the outstanding pioneers in the education of Negroes in this city, was placed in charge of a school for colored monitors.

In 1847 the Society for Promotion of Education Among Colored Children was formed. It established Colored Grammar School No 3 in Thomas Street and No 4 in Center Street. It attempted also to encourage education among Negro adults, and by 1852 had opened evening schools for males and females; it reported an attendance of 319 pupils that year. The view that education was the province of the government rather than of philanthropic individuals and societies brought the work of the Public School Society to a close. In 1853, all the schools, black and white, were brought under the supervision of the Board of Education of the City and County of New York, marking a new page in the education of New York Negroes.

"RAGGING AND BONING"

Despite the special training[21] given the blacks, there was not a single trade in New York in which Negroes were allowed to work beside white people. They were banished to the galleys of menial labor. From 1800 to 1827 a few Negro males were employed as carpenters, mechanics, shopkeepers; but most of them were found to be laborers, seafaring men, coachmen, caterers, butlers, waiters, cooks, and hairdressers. Most of the females were washerwomen, maids, cooks and needle workers. The large mass of unemployed,

---

21 M: "Where were they given special training?"

whose problem was heightened by foreign immigration, were found "ragging and boning."

Perhaps a chief reason why the blacks were given only menial jobs was the violent objection of white workers to Negroes being taught trades, whether they were slaves or freemen.[22] White labor[23] feared competition from this great reservoir of black workers. "When the carpenters struck work at New York," wrote E.S. Abdy, "some of the blacks got work from the masters—an additional reason for jealousy from the mechanics." The wage-earning whites emphasized their fears by heaping abuse upon the whole Negro race, although they barred Negroes from their labor organizations, and thus could hardly hope for their loyalty in the event of a strike. The barriers against Negroes extended to Federal jobs. It was not until March 3, 1825, that the Government permitted Negroes to carry or to handle the mails. So prevalent was color discrimination that public officials openly manifested it in performing their duties. An outraged traveler describes this attitude as expressed by a mayor of New York City:

> A poor fellow applied to the Mayor for a license to act as town carman, producing the requisite certificates of his fitness. The Mayor looked at the signatures, told the man they were satisfactory, but added that he would grant no license to any but a white; and thus the poor man was debarred from obtaining an honest livelihood by his labor, because he was not of the proper colour! . . . The Mayor excused himself, by expressing his fears that a compliance would endanger not only the man's safety but his own. He said the populace would likely pelt him as he walked along the streets, when it became known that he had licensed a black carman.

"A CATHOLIC UNCLE TOM"[24]

New York Negroes, as a whole, were industrious and thrifty and a few made imposing economic gains, despite adverse conditions. Foreign visitors to this city remarked that free Negroes were "as decently dressed and as well-behaved as their skin-proud countrymen." Some Negroes apparently wore unusual costumes, as Henry

---

[22] M: "Should be handled carefully."
[23] M: "At whose instigation? Douglass has something on this."
[24] Henry Binsse, "Pierre Toussaint, a Catholic Uncle Tom" *Historical Records and Studies* XII (1918).

Fearon, an Englishman visiting America in the 1820s, wrote, "One striking feature (of New York) consists in the number of blacks, many of whom are finely dressed, the females very ludicrously so, showing a partiality to white muslin dresses, artificial flowers, and pink shoes." He added, a bit facetiously, that he was unable to so compliment the white women.[25]

One of the more industrious Negroes was Pierre Toussaint, who was the most fashionable coiffeur in the city, and was extolled in many diaries and novels of the time. Mrs Lee, one of his biographers, wrote: "As a hair-dresser for ladies he was unrivalled . . . he had all the custom and patronage of the French families . . . [and] many of the distinguished ladies of the city employed him."[26] A brief resumé of Toussaint's personal history is important here because it reflects the manner in which, under the most trying conditions, some Negroes managed to acquire a measure of affluence.

Toussaint arrived in New York in 1787, the twenty-one-year-old slave of Jean Bérard, a French planter from Santo Domingo, who went back to Santo Domingo to look after his property and never returned. Madame Bérard was left stranded and Toussaint, who was already a popular hairdresser and had even managed to save some money, assumed full responsibility for her and her household. Even after her marriage to a Monsieur Nicolas, a Haitian refugee, he continued to support her.

After Madame Bérard's death, at which time he was given his freedom, Toussaint bought the freedom of his sister, Rosalie, when she wished to be married. In 1811, when Pierre himself planned to marry, he purchased the freedom of a comely slave girl, fifteen-year-old Juliette Noel, and made her his wife. Three years afterward Pierre adopted his sister's child, Euphemia, because of Rosalie's failing health. He educated her in the best manner of the day, engaging music and French instructors. Euphemia died in her early teens and Toussaint, grief-stricken, turned his efforts more and more toward religious and general benevolence.

Catholic church historians of the nineteenth century spoke of Toussaint as "the most conspicuously outstanding Negro Catholic in

---

[25] M: "Far too long."
[26] [Hannah F. S. Lee], *Memoir of Pierre Toussaint* (Boston, Crosby, Nichols and Co. 1854) 34.

the history of New York" and as "God's Image in Ebony." His many generous acts earned him these glowing titles. In response to an appeal on February 28, 1841, by the Monsignor de Forbin-Jasson, Toussaint gave the first subscription, the then imposing sum of one hundred dollars, for the erection of a Roman Catholic church (now St Vincent de Paul's on West 23rd Street) for French-speaking people of New York. He also gave regularly for the support of the Catholic Orphan Asylum for white children. The *Toussaint Papers,* a collection of letters, papers, and documents which he systematically kept during his lifetime, contain many interesting items, among them being four rent receipts for pew No 25 in St Peter's Roman Catholic Church at Barclay Street, of which he was a member; a prospectus for a school for Negro children, which was to be "an English and French school for Young Girls" and to be located on Canal Street; many letters of acknowledgment of sums received by white students in Rome, who were studying for the priesthood; and notes from Negro boys, whose freedom he had bought and whom he had given a start in life. Toussaint died at the age of eighty-seven and was buried, beside his wife, in St Patrick's Cemetery on Mott Street.

TOM MOLINEAUX[27]

In the early part of the last century one Tom Molineaux drifted into this city in search of employment. He obtained a job as porter at the Catharine Market, a place long frequented by Negroes of the sporting world. Here impromptu fights were held between blacks and adventurous sailors. Tom warmed to this environment and soon demonstrated that he was a master with his fists. In time he became the first acknowledged champion of America.[28] Newspaper references to Molineaux as champion first appeared in 1809. His ability to whip anyone in America established, a sea captain dangled before Molineaux's eyes the bait of great sums of money to be won if he went to England. The fighter yielded and worked his way across as a sailor. On his arrival in England he went directly to his compatriot, the Negro Bill Richmond, who became his sponsor and coach.

---

[27] M: "1-Negroes' place in city. 2-Cultural achievement, sports etc. 3-Back to Africa."
[28] M: "Too long!"

America's first bid for a place in the boxing world was made when Molineaux met the famous Britisher, Tom Cribb, December 10, 1810, at Caphorn, near Essex. The Englishman won after forty rounds of grueling battle. The "we wuz robbed" cry, still familiar in sporting circles today, was raised. Tom said afterwards that he would have won if Cribb's second had not bitten his thumb. Following another losing engagement with Cribb, ill-fortune dogged the steps of the black boxer, and he met death by violence in a barracks at Galway, Ireland, August 4, 1818, at the age of thirty-four.

There is considerable speculation as to how Molineaux gained his freedom. Information is scanty because he is believed to have been a runaway slave and as such had to hide his true identity to protect himself against preying kidnapers and zealous officials. In any case, when Molineaux was first seen in New York he was already the master of the city's brawlers. Records indicate that he was born in 1784 at Georgetown, Md, and was reared as a slave on a Virginia plantation. He began fighting at the time the sport was first introduced into America by the sons of the wealthy southern planters. In those days the young men of the well-to-do southern families went to England to acquire a final polish of refinement, and while abroad many acquired a taste for the vigorous sport. On returning to America, they often matched their slaves, and it is possible that Molineaux was one of those early slave-fighters.

BACK-TO-AFRICA SCHEME

What to do with the free Negroes became more and more of a puzzle as their numbers increased and unemployment heightened their plight. The South was afraid of them; the North did not want them;[29] New York tolerated them, hoping some day to be rid of them. It was out of this problem that a plan grew to eliminate free blacks from American life by deporting them to Africa. In 1816 the American Colonization Society was formed with such sponsors as Henry Clay, Andrew Jackson, Judge Bushrod Washington, and Francis Scott Key. Jefferson was one of its chief supporters and became president of its Virginia branch. The belief that blacks could never be incorporated into the life of the American people was so widely held that the society grew from five branches in 1817 to

[29] M: "I think you should show forces at work here. Other view too general."

twenty by 1824; at its high point, the society had one hundred and fifty auxiliaries throughout the country. One of its most active branches was in New York. Among its most powerful backers were the Protestant churchmen, who even disciplined Negro ministers for opposing the colonization plan. The character and aims of its membership were best described by John Quincy Adams:

> There are men of all sorts and descriptions in this society; some exceedingly humane, weak-minded men, who have really no other than the professed objects in view, and who honestly believe them both useful and attainable; some, speculators in official profits and honors, which a colonial establishment would of course produce; some, speculators in political popularity, who think to please the abolitionists by their zeal for emancipation, and the slave-holders by the flattering hope of ridding them of the free colored people at the public expense; lastly, some cunning slave-holders, who see that the plan may be carried far enough to raise the market price of their slaves.[30]

Many of the society's organizers sincerely desired to provide the free blacks with an asylum from oppression, and hoped through them to extend to Africa the blessings of western civilization and Christianity. But despite its widely advertised slogan that it was "an effort for the benefit of the blacks in which all parts of the country could join," the very conflict in interests of its various sponsors doomed it to failure.

Rumors that they were to be forcibly deported aroused widespread opposition among the free Negroes, who regarded themselves as Americans. Most of them were in fact two and three generations removed from Africa, and that continent held no charms for them. They held numerous protest meetings in New York and in other large cities. The Philadelphia meeting in January 1817 assumed the proportions of a national protest demonstration. Delegates from every large northern city were present. John N. Gloucester, a wealthy New Yorker, was appointed to the committee delegated to "open correspondence" with members of Congress. "Without one dissenting voice," resolutions were adopted, one of which characterized the Colonization Society's plan as "the circuitous route . . . to perpetual bondage":

---

[30] Memoirs of John Quincy Adams, ed. Charles Francis Adams, 12 vols. (Philadelphia, J. P. Lippincott and Co. 1875) IV 292.

WHEREAS Our ancestors (not of choice) were the first successful cultivators of the wilds of America, we their descendants feel ourselves entitled to participate in the blessings of her luxuriant soil, which their blood and sweat manured; and that any measure or system of measures, having a tendency to banish us from her bosom, would not only be cruel, but in direct violation of those principles which have been the boast of this republic.

Resolved, That we view with deep abhorrence the unmerited stigma attempted to be cast upon the reputation of the free people of color, by the promoters of this measure, "that they are a dangerous and useless part of the community," when in the state of disfranchisement in which they live, in the hour of danger they ceased to remember their wrongs, and rallied around the standard of their country.

Resolved, That we never will separate ourselves voluntarily from the slave population of this country; they are our brethren by the ties of consanguinity, of suffering, and of wrong; and we feel that there is more virtue in suffering privations with them, than fancied advantages for a season.

Resolved, That without arts, without science, without a proper knowledge of government, to cast upon the savage wilds of Africa the free people of color seems to us the circuitous route through which they must return to perpetual bondage.

The Negro had already chosen the role he wanted to play in American life. In the War of Independence he had fought willingly and bravely in defense of his country.[30] When the call for volunteers was made during the War of 1812, a "citizen of colour" called upon "the people of colour" to contribute their services to work on the fortifications because it "becomes the duty of every colored man... to volunteer" as "our country is now in danger.... Let no man of colour, who is able to go, stay at home." There was a gratifying response. More than a thousand Negroes worked without pay on the Brooklyn defenses. Commander James Lawrence said that "a full half" of his sailors in the victorious battle over the English warship *Hornet* were Negroes. Perry also added his praise for the bravery of the Negro sailors.

---

[31]M: "I think this should come first—then their protest?"

ONE WAY PASSAGE

Weary with the long struggle for freedom, and inspired, no doubt, by the success of the Republic of Haiti, some Negroes were lulled into believing that the colonization plan was a solution of their problems.[32] Two ships were outfitted by the government for the pilgrimage to Africa, one of which, the *Elizabeth*, left New York in February 1820 with eighty-six Negroes, forty of them New Yorkers. A day-to-day account of the voyage was kept by Daniel Coker, a Negro, whose first notation was "Thousands of people, both white and colored,"[33] came to see the ship sail. There were three white agents of the Colonization Society aboard. A convoy ship, the *Cyane*, set sail with the *Elizabeth*, but was soon lost sight of, and was not again seen until the migrants had reached Africa.

When *Elizabeth* was a few days at sea, a dog belonging to one of the Negroes bit a dog belonging to one of the white crew and the owners clashed. Tempers flared. A riot between the white crew and the black passengers was only averted when the captain drew his pistols. "I feared for a few moments," wrote Coker, "that there would have been several deaths." On their arrival in Sierra Leone, after a stormy voyage, one of the first sights that greeted the colonists was a ship with one hundred slaves in irons. Coker says that there was talk of seizing the vessel and freeing the slaves, but nothing further was recorded. His last entry is dated March 30, 1820.

> *We must save the Negroes,*
> *or the Negroes will ruin us.*
>
> —Samuel J. Mills.[34]

Between 1820 and 1860 a total of 10,586 blacks were expatriated, of whom more than six thousand were former slaves. A census of the colony taken in 1843 shows that 2.2 per cent of the colonists were from New York. But the unfavorable climate, the hostile chiefs, the fact that the emigrants were collected without regard to fitness, and the lack of adequate provisions, tools, and other supplies, to-

---

[32] M: "Too long."

[33] Daniel Coker, *Journal of Daniel Coker* (Baltimore, Edward J. Coale 1820) 10.

[34] A member of the American Colonization Society who, in the Society's Fiftieth Anniversary Report, is credited with the above remark.

gether with the promiscuous dumping of free men, newly-freed slaves, and recaptured Africans into a region strange to most of them, made it a hopeless venture. Nevertheless, the colony grew and on August 24, 1847, it became the Republic of Liberia, with the City Monrovia as its capital. Up to this time the colony had been administered by a white governor, appointed by the United States. Today Liberia is an independent republic with friendly relations with the United States.[35]

FIRST NEGRO THEATER[36]

Oblique evidence that Negroes had their roots in this country and had every intention of remaining here is the appearance of a Negro theater in New York at this time, to satisfy the growing cultural needs of the group. The Negro theater was inaugurated in 1821. Its first playhouse was known as the African Grove—sometimes as the Hotel—and was located in the vicinity of Bleecker and Mercer Streets, the section where blacks first owned land in New York. In its brief span from 1821 to 1829 the Negro theater became something of an institution to the black population of the city. Advertisements boasted that "neither time nor expense had been spared in rendering this entertainment agreeable to the ladies and gentlemen of color." A letter written in 1827 by an English visitor to this city, Mrs Anthony Trollope, sheds interesting light on the "Theatre in Mercer Street, in the rear of the 1 mile stone, Broadway":

> There are a great number of Negroes in New York, all free; their emancipation having been completed in 1827. Not even in Philadelphia, where the anti-slavery opinions have been most active and violent, do the blacks appear to wear an air of so much consequence as they do in New York. They have several chapels . . . and a theatre in which none but Negroes perform. At this theatre a gallery is appropriated to such whites as choose to visit it. . . .

---

[35] "The International Commission of Inquiry on Liberian Conditions made public its report today. The report finds that the 'ruling Americo-Liberians have inflicted virtual slavery upon the natives of the interior.' Kidnaping, pawning, fining, raiding, flogging and torture of all kinds are daily cruelties which the tribal Negroes patiently suffer. The 220-page report contains testimony of hundreds of witnesses regarding 'depopulation of whole villages and the wiping out of the men folk among certain tribes through wholesale deportation into forced labor, amounting to slavery'." —New York *Herald Tribune*, January 11, 1931.

[36] M: "This might be included on page 71."

The *National Advocate* of October 27, 1821, had previously noted that a partitioned section at the back of the house was reserved for white persons. In its handbill the company contended that the segregation was practiced because "whites do not know how to conduct themselves at entertainments for ladies and gentlemen of color." In 1829 the city authorities decided to prohibit further performances because of the danger of "civil discord." They referred to the increasing number of assaults on blacks during this period and for this reason were persuaded to close all places where Negroes were known to congregate.

Nevertheless, a number of Negro actors were launched on theatrical careers. One of these was James Hewlett, a native of Long Island, who was the outstanding personality of the African Grove. According to an eyewitness he "evinced a nice discrimination and tact which ought to recommend him to every lover of pure acting." While this praise may have been a shade extravagant, he did become identified with the title role of *Richard III*. Hewlett also wrote and danced the principal role in a Negro ballet which received critical praise in an issue of the *National Advocate* of September 1821.

"AFRICAN ROSCIUS"

Ranking far above early American thespians, black or white, was Ira Frederick Aldridge, who was born in New York in 1807, and who, in the 1850s, was famous in England for his interpretation of the Othello role. There is no record that Aldridge ever performed in the African Grove. The London *Journal* of that period found that "Mr. Aldridge... first caught the contagion of the theatrical malady from having seen (while a mere boy) the play of Pizarro, at a theatre in New York" performed by white people. The most reliable sources seem to indicate that Aldridge became the servant of Edmund Kean, the Shakespearean actor, and accompanied him to Enggland in the early part of the nineteenth century, and later became Kean's protégé. Handbills of that day referred to him as the "African Roscius." In his heyday, Europeans showered all manners of honors upon him.

NEW YORK EMANCIPATION

The high point of this epoch for New York Negroes was Emancipation Day, July 4, 1827. It caused no great stir in the white population, presumably because it had been anticipated since the legislative act of 1799. Most of the local newspapers made no mention of it. An upstate paper, the *Albany Argus and City Gazette* alone, on the morning of the Fourth, printed Governor Tompkins' message, carrying out the act calling for state-wide emancipation. Three days later there appeared in this paper a brief account of a parade and a meeting held by Albany Negroes celebrating the occasion.[37]

New York City Negroes, fully aware of the significance of the event, demonstrated accordingly. Since the Fourth was a Sunday, the celebration took place July 5, 1827, but on Sunday an "Oration" was delivered in the African Zion Church. The Rev. William Hamilton, a Negro said to be the illegitimate son of Alexander Hamilton,[38] was the speaker. For a really colorful and stirring description of the celebration next day, we are indebted to James McCune Smith.[39] In his sketch of the Negro abolitionist, Henry Highland . . . . [At least one page concluding the chapter is missing.—Ed.]

---

[37] M: "Placement?"
[38] M: "Do you have history of this?"
[39] M: "Rephrase."

CHAPTER VI[1]

SLAVERY'S RESIDUE[2]

NEW YORK, 1827-1831.—The Emancipation of New York Negroes did not solve all their problems.[3] Indeed, their plight in many instances became worse, for they were thrown into the world of competition with little training or skill to shift for themselves.[4] Though native-born, they were not so lucky as the white and the Creole refugees of the Haitian Rebellion, who had received land, tools,[5] and transportation at the City's and the State's expense to start life anew. With bitter hatreds and economic sanctions[6] facing them, many dropped to the lower depths of the social scale as a dismal, neglected group; and to exist fell into a life of crime and prostitution. The infamous Five Points Neighborhood, at the intersection which meets at Centre Street, where many of these unhappy people lived, became a symbol of their degradation.

FIVE POINTS NEIGHBORHOOD

The unsavory history[7] of Five Points began about the year 1820, when many of the old tenements of the neighborhood began to crumble, and became unsafe for occupancy. Respectable families had long since abandoned these clapboarded monstrosities for other more desirable parts of Manhattan and "their places were taken for the most part by freed Negro slaves and low-class Irish," who crowded indiscriminately into these old rookeries. By 1840 the dis-

---

[1] M: "2nd Draft."
[2] M: "Chap before speaks of rejoicing of Negroes at Emancipation."
[3] M: "Negative opening."
[4] M: "Sounds like slavery was better for Negroes."
[5] M: "Supplies?"
[6] M: "?"
[7] M: "Reputation?"

trict had become the most dismal slum area in America; its only
rival for vice and filth in that day was Basin Street[8] in New Orleans.
In the colonial days the area was chiefly marsh or swamp land,
which surrounded a large lake, and which was called Kalck Hock
(Chalk Point) Pond by the Dutch; the English called it Fresh
Water Pond, and finally it was named Collect Pond. In the center
of this pond was a little island which the English used as a place
of execution where scores of Negroes were executed after the Slave
Plot of 1741. It was here also that John Fitch sailed an early ex-
perimental steamboat in 1796.

Filling the Collect Pond and draining the surrounding marsh-
lands was begun by the city in 1802 in response to demands by the
unemployed for "bread and work." When completed it marked
the first public improvement in the history of the city. The drive-
way that resulted from this work was called Collect Street and
later it was named Rynders, in honor of the acknowledged king
of the Five Point gangsters, "Captain" Isaiah Rynders, Tammany
boss of the Sixth Ward. For almost fifty years afterward the thor-
oughfare was lined with bawdy houses and saloons, in what was
described as "one of the wickedest sections of the city." It was
finally named Centre Street after the dives had been closed and
rehabilitation of the area begun.

OLD BREWERY

In the wretched days of Five Points, its most notorious building was the Old Brewery, a dilapidated five-story brewing plant
which had been converted into a dwelling in 1837.[9] Its main entrance led into a great room called the Den of Thieves, in which
"more than seventy-five men, women and children, black and white,
made their home, without furniture or conveniences." Many of the
women were prostitutes and entertained their callers in the Den, in
full view of their neighbors. Another chamber of the building was
known as Murderers' Alley, where, as its name suggests, the most
ferocious criminals lived. The building housed more than a thousand persons "almost equally divided among Irish and Negroes,"

---

[8] M: "Source?"
[9] Five Points Mission (by the Ladies of the Mission), *The Old Brewery and
the New Mission House at the Five Points* (New York, Stringer and Townsend 1854)
44-49.

who crowded into some seventy-five makeshift chambers in the upper floors. Most of the blacks lived in the cellar. Miscegenation was the rule; incest not uncommon, and sexual promiscuity a prosaic matter between the races. The place swarmed with thieves, murderers, pickpockets, beggars, harlots, and degenerates of every type.[10] As a consequence murders were committed frequently. For more than fifteen years the Brewery averaged a murder a night, which made it as dangerous for a resident to venture out of his niche as it was for an outsider to enter this lair of cutthroats. "Once when a little girl was stabbed to death," relates Herbert Asbury in *The Gangs of New York,* "after she had been so foolish as to show a penny she had begged, her body lay in a corner for five days before it was finally buried, and then in a shallow grave dug in the floor of the building by the child's mother."

Though travelers to these shores rarely saw the seamy side of New York life, Charles Dickens, in his *American Notes,* mentioned the frightful living conditions of Five Points:

> Open the door of one of these cramped hutches full of sleeping Negroes. Pah! They have a charcoal fire within; there is a smell of singeing clothes, or flesh. . . . Here too are lanes and alleys, paved with mud knee-deep, underground chambers, where they dance and game . . . hideous tenements which take their name from robbery and murder: all that is loathsome, drooping, and decayed is here. . . .

DICKENS' PLACE

A few steps from the Old Brewery was an alley which came to a dead end, known as Cow Bay, which was "the battlefield of the Negroes and police," according to G. G. Foster's *New York By Gas-Light.* Here Negroes formed a large and controlling part of the population and "retained more consistency and force of character" than whites, despite their similar degradation. Many Negroes became housekeepers and landlords, and in one way or another managed to scrape together a good deal of money. Foster noticed that blacks associated upon equal terms with whites of the neighborhood, and that many of them either had white wives or white mistresses, sometimes both.

---

[10] M: "Is this what Emancipation brought for the Negro?"

One of the well-known dance halls of Five Points was in Cow Bay alley; a joint conducted by Pete Williams called "Dickens' Place," so named from the night the famous British author paid a visit there accompanied by two policemen. Pete, a man of varied talents, was described as "a middle-aged well-to-do, coal-black Negro, who made an immense amount of money from the profits of his dance hall," and who was to be found regularly gambling at the roulette tables. He was a passionate lover of the drama, and was in fact a first-rate amateur actor and critic. When there was anything "high" going on in the city's theaters, one was always sure to find Pete there. And there is no doubt that Pete was aggressively partisan in the feud between Forrest and Macready,[11] for it was said: ". . . he of course abominates Macready but 'hollers' on Forrest and goes to his death for 'Our Charlotte' [Cushman] . . . [and] delights in the Ravels and luxuriates over the ballet."

Admittance to Pete's place, a forerunner of the modern black-and-tan cabarets,[12] cost a shilling. Within its large, bare white-washed walls, a Negro band composed of a fiddler, a trumpeter, and a bass player beat out rhythms. An occasional show was performed on a rough platform without curtain or scenery. The visitors were served at little tables by waitresses who sometimes doubled as singers and dancers. The girls, both Negro and white, received no salaries, but were allowed to keep their tips, if any, and were paid a meager commission on all liquor sales; their principal rewards were the excellent opportunities for prostitution and stealing which their employment afforded. From ten to twenty prostitutes[13] were regularly attached to the dance house, and additional women were brought in from the streets when business was exceptionally brisk. Most of the white men who frequented this dive were well-to-do,

---

[11] One of the goriest incidents of the "Native American" movement took place on May 10, 1849, at the Astor Place Opera House. In this episode, known as the Astor Place Riot, true patriots demonstrated in favor of Forrest, the American actor, and against Macready, his English rival. More than two hundred persons were killed or injured before Macready's backers conceded that Forrest was the better actor.

M: "Connect note with Pete rather than 'Native American' movement."

M: "Note this deals with 1,000 people."

[12] Above this line was written "Too long All Negative," presumably referring to the whole paragraph.—Ed.

[13] M: "Prostitutes again."

and no doubt visited Pete's to escape from the puritanic strain[14] of uptown surroundings. The bawdy entertainment, the rowdy singing and dancing, and the frequent brawls, all of which overflowed into the better neighborhoods, occassioned much complaint from respectable citizens. But it is evident that Pete's catered to a "quality trade," for the only time it was closed was when, like the aristocratic establishments, it was shut up during the summer.

FUGITIVE

One of the legendary characters of Five Points was a Negro named Dusty Dustmoor, whose activities have been described by Manual Komroff in *A New York Tempest*. Dusty was the bouncer at Patsy Hearn's, a grogshop situated across from the Old Brewery and known as the Rat Pit. It was one of the lowest dives that ever existed in the city and was the hangout of the most vicious criminals and prostitutes. Its front was innocent enough, with a small bar serving red whiskey, but the back room, which was known as a "Men's sporting parlor," was the scene of cock-fights, boxing, and wrestling matches. This hall seated two hundred men on pine planks which surrounded a pit fifteen feet square. The pit was sunk about two feet below the level of the floor, and the spectators were protected from the violence in its center by a heavy railing on its rim. Almost every night contests of some sort were held here.[15]

Dusty's reputation in this community was identified with his job of preparing rats for the sport of rat killing, in which more than a hundred rats would be dropped into the pit to have their backs broken by terriers—a sport which was by far the most popular at Patsy's joint. The rats were kept in a cellar under the hall, which had a tin-lined pen in which Negro and white youngsters from the neighborhood would empty their large cagelike traps and received a swig of red whiskey for each catch of ten. Dusty was a big, overpowering tough who was a match for rats and rowdies alike. He lived in the Brewery and retained what might loosely

---

[14] "Gentility" was written above "puritanic strain," presumably as a suggested substitute, and "which confined them to the nice" enclosed in parentheses followed by a question mark.—Ed.

[15] "Too much out of key" was written in the right margin towards the end of this paragraph.—Ed.

be called his residence by the sheer strength of his arms. He had cut an opening in an old vat about ten feet wide and through this hole entered his lodging; it contained a mattress and a broken chair, furnishings which placed him in a class of luxury unknown to his neighbors. An old rouser chain, which was once used for stirring hops in the boiling process, was strung across the opening as a sign of ownership. Dusty was no mere penny-snatcher, but a bold runaway slave who, like many others, was banished to this area by fear of the long arm of the law.

BLACKBIRDERS

The unemployment of the large mass of blacks and whites made Five Points possible, but a more important element caused its continuance and shaded its desperation. Dusty was typical of that abandoned lot who lived in the neighborhood—he was constantly plagued by a gang of cutthroats known as the Blackbirders, who were engaged in a sort of hunt in which free Negroes were kidnaped and sold. Not all blacks were as capable in fighting off the Blackbirders as Dusty. So many were snatched from street or home, hustled to a boat at night, and shipped to the South where the lot was sold "as is" for sixty or seventy dollars a head. The Blackbirders themselves never sailed on the water, they merely delivered the "stuff" to the captains and slunk back to the grogshops and the back yards where they lived.

The violence and uncertainty of life produced a desperate crew of Negroes who, as runaway slaves, banded together to fight off the vicious Blackbirders. For weeks on end these Negroes never emerged from their dives, except to steal food, for fear of being snatched.[16] When the Fugitive Slave Law (1850) was enacted, providing that runaway slaves could be brought to court and legally returned to their masters, their vigilance increased, as somebody, perhaps some passing southern gentlemen, might recognize them and cast the net of legal proceedings over their heads. The fear of being returned South never left them, and in time the inmates of Five Points became so formidable as fighters that they certainly feared no palefaced snatchers of dark bodies nor transient Southerners.

---

[16] M: "David Ruggles' experiences."

UNDERGROUND RAILROAD

From the beginning of slavery in New York slaves sought to obtain their freedom by running away; but with state emancipation the thoughts of free[17] Negroes in New York turned to national emancipation of their people, and they beckoned Southern blacks toward greener pastures. Some intrepid ones ventured into the South, urged and assisted slaves to make their escape, guiding them by the North Star. Despite the presence of the slave agents, Blackbirders, corrupt officials, and all who preyed on the runaway, New York became a terminal, or rerouting point, for the famous Underground Railroad, as the system of smuggling Negroes out of the South was known.

The early history of the Underground Railroad is naturally lost in obscurity; in later years the penalties of the Fugitive Slave Law made it dangerous for the participants, hence, as in all matters of this kind, few records were kept. Historians have attempted to piece together the remaining fragments. From mere scraps one may gather that it existed as a sort of informal, cooperative effort, in which Negroes, long before history credits the existence of such organized traffic, assisted their black brothers to escape their white masters. During the dark, silent days of slavery, fugitives hid in swamps or forests for weeks on end, where food and information were brought to them by trusted friends or relatives. Messages were sent and received, and, when it was safe to proceed, they made their way to prearranged hiding places along the route. Those who actively aided these travelers became known as conductors.

HARRIET TUBMAN

One of the boldest and most sagacious conductors was Harriet Tubman, who stands out heroically. She was born a slave in Dorchester County, Maryland, one of eleven children of Benjamin Ross and Harriet Greene, both slaves. At an early age she became the victim of her master's rage, and suffered a skull injury from the impact of a heavy weight that he hurled at her. For the rest of her life Harriet was affected, suffering occasional sleeping spells. In 1849, when she was about twenty-two-years old, she ran away with

---

[17] M: "Conflicting after previous story."

her two brothers. After two days' journey her brothers lost heart and she went on alone. Sleeping days and tramping through woods and over back roads at night she made her way to New York.[18]

In her career as an Underground agent, it has been estimated that Harriet Tubman made more than nineteen trips into the South and assisted more than three hundred slaves—"pieces of living, breathing property"—in making their escape. She was a confidante of John Brown and Wendell Phillips, who relates that the last time he ever saw John Brown was when the latter came to his house and brought Harriet Tubman, saying: "Mr Phillips, I bring you one of the best and bravest persons on this continent—General Tubman, as we call her." She was several times a guest at the home of Ralph Waldo Emerson.[19] Her work was known and feared by the southern slave owners, and at one time there was an aggregate reward of forty thousand dollars offered by Maryland slaveholders for her capture—dead or alive. Because of her daring and experience, she was employed in the secret service of the Union Army during the Civil War.[20] After the war Harriet Tubman established an old folk's home for Negroes on property which William H. Seward had sold her in 1857 near his home at Auburn, New York. She was not idle long for she soon turned her thoughts to the rights of women. When asked if she believed that women should vote, she replied: "I suffered enough to believe it." Harriet Tubman lived to be more than eighty-years old and was strong and vigorous until her death on March 10, 1913.

TERMINALS[21]

The importance of the road in New York City dates from the early nineteenth century. Previous to that, fugitives escaping from the South had been content to settle in Ohio, Pennsylvania, and New Jersey, where large, protective Quaker populations resided. Kidnapers did a flourishing business in selling captured runaways,

---

[18] "Out" was written twice in the right margin of this paragraph and a line drawn through it. In the left margin was written: "No reference to N.Y. Seems there is some reference to her work in N.Y. somewhere."—Ed.

[19] M: "Ref.?"

[20] M: "Nurse also?"

[21] M: "You might mention David Ruggles' house as a terminal."

and also freedmen whom they had seized illegally. New York City, where the Negro abolitionists were particularly active,[22] was an important terminal of the railroad to freedom. Between 1800 and 1830 a continuous stream swelled the city's black population. Many were fugitives from the Gabriel Insurrection of 1800 in Virginia, the Denmark Vesey Uprising of 1822 in South Carolina, the Nat Turner Rebellion of 1831 in Virginia, and many other collective efforts to snatch liberty. New York was the focal point out of which several routes led overland to Philadelphia, New Jersey, Canada, and other sections north, and by boat to New England.

Though Negroes actively aided runaways from the start, there was always necessary aid from sympathetic whites. Not until the publication of Elias Hicks' work on *African Slavery* in 1814 did white cooperation assume positive form. In 1829 a significant boost was given to these activities[23] when the white abolitionist and Quaker, Isaac T. Hopper, who had been active in organizing the Underground Railroad in Philadelphia, moved to New York. Here, with the financial help of Arthur and Lewis Tappan, two of the city's leading merchants, Hopper continued his activities on a larger scale. But until the 1830s white helpers were comparatively few in number.

PRACTICAL ABOLITIONISTS

The Underground Railroad took official shape and substance with the formation of the New York Committee of Vigilance in 1835. Though mentioned but briefly by contemporaries, and then only in the most guarded language, it was one of the most fearless of the antislavery groups, and tirelessly combated the kidnaping of Negroes; abolition shock troops, so to speak. The committee was formed November 20, 1835, after a formal plea had been made to the "Friends of Human Rights" to halt the seizure of free Negroes in New York. It was composed primarily of leading Negro and white citizens. David Ruggles, a Negro, was appointed its director. He "commended" the committee "to the confidence of the people of color" and urged "friends of the colored brethren"

---

[22] A note points out that this information has already been given earlier in the chapter.—Ed.

[23] M: "?"

to aid in the fight to protect "unoffending, defenseless, and endangered persons of color . . . when arrested, under the pretext of being *fugitive slaves.*" That Negroes played a vital part in the activities of the committee is shown by an official reference to "those colored brethren whose financial and organizational cooperation, largely made its work possible." Three of Ruggles' prominent Negro colleagues in this enterprise were Charles B. Ray, Dr. James McCune Smith, and Philip A. Bell, the operator of an employment agency which found work for runaways.

The Vigilance Committee helped runaways to establish themselves, kept a watchful eye out for slave hunters and kidnapers, provided transportation, and furnished legal aid for Negroes tried in court as runaways. After a brief stay in the city, most of the fugitives were sent by water to Boston and Providence, and those who went northward were put on through trains to Syracuse, another important depot. At other times they went on foot to Albany and Rochester. From these places escape to Canada could be more easily and safely effected. The Vigilance Committee reported that in this way 366 fugitives had been given assistance in 1837. Although the Vigilance Committee had originally been formed "to protect persons of colour" from kidnapers, its records only vaguely implied its activity in the allied abolitionist field, the Underground Railroad; its published reports refer to the committee as "practical abolitionists," a name which was eventually to distinguish them from the moralists, the humanitarians, and the theorists.

FREDERICK DOUGLASS

One of those aided in his flight from slavery was Frederick Douglass. Born in a little town called Tuckahoe County on the Eastern Shore of Maryland in the month of February 1817,[24] he arrived in New York in 1838 a penniless fugitive. He was sheltered in the home of David Ruggles at No. 67 Lispenard Street, where he married Anna Murray, a free woman of Baltimore, after which he left with his bride by the Underground Railroad for New Bedford, Mass. From this union there were five children. His first wife, according to his daughter, Rosetta Sprague, "took a lively

---

[24] The exact date of Douglass' birth is unknown, even though he himself made a diligent search to ascertain the day.

interest in every phase of the Anti-Slavery movement." In a letter to his former Master, Thomas Auld, Douglass wrote: "Instead of finding my companion [wife] a burden she is truly a helpmeet." Anna Douglass died in 1861 in Washington of paralysis.[25]

CHURCH MILITANT[26]

The protective cloak for most of these underground activities was the Negro church, which in a sense was the backbone of the movement. It is safe to say[27] that one time or another before national emancipation, most Negro churches in the city were stations of the Underground Railroad and many Negro ministers conductors. Each church had its Dorcas Society, which was ostensibly a welfare group, but which was in fact an auxiliary of the Vigilance Committee, and as such gathered the necessary clothing and food for the passing runaway. Militantly antislavery, the Negro church was a source of constant embarrassment to the chaste white Fathers, because it had become the center not alone of the Negro's religious life, but also of his social and political life.[28] The period (1827 to 1860) is easily the most important in the history of the Negro church in New York. Because of its vital participation in the stern affairs of the black man's life, it became during this epoch a permanent, powerful institution with a definite field of service to its own members. And in this respect it supplemented and reinforced the work of the many lay organizations.

AGENT AT 67 LISPENARD ST

Before he started his activities as an agent for the Underground Railroad, David Ruggles had been a freedman in Norwich, Conn., and had migrated to the city in the early 1830s where he went into business. He is listed in Longworth's *New York Directory* for 1834-35 as "D. Ruggles. Books, 67 Lispenard." The scope of his work is suggested by his advertisement which appeared in the New York *Emancipator,* November 24, 1835:

---

[25] This paragraph has a line drawn through it with "Out" written above.—Ed.

[26] The opening of this paragraph has the following marginal note: "Put up front."—Ed.

[27] M: "Source?"

[28] M: "Were not white churches, too, inclined to antislavery sentiment?"

> Agency Office, 67 Lispenard Street, New York—The friends
> of Human rights are respectfully informed that in consequence
> of the destruction of my books, pamphlets, and stationery by
> fire, I am compelled for the present to discontinue the sale of
> books and the circulating library, but will abide in the same
> place, and continue my agency for all Anti-Slavery Publica-
> tions.[29]

Ruggles' broad interests extended to other fields, as is shown by
a December issue of the *Emancipator,* in which he advertised for
colored lads to learn the tanning business. This may well have
been just another blind for his underground activities. He continued his agency and is cryptically classified in the 1836-7 *Directory*
as "Agent-165 Chapel." In 1838, "because Negroes were not given
free privileges in the libraries of New York," he opened "a reading
room for the exclusive use of blacks." The *Directory* of 1838-9-40
bears evidence of this. It lists "David Ruggles (colored)" as having
a "reading room, 36 Lispenard, corner Church Street." In the next
issue, 1841-42, he is listed as "Editor, 62 Leonard St."

So effective was his work as a member of the Vigilance Committee that a punitive attempt was made to steal and sell him into
slavery, although he was then well over sixty-five years old and a
bad bargain as chattel. In the 1837 report of the Vigilance Committee, previously mentioned, an account of the attempted kidnapping, which occurred January 4, 1836, is recorded under Ruggles' signature. In the early hours of the morning, according to
his story, he was awakened by the sound of insistent knocking on
the door of the house in which he boarded. The caller, after trying
for some time to evade Ruggles' inquiries concerning the untimely
disturbance,[30] said he was "Mr Nash," and had come on business
of urgent importance. Ruggles refused to open the door, and Nash
went off cursing to get authority from the high constable to break
in. Returning a short time later with others, he battered down the
door, but when Nash and his gang rushed into Ruggles' room, they
found that the colored gentleman had made himself exceedingly
scarce; a fact which so enraged the intruders that they assaulted
the defenseless landlady to force her to disclose Ruggles' where-

---

[29] M: "Burned by proslavery mob."
[30] M: "Style."

abouts. Her brother Michaels came to her rescue, an impertinence for which he was promptly dragged to jail. The frustrated Nash was, in fact, able to produce a writ from High Constable Hays empowering him to seize Ruggles as a fugitive slave. The incident ended with inconvenience only to Mr Michaels.[31]

HENRY HIGHLAND GARNET [32]

It is obviously impossible to include in this story the hundreds who played important roles in the development of the underground system as many names were lost in protective silence. Prominent among the names that do remain, besides Ruggles and Hopper, are the Negroes, John J. Zuille, Henry Highland Garnet and Samuel Ringgold Ward; and their white comrades, Gerrit Smith and Arthur and Lewis Tappan. In this group of "practical abolitionists," Garnet was the most passionate in his hatred of slavery, and no doubt was the inspirational force in their activities. This feeling was instilled in him by his family's troubles, as its members, too, had had vivid experience with kidnappers.

In 1829 the Blackbirders broke into his father's house while Henry, yet a lad, was at sea. They seized his sister, Eliza, as a fugitive slave; the elder Garnet escaped by leaping from the roof of their two-story house and his mother quickly found refuge with a kindly white grocer. The Blackbirders were thwarted, however, for the case was tried in court through efforts of abolitionists, and Eliza was freed. Nevertheless, when the seafaring Henry returned shortly after these events, he became so enraged that he purchased a knife and dashed up Broadway in a menacing hunt for the kidnapers. Friends had to hurry him off to Jericho, Long Island, to save his life. It was here that he had the good fortune to meet Elias Hicks, the veteran Quaker abolitionist, and a warm friendship resulted. Garnet returned to the city a constructive abolitionist.

The Garnet family had, in fact, arrived in New York five years before as runaways from New Market, Maryland. His father immediately began to work at his trade as a shoemaker and young Henry was placed in the African Free School, No 1, where he became a classmate of Rev Samuel Ringgold Ward, Rev Alexander

[31] M: "How about landlady?"
[32] M: "Check."

Crummell, Dr James McCune Smith, Prof Charles L. Reason, Patrick Reason, the engraver, and Ira Aldridge, the actor. In 1828 his studies were interrupted when he made two voyages to Cuba as a cabin boy. Two years later he suffered an injury while working as a farm laborer which caused the loss of a leg. He returned to his studies and prepared for the ministry, entering the Canaan Academy at Canaan, New Hampshire, in 1835. Prejudice against the education of Negroes was so great in this rural town that shortly after Garnet arrived with his two companions, Alexander Crummell and Thomas S. Sydney, the academy was destroyed by an infuriated mob. He finally completed his studies at Oneida Institute.

Garnet entered public life early. Prior to his graduation in 1840, he made his maiden address before the annual meeting of the American Anti-Slavery Society. In 1842 he was licensed to preach and was given the Liberty Street Presbyterian Church in Troy, New York, as his charge. Later he became pastor of the Shiloh Presbyterian Church in New York City, a pastorate he held for more than forty years. During his entire career Garnet agitated constantly for militant action. At the National Convention of Negro Citizens, held in Buffalo, New York, in 1843, he alarmed the fainthearted when he exclaimed:

> Brethren, arise, arise! Strike for your lives and liberties. Now is the day and the hour. Let every slave throughout the land do this, and the days of slavery are numbered. You cannot be more oppressed than you have been—you cannot suffer greater cruelties than you have already. Rather die freemen than live to be slaves. Remember that you are four Millions!

EMERGENCE OF NEGRO PRESS

Moving along under tremendous momentum at this time, 1827,[33] · the American Colonization Society was making many new and important converts to its plan to eliminate the free Negroes from American life. Its organized campaign, making use of churches and newspapers, even won over some friends of the Negro.[34] The society's scheme loomed alarming by dark. But Negroes were faced with fighting more than propaganda; indeed, the foe was now the

---

[33] A line links this date to the previous one—1843—given above.—Ed.

[34] M: "Won some Negroes, too?"

prosperity of a feudal South[35] whose economy needed slaves to survive. The industrial development in the North had increased the need for cotton, and New York merchants found in southern plantations a lucrative investment for their capital. They were therefore anxious to remove any threat to their gains, which free Negroes had traditionally provided. The Colonization Society's ranks were swelled by these forces; in fact, the society was mainly composed of these mercantile forces in the North. Worse still, the political life of the nation was greatly influenced by the slave interests; in New York the Federalist power had waned and antislavery sentiment was at a low ebb. Negroes saw the immediate need for organizing public opinion against slavery to force action for its destruction, but few would listen to their pleas, few periodicals would print their speeches or announce their mass meetings. A Negro newspaper was therefore a necessity, as they saw it.

FREEDOM'S JOURNAL

The first Negro newspaper in the United States made its appearance in New York City, March 20, 1827—the same year that New York State abolished slavery, four years before William Lloyd Garrison published the *Liberator,* and six years before the organization of the American Anti-Slavery Society. The paper was named *Freedom's Journal,* and under its first editors, Samuel E. Cornish and John B. Russwurm,[36] it was in every sense an organ of propaganda which fought to end slavery and to secure citizenship for the Negro. Among its contributors were James Varick, Richard Allen, Peter Williams and David Walker.

Though *Freedom's Journal* was in a very special sense a "race paper," it also advocated the unity of Negroes and whites, the universal welfare of mankind, and the elevation of all races and people. Cornish, its leading spirit, explained that it was only a "strange necessity" that forced the editors to emphasize the racial aspects of the Negro's problems. The aim of these leaders, as they themselves expressed it, was "to hook together by one solid chain,

[35] M: "Foe = prosperity? Foe = feudal South?"

[36] John B. Russwurm, a native of Jamaica, B.W.I., was the first Negro graduate from a college in the United States. He was a student at Bowdoin College from which he received a degree in 1826.

the whole free population so as to make them think, and feel, and act, as one solid body, devoted to education and improvement."

Soon after the emergence of this periodical, numbers of other papers sprang into existence, all in a fighting fury for the over-throw of slavery. In the period between the founding of *Freedom's Journal* and the signing of the Emancipation Proclamation, some two dozen newspapers were published by Negroes in various north-ern states; of these papers, twelve appeared in New York State, of which eight were in New York City. One of the most articulate papers was the *North Star,* which was first issued in 1847 in Roch-ester, New York, by Frederick Douglass and his two sons. As one of the more advanced papers, it boasted of correspondents in Europe, the West Indies, and throughout America. Its readers were both white and Negro. When its editor-proprietor rose to national prom-inence its name was changed to *Frederick Douglass' Paper,* and as such it had increased prestige and influence.

Between 1848 and 1861 Negro newspapers came and went, but most profound and lasting in their effect were *Freedom's Journal,* the *North Star,* the *Impartial Citizen,* the *Colored Man's Journal,* and the *Anglo-African* magazine. These papers centered their at-tacks principally against the colonization scheme, and all undemo-cratic repressions and discriminations. They sought also to encom-pass the whole life of the Negro by carrying articles on the history of slavery, the contributions of Africa to world culture, poems by Negro authors, and inspiring essays by Negro leaders. Education was advanced as a cure-all for economic ills. But their most impor-tant contribution was the development of a concrete and uniform antislavery sentiment among Negroes. The result of this agita-tion was early apparent, for the 1830s were marked by the rapid formation of mass organizations to wage war on slavery. It was *Freedom's Journal,* in particular, that called for a national con-vention of the people of color to coordinate Negro forces into such a fight, although Hezkiah Grice, a Baltimore Negro abolitionist, is credited with having suggested holding this meeting.

MASS ACTION

The First Convention of the Colored People of these United States was held in Philadelphia, September 15, 1831, circulars for which were widely distributed in New York. It was apparent from the beginning that there was a strong feeling for the need of unity as the convention was well attended, with all sections of the country represented. The New York delegation included Henry Sipkins, Thomas Hamilton, Thomas L. Jennings, Thomas Downing, and Samuel E. Cornish, who were present to "devise ways and means for the bettering of our condition" and "to somewhat combat the lack of government recognition and equal opportunities." The most distinguished of the white visitors were the Rev R. R. Gurly, Arthur Tappan, Simeon Jocelyn, and William Lloyd Garrison. One of the proposals brought before the convention was the establishment and erection of a college for the proper education of Negro youth, which was to be located in New Haven, Conn. In particular, the convention passed resolutions sharply condemning the American Colonization Society. One of its resolutions concluded: "We claim this country, the place of our birth, *and not Africa* as our mother country and all attempts to send us to Africa we consider as gratuitous and uncalled for." Thus was launched a determined fight of all forces, white and black, against the slavery institution.[37]

---

[37] M: "Material for this chap. should be made from sections Underground Railroad to Mass Action leaving out Old Burney to Blackbirders which only negatives your story, also the different theme contradicting one another."

CHAPTER VII

RADICALS OF COLOR

New York, 1831-1860.—When in 1829 David Walker, a free Negro of some education and travel, published a pamphlet, calling upon the slaves to rise in violence against their masters, the country was alarmed and systematic attempts were made to suppress the pamphlet. The first Negro newspapers, though they were frankly organs of agitation and propaganda, had been calmly received by the pro-slavery public. But an unprecedented stir was caused by *Walker's Appeal in four articles together with a Preamble to the Colored Citizens of the World, but in particular and very expressly to those of the United States of America.*

This seventy-page work analyzed the conditions and problems of Negroes. It ran to three editions, each one more outspoken than the last, and was distributed in all parts of the South, where it caused consternation among the slaveholders. Immediately after its publication two southern states enacted laws prohibiting the circulation of "incendiary" publications and forbidding the teaching of slaves to read and write. *The African Repository,* organ of the American Colonization Society, spoke approvingly of the arrest of four Negroes charged with circulating the "diabolical Boston Pamphlet" in New Orleans. Not even white men were allowed to have it in their possession. Elijah Hinsdale Burritt, (brother of Elihu Burritt, the "learned blacksmith"), who edited a newspaper in Augusta, Georgia, was mobbed and driven from the state in 1830 for having received a package of the pamphlets. The extent of the attention that the *Appeal* received in that day may be estimated from the fact that the Negro newspapers of New York republished it. And it continued to be republished at frequent intervals by various Negro newspapers until 1860.

Little except the barest facts are known about David Walker's life. He was born free in Wilmington, N. C., September 28, 1785, of a free mother and a slave father. Traveling widely in the South, he developed a deep sympathy for the enslaved members of his race. In his reading, which was chiefly history, he sought parallels to the American Negro's situation in the recounting of the enslavement and oppression of other peoples. His first articles appeared in *Freedom's Journal.*

In 1827 Walker moved to Boston where he opened a second-hand clothing business in Brattle Street. He was thus in complete obscurity when the *Appeal* was first published. Many unsuccessful attempts were made by southern authorities to have Walker punished for its publication. When he died mysteriously in 1830, suspicion of assassination arose among the Negro population of Boston and throughout the nation. Henry Highland Garnet, who wrote a brief sketch of his life in 1848, says simply that Walker married a "Miss Eliza—." The only child of the marriage, Edwin G. Walker, born posthumously, was elected to the House of Representatives of the Massachusetts Legislature in 1866.

FALL FROM GRACE

Walker directly addressed the educated and wealthy Negroes, who because of their condition were able to make some progress and to escape much that those less fortunate could not. He reminded this group of its responsibility. Some of them he condemned as being ". . . in league with tyrants," and as receiving " a great portion of their daily bread, from the moneys which they acquired from the blood and tears of their more miserable brethren, whom they scandalously deliver into the hands of our natural enemies."

Walker had touched the core of a growing division of interests among the Negroes, which had led to the suspension of publication of *Freedom's Journal* in 1829. Living in a period of American life when "rugged individualism" was growing into a popular philosophy, some Negroes, no less than other men, were only intent upon their own interests. Russwurm, one of the editors of *Freedom's Journal,* capitulated to the colonization scheme. His action deeply disappointed those who looked to him for leadership. Publication of the paper was suspended for two months. Then it reappeared as *The Rights of All,* with Samuel E. Cornish as editor. Russwurm was sent to Liberia by the Colonization Society, where he was made editor of the *Liberian Herald.* Later he became governor of Cape Palmas, West Africa, leaving no doubt in the minds of American black men that he had betrayed them.

Though in 1830 he delivered the first address by a New York Negro which protested vigorously against the wrongs of his people, Peter Williams, Jr, pastor of St Philip's Protestant Episcopal Church, then on Centre Street, openly broke his ties with the abolition movement under pressure from his white bishop. His formal resignation from the Board of Managers of the New York Anti-Slavery Society appeared in the *African Repository,* the Colonization Society's paper, July 14, 1834, and was addressed "To the Citizens of New York:"

> My Bishop, without giving his opinions on the subject of Abolition, has now advised me, in order that the Church under my care "may be found on the Christian side of meekness, order, and self-sacrifice to the community," to resign connection with the Anti-Slavery Society, and to make public my resignation. . . . By the transaction of last Friday evening, my Church is now closed, and I have been compelled to leave my people. Whether I shall be permitted to return to them again, I cannot say, but whether or not I have the satisfaction of feeling that I have laboured earnestly and sincerely for their temporal and spiritual benefit, and the promotion of the public good . . . Having given this simple and faithful statement of facts; I now, in conformity to the advice of my Bishop, publicly resign my station as a member of the Board of Managers of the Anti-Slavery Society, and of its executive committee, without, however, passing my opinion respecting the principles on which that society is founded.

Peter Williams had bowed to the demands of the white churchmen in order to maintain connection between the black and white branches of the Protestant Episcopal Church. Negro newspapers immediately started an attack upon white Christian leadership.

SOUTHERN CHURCH SECEDES

The coercion used against Peter Williams by the white churchmen was a reflection of the struggle which was raging within the white churches, and which finally culminated in the split of the leading denominations into northern and southern branches, fore-shadowing the crisis of 1860. The manner in which the slavery issue came to a head at the General Conference of the Methodist Episcopal churches in May 1844, held at Baltimore, Md, is typical of its rise in other denominations. The northern delegates had asked that Bishop Andrew, who had come into possession of slaves by inheritance and by marriage, be "respectfully and affectionately re-quested to resign." The case was heatedly debated for more than a week, after which a resolution was offered by a northern delegate that "Whereas, Bishop Andrew has become connected with slavery both by marriage and otherwise . . . it is the sense of this General Conference . . . that he desist from the exercise of his office, so long as this impediment remains." [1]

The measure never reached a vote, but it resulted in a positive declaration by the southern delegates that the action taken in the case of Bishop Andrew and the continual slavery agitation by the northern section of the Church "rendered the continuation of the Conference jurisdiction over the southern area inconsistent with the success of the ministry in the South." Formal steps for the divi-sion of the Methodist Episcopal Church were then begun, and a "Plan of Separation" was adopted and carried out, it is reported, amid great excitement. Thus, the Southern Church seceded from the general church body, foreshadowing the secession of the south-ern states. This split lasted until 1939, a period of almost one hun-dred years, when the followers of John Wesley were finally reunited, doing away with southern and northern divisions, but establishing Negro and white divisions.

The Southern churches remained aggressively proslavery up to the Civil War. The Northern churches attempted to straddle the issue; they were in favor of restricting the slave trade but were silent on the question of abolishing slavery. Under this condition the white churches of New York had no settled policy toward the Negro. All the religious discriminations that had long irked Negroes continued. Separate pews marked "B.M." (black members) re-mained. Many individual churchmen denounced the principle of

<hr>

[1] "The Debates of the General Conference of the Methodist Episcopal Church," comp. by Rev. Luther Lee and Rev. E. Smith, *Journal of the General Conference of the Methodist Episcopal Church 1844.*

slavery, but very few were actual abolitionists. One church historian has said that some ministers of commanding talents and influence, as Henry Ward Beecher and Theodore Parker, were on the side of the abolitionists, but that, generally speaking, the great men and the great churches were enemies of the abolitionists.

ANTISLAVERY AGITATORS

The defections of Peter Williams and John B. Russwurm were keenly felt by the Negro people. Frayed nerves and wounded feelings contributed much toward the severe denunciation of these men. Negroes were not disappointed in all their leaders, however. Men of character, wisdom, and courage soon took the helm and became effective antislavery agitators and leaders. Their activities carried them even beyond the borders of the American Negro world. Some went to England, Germany, France, and Haiti to preach and to kindle antislavery sentiment. The advanced character of their leadership is shown in their attempt to draw the Hungarian revolutionist, Louis Kossuth, into the antislavery ranks. When Kossuth arrived in New York City in 1851, a "deputation of coloured persons" was among the first to meet him with an address of greeting. The Pulszkys, who reported this incident, were part of the Kossuth party traveling in America. They particularly noticed that the New York *Herald* ". . . immediately seized the opportunity for identifying Kossuth with the abolitionists . . . and hinted that he was most heartily received by the Freesoilers and Woolly-heads [Negroes]." They characterized the *Herald* as a paper of the planter South and said:

> It was easy to be seen that the New York *Herald* desired to dam the tide of popular enthusiasm. It is a paper conducted with surprising tact; it has no principles whatever; . . . the Editor, Mr. Gordon Bennett . . . . is a Scotchman, who hates England, and has no love for America . . . His boast is, that he is the enemy of all *isms,* as he calls it; and there are many . . . narrow-minded men in America, who, repeating this slang, think they protest only against mesmerism, socialism, communism and abolitionism not aware that the *Herald* includes in these isms, republicanism, protestantism, and patriotism.[2]

---

[2] Francis and Theresa Pulszky, *Red, White, and Black: Sketches of American Society in the United States* (New York, Redfield 1853) 82.

Most of the New Yorkers who entered the fight for Negro freedom were fairly well-educated, powerful speakers, and intelligent leaders—and as a group, a menace to the established order, and were, in the proslavery view, radicals to be dealt with by rigorous measures of repression and reprisal. The more important of the group were Frederick Douglass, Samuel Ringgold Ward, Henry Highland Garnet, James W.C. Pennington, James McCune Smith, David Ruggles, Samuel E. Cornish, and Theodore S. Wright. Indeed, the most distinguished of them, Frederick Douglass, was the victim not only of verbal denunciation but, according to newspapers of that day, of actual violence.[3]

Douglass was brought to the antislavery movement in the summer of 1841, at a meeting in Nantucket being addressed by William Lloyd Garrison. Someone who had heard of his escape from slavery asked him to speak: "When the young man Douglass closed late in the evening," Parker Pillsbury, an eyewitness, wrote, "none seemed to know or care of the lateness of the hour. The crowd had been wrought up almost to enchantment as he turned over the terrible apocalypse of his experience in slavery." Soon afterwards he accepted a position with the Massachusetts Anti-Slavery Society.

The demands of people to know the whole story of his life made him publish a narrative of it in 1845. He later wrote a moving autobiography entitled, *The Life and Times of Frederick Douglass, Written by Himself.* After the narrative appeared his friends feared his former master would capture him and return him to slavery, and he was persuaded to leave the country. Douglass wisely sailed for England, arriving there at an opportune moment. The great fights for the repeal of the Corn Laws and the dissolution of the union between England and Ireland were on, and he met such men as O'Connell, Cobden, and Disraeli, the chief supporters of these issues. Douglass cherished a particular affection for Daniel O'Connell, orator and leader of the Irish people, and appeared with him on platforms in Ireland and Germany.

Douglass returned to New York in 1847. Feeling the need for a newspaper of his own, he published the *North Star,* with an editorial policy that followed Boston abolitionists like Garrison, who

---

[3] London *Times* June 11, 1850 (quoting a writer of the New York *Globe*)

were opposed to any political action against slavery because they regarded the Constitution as a sinful document which protected the institution. After an association with "practical abolitionists," like David Ruggles, Samuel Ringgold Ward, and Samuel Cornish, Douglass began to look upon the Constitution as "a pure warrant for the abolition of slavery in every State of the Union," and he took the struggle into the political arena. This idea, the central theme of his messages to the Nation during the Civil War, caused him to align himself with the Republican Party, a party in which he came to have unlimited faith during the war period.

SOJOURNER TRUTH

One of the most inspiring of the Negro leaders was Sojourner Truth, called the "Libyan Sibyl" because of her alleged gift of prophecy. She was born a slave in Ulster County, New York, about 1797, and named Isabella. As a youngster, she experienced the ignominy of being sold three times. She bore six children in a slave marriage. In 1827, when the State abolished slavery, Isabella became free and two years later drifted into New York City.

Soon after her arrival, she joined the African Methodist Episcopal Zion Church, where she attended classes for adult ex-slaves. Responding to religious hysteria which engulfed New York at this time, Isabella rose up one night and announced herself to be "Sojourner Truth": the Lord had commanded her, she said, to travel throughout the land to declare Truth. Comely, black, very tall, and of striking figure, she became one of the most effective speakers of the Anti-Slavery Society. Though a fervent antislavery pleader, her appeals also included women's rights, and she later became an important figure in the women's suffrage movement.

Sojourner Truth was a source of inspiration and confidence to the Negro radicals with whom she worked. The white abolitionists were not less impressed. During her preaching tours, she stopped in Northampton, Mass., where she later went to live, and Parker, Whittier, Garrison, and many other noted abolitionists, contributed to a fund to build her a home. After a life well spent in the service of mankind, Sojourner Truth died at Battle Creek, Michigan, November 26, 1883.

ASSOCIATION OF GENTLEMEN

The white citizenry of New York was slow in taking up the struggle to end slavery throughout the United States. Even when the institution was becoming the central issue in American politics, its first steps were timid and uncertain. The Manumission Society, which had worked so effectively to secure the emancipation of New York Negroes, was no longer a force in the antislavery movement. In fact, the society officially ended its activities in 1834 when the African Free Schools, which the society had supported since 1785, were turned over to the city. Arthur Tappan, a leading abolitionist, wrote in later years that the Negro membership of the Vigilance Committee had impatiently accused their white friends of being "idealists" rather than "practical abolitionists." They declared, according to him, "Now, it is time for the white abolitionists to lend their aid," if the battle is to be won.

Shortly after Garrison's *Liberator* had carried the now famous antislavery *Manifesto,* Arthur Tappan and his brother, Lewis, set about forming the American Anti-Slavery Society, with Negro and white members. Though the Tappans undertook this mission with religious zeal, they felt that antislavery sentiment, which was then languishing in New York, could not be firmly welded until the British Government abolished slavery within its dominions. This thought was prevalent among most of the early white abolitionists. The Tappans dropped their activities and permitted interest in the American Anti-Slavery Society to wane. Other members of the society, a number of them wealthy merchants, decided to continue as the Association of Gentlemen, more commonly known as the New York Committee.

For two years (1831-33) the New York Committee carried on as inconspicuously as possible. When, however, George Thompson, a prominent member of London's Wilberforce Society, arrived in this city in 1834, and emancipation in the British West Indies had been won, kindred abolitionists in the United States felt the time to act was ripe. Garrison, who was on a whirlwind tour to organize groups for a national call, returned to New York and urged the influential Tappans to reorganize the New York Anti-Slavery Society.

The society was formed in the face of bitter opposition from the proslavery ranks, an opposition which on occasion broke out in violence. On the evening of the society's first meeting, the doors were suddenly broken open, and in stormed a mob of more than four hundred men. A wretched-looking black man was seized by them and dragged to a bench, upon which he was mounted and installed as "chairman." Amid the derision of these hoodlums, mock resolutions were passed, and the poor black who had thus been handled was insulted and abused for aspiring to be a free man. He was, the accounts say, not without a sense of the ridiculous, for he played his role by "humoring the scene."

"FRIENDS OF IMMEDIATE ABOLITION"

The Tappans accepted Garrison's leadership and then announced a meeting to be held at Clinton Hall, October 2, 1833. On the scheduled night, a mob hostile to the antislavery group gathered before the hall. The abolitionists changed the meeting place to the Chatham Street Chapel, and again formed the New York Anti-Slavery Society. The rage of the mob increased when it found the abolitionists had flown the coop. Unable then to vent its spleen upon the Tappans, the hoodlums withdrew to Tammany Hall, where a formal resolution was passed to wage a fierce battle against the antislavery "fanatics.'

Two months after the formation of the New York group, the first national convention of anti-slavery societies was held at Philadelphia, December 4, 1833. The New York delegation included its two Negro executive members, Samuel E. Cornish and Theodore S. Wright. The convention immediately started formulating a declaration of principles which would embody all the purposes and beliefs of their organization, thenceforth to be known as the American Anti-Slavery Society with its main office in New York City. Its declaration fairly bristled with denunciation of slavery and the colonization scheme:

> But those, for whose emancipation we are striving,—constituting at the present time at least one sixth part of our countrymen,—are recognized by the law, and treated by their fellow-beings, as marketable commodities—as goods and chattels—as brute beasts; are plundered daily of the fruits of their toil with-

out redress; really enjoying no constitutional nor legal protection from licentious and murderous outrages upon their persons; . . . for the crime of having a dark complexion, they suffer the pangs of hunger, the infliction of stripes, and the ignominy of brutal servitude.

We regard, as delusive, cruel, and dangerous, any scheme of expatriation (Colonization Plan) which pretends to aid . . . . in the emancipation of the slaves, or be a substitute for the immediate and total abolition of slavery.

MOB VIOLENCE

This formal denunciation aroused the expected opposition against the "abominable doctrines" of abolitionists. Various groups in the country who espoused the colonization plan immediately attacked the American Anti-Slavery Society as a group of fanatics and traitors. Their wrath was increased by the fact that many such abolitionists as Garrison and Gerritt Smith originally had been members of the Colonization Society. Arthur Tappan's home was stoned by mobs. Many dwellings of Negroes and a Negro school were the targets of the mob's fury. On July 4, 1834, St Philip's Protestant Episcopal Church of which the Rev Peter Williams, Jr, was the pastor, was broken into, and for two hours the mob continued the work of destruction unmolested. In spite of such manifestations, the society, from its offices in Nassau Street, continued to pour out pamphlets, letters, and newspapers.[4]

Meanwhile, southern demands in Congress grew stronger for some more efficient method of Federal assistance in halting the increased activities of the antislavery groups. Petitions urging Congress to abolish slavery within the District of Columbia were gagged by law. Angry proslavery mobs in the South raided post offices and destroyed abolitionists' mail. Postmaster-General Amos Kendall gave orders to the New York postmaster not to handle the mail of the American Anti-Slavery Society. Slavery supporters put pressure on public officials, North and South, to intensify control over abolitionists. Even President Van Buren, in his Congressional message, buck-

---

[4] Robert Everest, an English minister who visited New York City during this period, observed that "the opinions of the abolitionists are only the doctrines of the 'Declaration of Independence,' and the 'Rights of Man,' applied to the case of the Negro."

led under to proslavery demands and condemned the Anti-Slavery Society:

> I must invite your attention to the painful excitement produced in the South by attempts to circulate through the mails inflammatory appeals, addressed to the passions of the slaves, in prints and in various sorts of publications, calculated to stimulate them to insurrection, and produce all the horrors of a servile war.

By 1835 the American Anti-Slavery Society was in full swing with two hundred branches scattered throughout the country. But violence against its members continued. James G. Birney, publisher of the Cincinnati *Philanthropist,* a militant abolition paper, was forced to leave the city in 1835. He came to New York after his press was wrecked and his life threatened. After being forced to leave St Louis for criticizing the burning of a Negro at the stake, Elijah P. Lovejoy, another publisher of abolition fame, was killed by a mob in Alton, Illinois. Casualties in antislavery ranks became more and more frequent. The refusal of the society to participate in any political party, because of its belief that the Constitution supported and protected slavery, led to the charge that its members were disrupters of the Union. Eventually, this very issue was to cause a split in the ranks of the abolitionists themselves.

IMMIGRANT IRISH

The fight for equal rights for free Negroes did not help the Anti-Slavery Society's case with white labor, who saw in Negro emancipation a flood of cheap labor which would tend to lower further the already degraded position of white workers. Particularly antagonistic to Negroes were the newly arrived Irish, the bulk of whom immigrated around 1848 after the famine in Ireland. They had arrived in New York a desperate and despised lot. In their own country they had little or no experience in political responsibility but they were held together by strong religious and nationalistic sentiments. Unlike the German immigrants, who were in the main political refugees with trades, the Irish were mostly peasants without trades or skills.

As Tammany was not long in appreciating the value and numbers of the newcomers, the Irish were greatly to affect the political history of this city and the political fortunes of Tammany Hall, and therefore, also, the life of the Negro. The Irish expressed their hatred of Negroes politically through the Tammany organization, and Tammany became an instrument of oppression to Negroes. The Irish, most of whom were Catholics, had arrived in a predominantly Protestant country, and were subjected to persecution especially between 1851 and 1860, when the "Know Nothing" party flourished in all parts of the United States. The Roman Catholic Church in America was therefore chiefly concerned with fighting for its life and in defending the Catholic Community against sporadic outbursts of prejudice. Individual priests, however, spoke out freely against slavery. But the crux of the problem was that the Irish were thrown into competition for jobs with slaves and free Negroes. Out of a fierce economic struggle came a new enemy of the New York Negroes—these Irishmen who were directly competing with them for bread. These conditions undoubtedly made the New York Irish proslavery despite the appeals sent to them by the Irish patriot, Daniel O'Connell, strongly urging them to support the antislavery cause, and also caused their participation in the bloody Draft Riots in 1863.

JIM CROW

The Colored National Convention held in Rochester, New York, in 1853, recognized this problem and said in one of its resolutions: "Even the intelligent foreigner, who, when cast upon our shores, is at first astonished at not finding us agriculturists, artisans, mediums of traffic—engaged only in a few callings of an elevating character—soon settles down in the false conviction of our incapacity for these pursuits." They boldly proclaimed: "For, with the single exception of the Jews, under the whole heavens, there is not to be found a people pursued with a more relentless prejudice and persecution, than are the Free Colored People of the United States."

Negroes bitterly condemned the Jim Crow "branding" of Negro citizens, a restriction which operated, as they said, in every saloon, church, theatre, school, and even the labor unions, making freedom there impossible for even a moment. Heaped on these insults and humiliations was the fact that the Negroes were not permitted to ride in the street cars in New York, except in certain cars which bore a banner on both sides proclaiming: "Colored People Allowed in This Car."

In 1853 the Sixth Avenue Railway Company (one of the several street railways drawn by horses) was sued by the Rev W. C. Pennington for throwing him from one of their cars. In charging the jury, Judge Glossen ruled that a common carrier had a right to prescribe reasonable rules and regulations for the management of its business. After two hours of deliberation, the jury found a verdict in favor of the company. An end was brought to this particular type of humiliation in 1854 by a plucky Negro woman, Elizabeth Jennings, a teacher in one of the Negro public schools, who on being ordered out of a car clung to her seat until she was dragged away and thrown off. She took her case into the court, with Chester A. Arthur, who later became President of the United States, as one of her lawyers. The court not only awarded her $225 damages, but ruled that the Jim Crow law was unconstitutional.

LIBERTY PARTY

The growing opposition to slavery among the northern industrialists plus the activities of the more practical abolitionists finally led to the formation of the Liberty Party to combat the proslavery politicians of the North. Its supporters had elected Joshua R. Giddings to Congress, and chose James G. Birney as the party's presidential candidate. In the meantime the New York Anti-Slavery Society had split because of the wrangling that arose when Garrison objected to political action. The New York group, which favored political action, split off and formed the American and Foreign Anti-Slavery Society. Garrison, as a representative of the Boston group and of the humanitarians who had led the original antislavery societies, found himself at odds with the political-action group led by Birney, now of New York. Theodore S. Wright was leader of the Negro faction which supported Birney's stand. By 1840 the cleavage was so wide that the story of the next stage of the antislavery movement is no longer the story of the American Anti-Slavery Society alone. But rather it is the story of the Negro's struggle, led by Negroes, and of the great political conflict between the agrarian South and the industrial North.

UNCLE TOM'S CABIN

An event that aided in preparing the public mind for the ending of slavery was the publication of Harriet Beecher Stowe's *Uncle Tom's Cabin* on March 20, 1852, after it had been running serially in the *National Era*. Immediately it hurled this small, pious woman to international fame. No one was more surprised than Mrs Stowe to find herself a leader of radicals.[5] Vainly she waved the white flag, saying that her book was only "the great pacificator" between the North and the South, but the moral indignation it aroused helped to bring on the war. The effect of this work was to awaken the strongest compassion for the Negro slaves and the utmost abhorrence of a system which was grinding them under its heel.

By the summer of 1852, both sides flanked *Uncle Tom's Cabin* in pressing formation. The proslavery newspapers of this city damned it as "a ridiculously extravagant spirit of generalization," and that "her black people" were "too white and her white people too black." The abolitionists greeted it in the manner of Whittier who wrote: "Ten thousand thanks for thy immortal book"; and of Thomas Wentworth Higginson who declared it to be "the most powerful of contemporary fiction and the most efficient . . . . anti-slavery tract(s). . . . This country has heretofore seen no parallel." It was forceful propaganda which caused people to array themselves on one side or the other of the slavery question. A graphic illustration of the public reaction occurred when an envelope was received at the Stowe home, which "contained a Negro's ear, pinned to a bit of card-board. Accompanying this sickening thing were a few words scrawled, which hinted that this was one of the effects of her would-be defense of the 'D—n niggers.'"

This story of slavery received such universal interest that Mrs Stowe was swamped with proposals to dramatize and present her masterpiece on the stage. Violently opposed to the theater as an instrument of the devil, she positively refused to be tempted, but she had neglected to secure the dramatic rights to her work. Immediately many versions were prepared and presented. The first·

---

[5] Vernon Louis Parrington, *Main Currents in American Thought* 3 vols (New York, Harcourt, Brace and World 1930) II 371-378.

in New York was a timid offering by C. W. Taylor in which the names of all the characters with the exception of Uncle Tom were changed, and which had its premiere March 1, 1852, at the Broadway Music Hall. George L. Aiken's version became the most popular one, and Mrs Stowe, heavily veiled, was persuaded to witness it. It is reported that she was shaken to the point of tears at the sight of her characters coming to life before her eyes. This production opened in New York, July 18, 1853, at Purdy's National Theatre, and ran almost daily until April 19, 1854.

Its long and prosperous run was not without considerable excitement. The ill-feeling which so far had only taken the form of heckling was brought to a head when a parquet was installed for colored patrons on August 15, 1853. Laughing derisively at the tender passages and cheering the villain, Simon Legree, the hecklers descended upon Negroes in the audience in a furious attack. The gentlefolk saw their women to their carriages and returned to battle. The riot overflowed the auditorium and spilled into the street and alley. Policemen who rushed to the scene joined in the fracas. This they did with care, however, for they were loathe to risk their jobs by handling too roughly some wealthy and important individual. This meant that only white persons who were poorly dressed could be attacked, as any Negro there might be the servant of some frockcoated protector and champion. The riot ended in the rout of the hecklers, and proved to be a great advertisement for the already well-attended play.

DRED SCOTT

In the midst of heated controversies over slavery, the United States Supreme Court handed down the far-reaching Dred Scott decision in 1857, the culmination of all the legal devices of the proslavery forces to make the slave system secure and permanent. The case arose over Dred Scott, who was a slave in Missouri and whose master had on several occasions taken him into free territory. Back in Missouri, Scott brought suit to gain his liberty on the ground that he had lost his status as a slave through his residence in territory where slavery was prohibited. After nearly ten years of litigation his case reached the Supreme Court where it was finally decided. The decision rendered by Chief Justice Taney not only settled the issue raised by Scott but went far beyond and attempted to make every foot of American soil safe for the slaveholder. It opened up the vast western section to slavery by declaring that Congress had no constitutional authority to abolish slavery in the territories. Its importance to New York was the fact that it dealt a direct and staggering blow to the free Negro population by laying down the doctrine that "the Negro had no rights which the white man was bound to respect."[6]

The Dred Scott decision proved to be the beginning of the end of slavery. But it was only one of the series of events that followed in portentous succession. In 1859 John Brown attempted the daring raid at Harper's Ferry, which served more than any one act to bring to a climax the political and sectional differences between the North and the South. When John Brown was captured and rushed to Charles Town, Virginia, October 25, 1859, and placed on trial for his life, cries of vengeance went up from all the slaveholders, and all who were in any way connected with him were hunted down. Congress appointed an investigating committee.

Brown was found guilty and was executed December 2, 1859. Fourteen days later four of his followers were hanged, and, March 16, 1860, two others, the Negroes, Shields Green and John Copeland, were executed. Of the Negroes who participated in the raid, only Osborn P. Anderson escaped. Dangerfield Newby and Lewis S. Leary were killed at Harper's Ferry. Papers found on Brown involved Frederick Douglass, who fled to Canada and thence to England, just in time to avoid arrest under an order issued by Governor Wise of Virginia.

The executions aroused the whole civilized world against American slavery. Demonstrations and meetings of protest against it were held all over the country. John Brown's deed had awakened the country. "From 1859 to 1860," wrote Douglass, "the whole land rocked with this great controversy."

---

[6] *The Case of Dred Scott in the United States Supreme Court* (New York, The Tribune Association 1860) 9-11.

CHAPTER VIII

THE CIVIL WAR

New York, 1860-1865.—A dismal period in American life set in on the eve of Lincoln's election. Proslavery forces in New York spoke openly of armed resistance at any attempt to end slavery; many in that camp even clamored for the city to secede from the Union in such an eventuality.[1] Lincoln's election, it was said, would "inaugurate a reign of terror, anarchy, and bloodshed without precedent in the annals of civilized nations." The campaign against Lincoln degenerated into frank appeals to prejudice and passion. A typical appeal in James Gordon Bennett's *Herald* was addressed unblushingly to "Irish and German Laborers!":

> If Lincoln is elected today you will have to compete with the labor of four million emancipated Negroes. His election is but the forerunner of an ultimate dissolution of the Union. The North will be flooded with free Negroes, and the labor of the white man will be depreciated and degraded.

In 1860 Lincoln, candidate of the newly formed Republican Party, was elected President. The election was greeted with much joy by the Negroes and the white antislavery leaders of the city who looked forward to a brighter future. William Cullen Bryant declared in the New York *Evening Post,* "The old order of things is passed away, never, let us hope, to return."

NEGROES VOLUNTEER

The news of the bombardment of Fort Sumter on the morning of April 12, 1861, the beginning of the "irrepressible conflict" so

---

[1] Mayor Fernando Wood, a Tammany Democrat, sent a message to the Common Council, January 29, 1861, proposing that New York secede from the Union and become a free city to be called Tri-Insula.

many times prophesied by William H. Seward, was received with mixed feelings in New York. The proslavery group said it was murder. The abolitionist hailed the war and seized the opportunity to demand the freeing of the slaves. A police guard had to be assigned to Henry Ward Beecher, the Brooklyn abolitionist, when he spoke at Cooper Union on the second anniversary of John Brown's death. The war's greatest effect was on the various antislavery factions who came together in a united front.

The arrival of survivors from Fort Sumter was marked by joyous demonstrations by the antislavery forces, and Negro New Yorkers formed a military club and drilled until stopped by the police. They then pleaded with the Government for a chance to do their share of the fighting. Negroes even offered the state, July 26, 1861, three regiments of Negro troops, "their arms, equipment, clothing and pay while in the service would be provided by the colored population of the State." The governor refused the offer, saying he was not authorized to enroll blacks.

The declared objective of the war was "to save the Union," but Negroes and their white friends saw that it would lead to emancipation. Frederick Douglass, one of the first antislavery leaders to see this, more strongly than ever demanded emancipation and urged the enlistment of Negroes. Concerning this he afterwards wrote:

> From the first I reproached the North that they fought the rebels with only one hand, when they might strike effectively with two—that they fought with their soft white hand while they kept their black iron hand chained and helpless behind them—that they fought the effect while they protected the cause, and that the Union cause would never prosper till the war assumed an antislavery attitude and the Negro was enlisted on the Loyal side.

Although leading abolitionists agreed with Douglass and said so in firm and certain terms, the administration leaders and the Union commanders in the field feared his proposal. In New York general sentiment was opposed to it. The opinion was held that such a step would transform the conflict into an abolitionist war and drive the wavering border states into rebellion. Those who bore a tender consideration for the rebels declared that it would exasperate and intensify southern feeling, thus making more difficult the return of amity between the two sections of the country. A few whites even declared that black troops would wilt under fire.

Early defeats of the Union forces spread discontent in the North. The Republican administration became less popular; and New York elected Democrats in the State elections. At the same time the anti-slavery forces were pressing the administration anew for a positive policy on arming the blacks. While the North was gingerly handling this problem, the Confederates were making effective use of Negroes as laborers and soldiers. The New Orleans *Picayune* of February 9, 1862, speaks of "companies of free colored men, all well-drilled, and comfortable uniformed" in the ranks of the southern forces. Horace Greeley's open letter to Lincoln of August 22, 1862, known as "The Prayer of Twenty Millions," berated the administration for catering to the slaveholders and strongly urged cutting off the South's economic power in slaves to end the war. Lincoln was hesitant and wrote to Greeley the now historic letter:

> My paramount object in this struggle is to save the Union, and is not whether to save or destroy slavery. If I could save the Union without freeing any slave, I would do it; if I could save the Union by freeing some and leaving others alone, I would also do that. What I do about slavery and the colored race, I do because I believe it helps to save the Union. . . .

Though many Negroes had volunteered, it was almost two years after the beginning of the war before the administration took its first timid step toward accepting them. Nevertheless, unofficially a number of Negroes had been fighting in the Union armies during these years; certain commanders had been using them on their own initiative. Many others were active throughout the conflict in Union espionage. Negro fugitives were sent back as agents to the South, whence they had fled at the outbreak of hostilities. A southern planter wrote a friend in New York that four of his runaway slaves had returned voluntarily after a spell of "Yankee freedom." But several months later he complained bitterly that the same four had run away again—this time taking with them two hundred other slaves. Attempts at insurrection in Confederate territory were frequent. On one occasion the whites in South Carolina became very suspicious about the increasing number of Negro funerals and trailed a group of mourners to a cemetery where it was discovered that the coffin contained arms which were being removed and hidden in a vault. Nineteen of the most "intelligent" conspirators were executed.

The first official act to enroll black men into the Union forces took place in July 1862 when Congress passed a bill of Senator Preston King, a New York Republican, to accept "Persons of African descent for the purpose of constructing entrenchments, or performing camp service, or any war service for which they may be found competent." Lincoln signed the measure, but not before Senator Davis of Kentucky cried out for the border states, "We will not give our sanction and approval." While it was not a direct order for mustering black troops, it was interpreted as such; the men were to receive ten dollars a month, of which three dollars were to be used for clothing. The pay of the white soldiers was thirteen dollars a month besides clothing.

EMANCIPATION

Shortly after the adoption of Senator King's proposal the movement for recruiting blacks with the status of full soldiers gained momentum. The administration was influenced in this step by two principal factors. In the spring of 1862 the government had made earnest appeals to the border states to favor "compensated emancipation"; they had declined; the alternative, according to Lincoln, was "either surrendering the Union and with it the Constitution, or laying strong hand upon the colored element." Later General Lee's progress towards the capital in the late summer of that year became so threatening that the need for Negro soldiers increased. On September 22, 1862, Lincoln signed the Emancipation Proclamation, effective January 1, 1863, "as a fit and necessary war measure for suppressing said rebellion." It decreed that all persons held as slaves were to be freed and those of suitable condition were to be "received in the armed service of the United States."

New York's Negro population celebrated Lincoln's Proclamation with a great burst of joy. Men, women, and children jammed Cooper Union Hall where they cheered "Lincoln, our native land, the Stars and Stripes, and the abolitionists who for thirty years have operated on the heart of the Nation." Hastily composed poems were read, songs were sung, one of them to the music of "John

Brown's Body." The high point of the celebration came when Henry Highland Garnet formally intoned the Proclamation. "For the purpose of keeping away proslavery white men who might desire to be present and undertake to create a disturbance," admission was charged to the affair. The Proclamation was on the lips of every Negro in the city and was read and acclaimed in the churches. Henry Ward Beecher called it a "redeeming of the Constitution from the refuge of lies and false interpretations."

LINCOLN DEPORTS BLACKS

Strangely enough, the promulgating of the Emancipation Proclamation was followed by a new colonization scheme.[2] This time the plan was not to send Negroes to Africa, but to South America and the West Indies. The *Tribune* of August 14, 1862, quoted Lincoln as saying to a protesting committee of colored men:

> This physical difference [color] is a great disadvantage to us both, as I think your race suffer from your presence. In a word, we suffer on each side. If this is admitted, it affords a reason at least why we should be separated. . . .

Soon afterwards Congress, at Lincoln's urging, voted six hundred thousand dollars as the first installment on the colonization project which was estimated would cost more than twenty million dollars. Lincoln signed a contract with Bernard Kock, a white adventurer, who had secured a lease on the island of Vache, off the coast of Haiti. Kock agreed initially to colonize five thousand Negroes for a compensation of $125,000. The agreement also stipulated that the migrants would be provided comfortable houses, substantial food, garden lots, medical care, schools and churches. For their labor, minors and women were to be paid four dollars and men ten dollars monthly for four years. With a plan to grow cotton there, Kock had little difficulty in interesting capitalists of New York and Boston in this scheme. But after collecting considerable money, Kock turned out to be "an irresponsible and untruthful adventurer." Lincoln cancelled Kock's contract when he discovered

---

[2] John G. Nicolay and John Hay, *Abraham Lincoln, a History.* 10 vols (New York, The Century Co. 1890) VI 354-367. Abraham Lincoln, *Complete Works: Comprising His Speeches, Letters, State Papers and Miscellaneous Writings.* Ed. by John G. Nicolay and John Hay 2 vols (N.Y., The Century Co. 1894) II 477.

that he planned to hand over the Negroes to Captain Semmes, the Confederate privateer, who would return them to slavery in the South.

A new agreement was signed on April 6, 1863, with several reputable business men, and that month the *Ocean Ranger* sailed with the first contingent of between "411 and 453" Negroes, about a third of whom were women and children. More than twenty of them died during the voyage. So great was the haste to get these people out of the country that no houses, hospitals, or other accommodations had been provided. On their arrival, the Negro settlers were forced to erect and live in rude palm-leaf huts. Kock, despite his reputation, had been sent along to govern the colony. Though his authority was nominal, he "put on the air of a petty despot and by neglect and oppression rendered himself so obnoxious to the colonists that they finally drove him from the island." The colony was a miserable failure and many died. D. C. Donnohue, a special agent sent by Lincoln to investigate conditions, arrived December 15, 1863, and found only some three hundred of the colonists alive. Lincoln was forced to bring survivors back to America. They sailed March 4, 1864, aboard the *Marcia C. Day* and arrived in Alexandria, Va., sixteen days later. The bill for Negro deportation was repealed by Congress, July 2, 1864, ending Lincoln's dream of settling Negroes outside the United States.

"NIGGER WAR"

In the meantime the Confederates had made further gains, and the enrollment of Negroes in the Union Army began in earnest. On March 3, 1863, the day after Frederick Douglass had issued his historic call, "Men of color, to arms . . . better even die free than to live slaves!", the Government passed a national conscription law designed to strengthen the Draft Law of the previous year. The next month a troop of Illinois mutinied in protest against the "employment of Negroes as soldiers." It became increasingly apparent, however, that the use of the Negro as a soldier was a necessity.

The enlistment of black men had a decided effect upon the Negro himself and on the Nation generally. More and more, as the war went on, the truth emerged that under the ostensible issue of preserving the Union was the fundamental issue of abolition. White men, who were eager to fight and even to die to the slogan "Save the Union!," were not so moved to sacrifice for the freeing of the slaves. But sentiment for the Negro and his cause was strengthened by the fact that black men were willing to fight and to die, not only to free the slaves but also to save the Union. And by the same fact new strength and dignity were given Negro leaders in the North. They had an unshakable foundation upon which to base further demands and these they continued to make.

Conscription was nowhere popular. In New York City it met with open hostility and violence. It was attacked in forums, in the press, and in the barrooms of the city. It was said that Negro suffrage was being manipulated for Republican Party gains. At the outbreak of the Civil War the investments of New York residents in southern industry amounted to more than two hundred million dollars, a sum the business interests of the city did not wish to lose even for the most patriotic ends. The close economic tie between New York's merchant and banking class and the slaveholders of the South formed a powerful opposition. The wealth of this class gave it considerable control of public opinion, and its views were reflected by most metropolitan newspapers. After a meeting of New York editors on June 3, 1865, the proslavery newspapers began a relentless attack on the conscription law. The *World* said it was "wholly repugnant to the habits and prejudices of our people." The *Daily News* contended it aimed at lessening "the number of Democratic votes at the next election . . . to kill off Democrats, stuff the ballot box with bogus soldiers' votes, and deluge recusant districts with Negro suffrages." The *Journal of Commerce* declared conscription was "murder" and the Government's efforts to suppress slavery were "criminal." The editors of these papers adopted resolutions criticizing the National Government. They opposed any limitations on their "critical attitude," and plainly labeled the conflict a "nigger war."

The Tammany Society, for all its expressed leanings toward loyalty, did not cooperate with the National Administration. Fernando Wood, a Tammany brave and former mayor of New York, called a peace meeting in New York. The Democratic Governor Seymour said on Independence Day, 1863, that "the Democratic organization looks upon this administration as hostile to their rights and liberties."

The match that was to set off the explosion, an explosion that soon became a blazing insurrection, was the exempt clause in the new Draft Law. It provided that any one who paid three hundred dollars, or offered a substitute, was exempt from military service. Naturally the sons of the wealthy families were able to supply substitutes and thus avoid service. Matthew Josephson in *Robber Barons* quotes Judge Thomas Mellon, a typical member of the northern business class, as sternly forbidding one of his sons to enlist even for service behind the lines:

> I had hoped my boy was going to make a smart, intelligent business man and was not such a goose as to be seduced from duty by the declamations of buncombed speeches. It is only the greenhorns who enlist . . . All now stay if they can and go if they must. Those who are able to pay for substitutes do so, and no discredit attaches. In time you will come to understand that a man may be a patriot without risking his own life or sacrificing his health. There are plenty of other lives less valuable of others ready to serve for the love of serving.

From the other side of the tracks, the story of Mrs Malaprop, who had her say on this point, survives to this day:

> "Has your husband gone to the war?" someone asked her.
> "Oh, no; he couldn't go," she replied, "But he sent a prostitute."

DRAFT RIOTS

The first drawings took place, Saturday, July 11, 1863, in the Ninth Congressional District at the corner of Forty-seventh Street and Fourth Avenue. The next morning the names of those chosen were published in the newspapers. Some newspapers utilized this opportunity to make inflammatory comments against the Draft Law. Everywhere groups of men met to discuss the exemption clause. By early Monday morning a mob had gathered in the streets, marched northward to a vacant lot east of Central Park, where it was harangued by agitators. The main body went along Eighth and Ninth Avenues, while small detachments spread into the side streets where they visited factories in an attempt to induce or force other working men to join them in protest.

Furiously pushing, yelling, and milling, the mob stopped and searched streetcars and private carriages, while telegraph poles were shrewdly torn down. It was reported as a solid mass of men, women, and children that completely filled the streets, shouting: "Down with rich men," "Down with the police," and "Down with the draft." Gathering their numbers in a mighty push, the rioters swept into the government draft offices, drove off the police, killed the marshal and several of his aides, and set the building afire. Firemen called to the scene were beaten back. The Superintendent of Police, John A. Kennedy, who was unlucky enough to be in the vicinity, was recognized, beaten, and barely escaped with his life. The mob then attacked a detachment from the Seventh New York Regiment sent to quell it, killed the officers, routed the soldiers and seized their guns.

But the attack was soon diverted to Negroes, for the rioters saw in them the main reason for the enactment of the Draft Law and the war. Dividing into small groups, the rioters surged across Manhattan, hunting down, beating, and hanging every Negro who could be found. The attacks spared neither infants nor old folk. Establishments that employed Negroes were raided and wrecked and blacks were dragged to the streets and beaten or hanged from lampposts. Thompson Street, which seethed with poverty-stricken Negroes, was burned to the ground. The Negro tenements on Sullivan and Roosevelt Streets met the same fate. The mob danced and howled while the store of a German, who traded with Negroes, went up in flames. The police files of the period are revealing:

> 3:15 P.M. From the Twenty-fourth Precinct. Mobs are firing the building on Second Avenue near Twenty-eighth Street. Houses occupied by Negroes, who are fleeing for their lives.
>
> 3:30 P.M. From the Twenty-first Precinct. There is an attack on the colored people on Second Avenue, between Twenty-eighth and Twenty-ninth Street.
>
> 4:00 P.M. The mob has captured some five or six Negroes, and are preparing to hang them; be quick with reinforcements.
>
> 4:30 P.M. From the First Precinct. Riot at Pier 4, North River; they have just killed a Negro there.

In these four frightful days, the police stations proved of little use as refuges to defenseless Negroes, because the police themselves feared for their own lives. When a frightened Negro broke away from his attackers and ran for his life, with no place of safety in view, he headed toward the river, preferring to take his chances in the water rather than face the murderous mob. An investigator of the riots wrote:

> The sight of one in the streets would call forth a halloo as when a fox breaks cover, and away would dash a crowd of men in pursuit. . . . . At one time there lay at the corner of 27th Street and Seventh Avenue the dead body of a Negro stripped nearly naked, and around it a collection of Irishmen dancing and shouting like wild Indians. . . . . The hunt for these poor creatures became so fearful, and the impossibility to protect them in their scattered localities so apparent, that they were received into the police stations. But soon this proved inadequate and they were taken to the arsenal where they could be protected against the mob. Here the poor creatures were gathered by hundreds and slept on the floor and were regularly fed by the authorities.[3]

RAZE COLORED ORPHAN ASYLUM

Violence against individual Negroes was frequent and vicious, but the rioting reached a point of unrivaled savagery when the mob marched on the Colored Orphan Asylum at Fifth Avenue, situated between Forty-third and Forty-fourth streets, just north of the present Public Library. It was a four-story brick structure with two wings of three stories each and housed more than twelve hundred Negro children under the age of twelve. The superintendent and the matrons, who had been watching through hours of terror, managed to barricade the front doors before the rioters arrived. The children had a clear view of all this from the windows of the orphanage. The superintendent, William E. Davis, working hastily with a staff of fifty, stealthily led the children out by the rear door as the mob broke through the front, and they toddled west to Eighth Avenue, where they were hastily packed into a police station. Thomas H. Barnes, who was one of the orphans and the only living person who was an inmate of the institution, says that they saw several Negro victims of the mob hanging from lampposts on their

---

[3] J. T. Headley, *Pen and Pencil Sketches of the Great Riots* (New York, E. B. Treat 1882) 207-209.

way to the police station.[4] For three days and nights the children remained barricaded in the police station, receiving only such food as could be smuggled through by Roman Catholic priests. Finally a regiment of Zouaves arrived, and the little refugees were removed between lines of bristling bayonets to Blackwells Island where they were safely quartered for the next three months. "I wanted to put my arms around those soldiers then and many times since," says Barnes of that day.

The children had barely left when the doors of the Asylum were battered from their hinges and the howling mob poured into the building. The rioters destroyed the furniture with hatchets and axes and killed a little girl who had been overlooked in the hurried exodus and had sought refuge under a bed. After looting the building, even to the taking of the children's toys and trinkets, the mob set it afire in half a dozen places.

Groups of Negroes did offer successful resistance, however. When the rioters attempted to burn the Fifth Precinct Police Station in which some four hundred Negroes had taken refuge, they demanded arms to defend themselves; in the face of firearms the mob retired. The *Evening Post* of July 21, 1863, told of Negro residents of the Eighth Ward "fortifying and strengthening" themselves in anticipation of new attacks. Several attacks were made, but the rioters "evidently became satisfied that the position was too strong, as the Negro skirmishes caused them to skedaddle with fleas in their ears." Negroes who lived through those days tell of defending themselves by throwing hot water down on the mobs from rooftops and heaving bricks at armed bands.

Not all doors of white people were closed to Negroes during those hectic days. Newspapers report the many acts of bravery on the part of whites in defense of Negroes. The *Evening Post,* July 18, 1863, speaks of a white butcher who saved the lives of two Negroes hotly pursued by rioters by hiding them in the loft of his slaughter pen. Another story is told of a white woman who bravely hid a Negro Methodist elder in her cellar. One of the more heroic deeds was that by John J. McGovern, a fireman, who rescued single-handed a crippled Negro boy who had been knocked down by a band of

---

[4] Interview with Thomas H. Barnes, June 30, 1939, now residing in Olean, N.Y.

ruffians intent upon killing the boy. He lifted him from the gutter where he lay in a pool of blood and carried him to the home of a German family, but a few days later the child died of his injuries.

"STATE OF INSURRECTION"

The cry "Down with rich men!" was often heard as the mobs swept through the streets of New York and it was as dangerous for anyone of presentable appearance to be seen on the streets as it was for Negroes and white abolitionists. The homes of Postmaster Abram Wakeman, Colonel Robert Nugent, the Assistant Provost Marshal, and those of several other wealthy citizens, were burned. Mayor Opdyke's residence was saved only by the timely arrival of a defense corps. The house in which J. S. Gibbons, a cousin of Horace Greeley's, lived, was attacked and sacked. Much property, including a large mill at Third Avenue and 129th Street and a grain elevator in Brooklyn, was destroyed. The block of buildings on Broadway, between Twenty-fourth and Twenty-fifth streets, was burned to the ground.

Perhaps no other person was more hated by the rioters than Horace Greeley. While other papers had challenged or lukewarmly criticized the Draft Law, Greeley's New York *Tribune* had not only urged the authorities to enforce the law but at the outbreak of the rioting he demanded forcible suppression of the mobs. On the first evening of the riot, a mob besieged the Tribune building and after overpowering the police who tried to defend it, rushed inside and set it afire.

The riot had been raging within the city for three days before Governor Seymour proclaimed a "state of insurrection." At the same time Seymour assured the rioters he was doing everything to suspend the draft; adding, that it was possible the Supreme Court would declare the law unconstitutional. The following day regiments of National Guards and United States regulars, hastily summoned from the front, began to arrive. The insurrection was put down by Friday, July 17, with bayonets and cannons.

Property valued at more than two million dollars was destroyed. Between three and four thousand persons were killed and a thousand wounded, according to the *Tribune*. The Merchants' Committee for the Relief of Colored People Suffering from the Riots, which included among its workers the Negroes, Henry Highland Garnet, Charles B. Ray and John Peterson, reported that it gave aid to more than ten thousand victims.

Though the riots were followed by a show of kindly feeling towards Negroes and indignation against the lawless elements, new obstacles were thrown in the path of black men. Streetcar companies refused to transport Negro workmen who still had jobs and merchants in fear of future damage to their property refused to re-hire Negroes.

UNION LEAGUE CLUB

Four months after the Draft Riots the Union League Club asked the government for permission to organize a Negro regiment. Governor Seymour's cooperation was sought, but he excused himself, saying that the matter rested with the War Department. Through the efforts of Senator E.D. Morgan, a New York Republican, approval of the proposal for a New York Negro regiment was received from Secretary of War Stanton. The regiment was to serve three years and was to be known as the Twentieth Regiment United States Colored Troops. A committee of seven headed by Alexander Van Rensselaer (chairman), James A. Roosevelt (treasurer), and George Bliss, Jr, (secretary) was set up to direct this work.

The committee's offices hummed with enthusiasm as blacks eagerly volunteered for service. Town supervisors throughout the state were notified to urge Negroes to enlist in New York instead of Massachusetts, Rhode Island, and Connecticut, as they had previously been doing. Recruiting agents were engaged to promote this work, some of whose activities were not without blemish. A large number of cases of dishonest agents and "bounty runners" were reported. The "runners" were groups of men who roved the city recruiting Negroes and keeping the bounty that was appropriated by the state and county for the impoverished families of the recruits. The practice became so scandalous that recruiting dropped off seriously. The Negro leaders came to the aid of the recruiting committee by holding rallies in the Negro churches, and the Negroes were informed of the true amount of the bounty and the right of their families to receive such relief. Through the work of Henry Highland Garnet, evidence was obtained that enabled the authorities to act against the "runners." It was undoubtedly this phase of his activities that caused the Negro minister and two friends to be attacked at this time while crossing the Hudson River on the Cortlandt Street ferry.

Although tension over the draft had eased somewhat and the city had appropriated a palliative of $1,500,000 to pay claims, an unfriendly feeling towards Negroes was still in evidence after the riots. Steps had to be taken to protect the families and friends of the Negro recruits. It is no wonder then that a feeling of uneasiness swept over the city on the morning of May 5, 1864, after it had been announced that the Twentieth Regiment, composed of Negro troops, was to leave for the front. Though many feared an attack would be made upon them, the parade took place without incident. An impressive scene greeted the men as they landed at the foot of Twenty-sixth Street. A cordon of police surrounded the dock while outside a large number of Negroes, most of them women, carried baskets filled with delicacies for the soldiers. An eyewitness said, "Broadway became a dusky river flowing between banks of white faces and waving handkerchiefs," as the Negro soldiers marched to Union Square.

All the metropolitan newspapers reported the warm reception given the Negro soldiers, except Bennett's *Herald*. Seizing upon the fact that a flag was bestowed on the troops as "an emblem of love and honor from the [white] daughters of this great metropolis to her brave champions," the *Herald* declared: "This is a pretty fair start for miscegenation. Why, the phrase, 'love and honor' needs only the little word 'obey' to become equivalent to a marriage ceremony."

BLACK PHALANX

Meanwhile the Union Army was dealing effective blows at the South. Lee was turned back at the Battle of Gettysburg. Black soldiers had planted "the star-spangled banner on the blazing parapet of Fort Wagner," September 4, 1863, forcing its evacuation by the Confederates. By September 9, the Union forces had occupied Chattanooga, Tenn. Even before these victories President Lincoln had written to James C. Conkling of New York that "some of the most important battles would have been lost if the Negro soldiers had not flocked into the Northern Army." The second regiment of Negroes—the Twenty-sixth—which was organized in this city left for the South on March 27, 1864. Efforts were made to organize a third—the Thirty-first—but the number of eligible recruits had decreased considerably.

Despite the acknowledged courage and bravery of the Negro troops, popularly known during the war as the Black Phalanx, Frederick Douglass found it necessary toward the end of 1863 to write to President Lincoln for an interview "to secure to the colored troops then fighting for the country, a reasonable degree of fair play." The major grievances of the Negro troops were inequality of pay, lack of protection for captured soldiers who were being mutilated by the Confederates, and failure to cite black men for distinction. Douglass' interview with the President must have allayed his fears for he left "determined to go on with the recruiting."

The black regiments from New York particularly distinguished themselves in an attack upon John's Island, Beaufort, S.C. A *Tribune* correspondent who witnessed the battle wrote:

> They go forward with a will and a loud shout. And never have I seen troops, old or new, set with cooler determination, although they were heated by fatigue and the sun. They went forward as though they were certain there were no rebels at their front. They advanced under a heavy fire of musketry and artillery . . . . while missiles of death were laying many a poor fellow low.

Of the more than two hundred thousand Negroes who enlisted in the Union Army, eighty thousand died in battle; New York's dead totaled 877.

SAGE OF ANACOSTIA

Many New York Negroes remained in the South after the war to aid in the arduous task of reconstruction. Others returned to the city to share in the expected abundant life. The agencies for emancipation found themselves without a cause, and it was proposed that the American Anti-Slavery Society be abolished, but Frederick Douglass said, "The Negro still has a cause and he needs my pen and voice to plead it." He left New York in 1869 and went to

Washington, where he devoted his chief interests to the condition of the ex-slave and to the Freedman's Bureau. It was then that he distinguished himself as one of the ablest of the reconstruction leaders.

Not yet fifty at the time, he was, according to James Weldon Johnson, "a tall, magnificent man, with a leonine head covered with a mass of hair, which later became a glistening white mane" and gave him a striking resemblance to Karl Marx. He walked with the great men of his day and was a friend and adviser to Lincoln. Though he almost slavishly followed the Republican Party during the war, he remained at all times realistic, for he often said, "The Republican party is not perfect . . . but it is the best friend we have." Twenty years after the war, during the administration of the Democratic reformer Cleveland, a note of disillusionment crept into his public utterances: "Their [the Negroes'] condition seems no better and not much worse than under previous [Republican] administrations. Lynch law, violence, and murder have gone on about the same as formerly, and without the least show of Federal interference or popular rebuke."

In the decades following the war, Douglass' activities brought him many honors and distinctions. In 1872 he was named elector-at-large by the Republican Party in New York, and upon Grant's election was chosen to take the electoral vote of the State of Washington. The same year the Equal Rights Party, which met in New York City and nominated Victoria G. Woodhull for the Presidency, named Douglass for the Vice-Presidency. During Grant's administration he was appointed Secretary to the Santo Domingo Commission, which attempted to negotiate a treaty with the island republic for its annexation to the United States. He held, in turn, the positions of Councillor of the District of Columbia, Recorder of Deeds for the District of Columbia, and Minister to Haiti.

Three years after the death of his first wife, Douglass had married Helen Pitts, a white woman who was spoken of as a lady of refinement and education and possessed of pleasing manners. This man, who had lived in a period of war, controversy and strife, spent his last days healthy in body and mind. On Sunday evening, February 2, 1895, after attending an all-day session of a meeting held by the Council of Women, Douglass returned home in fine spirits, enthusiastic about the progress of the meeting and prepared to make an address that same night. His carriage was waiting. While passing through the hall of his home he fell slowly to his knees and died. Forty years of work on behalf of his people had ended. He was reputedly worth a quarter of a million dollars at his death; but his property was only assessed at eighteen thousand dollars. His old homestead in Anacostia, D. C., is now a national shrine, maintained by the National Association of Colored Women's Clubs. It was restored through the efforts of Mrs Mary B. Talbert of Buffalo, New York, one time president of the association.

Douglass probably died a disappointed man for he lived to see many of the highest hopes and dreams of his race trampled.

BOOK THREE

(1865 – 1910)

CHAPTER IX

NEGROES IN AN AGGRESSIVE AGE

NEW YORK, 1865-1890.—Negroes of the North dropped into a place of insignificance nationally soon after the close of the Civil War— a position from which they did not emerge to any appreciable degree until the United States entered the World War. The arena for the Negro had shifted from the North to the South. So far as the Nation was concerned with the Negro, the status and the future of the newly freed slaves occupied its attention to the exclusion of the rights of the free Negroes of the North. The controversies in Congress and throughout the country surged around the War Amendments and Reconstruction, with four million exslaves as the center of the storm.

New York Negroes had slackened their racial projects. The passage of the Thirteenth Amendment (1865) ending involuntary servitude; that of the Fourteenth Amendment (1868), giving the rights of citizenship to Negroes; and the Fifteenth Amendment (1871), giving Negroes the vote, contributed much to a sense of security. The Negro newspapers suspended publication, not to reappear until 1880.

"BIG WHITE BOYS"

The Nation had recovered from the panic of 1873, an aggressive age had set in, and Negroes were swept along on the compelling tide of this new development. New York's wealth came from new sources. Manufacturing in particular had increased at an astonishing rate; inventions of every sort had served to accelerate the modern growth of New York. The mighty rush for dollars consumed most of the energy of Negroes.

When those men who "built up the country" arrived on the scene during the Civil War, the United States was a mercantile-agrarian democracy. When they departed, the Nation was a unified industrial society, with its control more or less in their hands. Under their molding, the social philosophy of the Nation and the city changed. The East became the center of American culture and New York the "social capital," its "400" the charmed circle of the "polite world."

The mode of living and the customs of New Yorkers changed accordingly. The rapid increase in the population, the concentration of enormous riches among a few individuals, and the increased antagonisms toward the immigrant, all were part of this change.

Foreign visitors to the city were struck by the "arrogant display of riches." On holidays, especially Easter Sunday, these people paraded Fifth Avenue, garbed in "five hundred dollar gowns and fifty dollar hats." Often they were seen riding through Central Park in magnificent carriages, driven by Negro coachmen wearing white linen trousers, plain black coats, and high hats. The poor people were banished to the elevated railway and horse-drawn cars, which carried passengers to and fro for ten cents each way, and which were said to be "a favourite resort for pickpockets." The journey was not without distinction, though, for the small locomotives which pulled these trains were apt to be named Aristotle or Pericles or Jay Gould or Chauncey M. Depew. One of the chief worries of the fashionable people was the servant problem. The poor people complained against the tyranny of landlords.

The newly rich, though lawless and naive, enjoyed the public esteem. Occasionally they were the targets of the yellow journalists, but, on the whole, the pulpit and press ecstatically heralded their triumphs in the markets of beef and sausages. They were referred to inspirationally as "nature's noblemen." Their princely philanthropies extended to the schools and churches of every denomination; and Negroes shared in this munificence through Jim-Crowed southern education.

BOSS TWEED

The decade following the Civil War saw the sudden attempt of "Boss" Tweed to bring Negroes into the Democratic Party. While his organization had been aggressively proslavery during the Civil War and spoke of the "political supremacy of the white race,"

Tweed had been shrewdly contributing money to the Anti-Slavery Society and had been seen on the platforms with abolitionists. He represented a body which became known as the "Tweed Ring," a band of politicians who had an astute understanding of "the most subterranean phrases of ward politics." Its system of "wholesale repeating at the polls" worked a particular hardship on the Negro population of the city. In the May 1870 judiciary election in one of the wards where about 1,100 Negroes were registered, Negroes were bewildered to learn, on going to the ballot box, that white repeaters had already voted upon nearly five hundred of their names. When these Negroes insisted upon their right to vote, they were promptly arrested as "repeaters." [1]

The Tweed Ring, which by 1871 had plundered the city of a sum estimated at $74,000,000, extended its fingers into the "two-bit joints" conducted by Negroes in Church, Duane, Leonard, Bleecker, and the neighboring streets. In time these sections became "a hot-bed of vice." Under the benevolent eye of Tweed's organization tribute was exacted from the Negroes who operated these gambling clubs and dance halls, and "protection" given in return.

For many years Minetta Lane and Baxter and Thompson Streets were noted for their galaxy of Negro criminals who strode about with the arrogance of those sheltered by the law. Negro characters such as "No-Toe" Charley, "Bloodthirsty," "Black Cat," and "Jube" Tyler gained at least neighborhood reputations because of their dexterity in the use of the knife and the razor. Hank Anderson, Negro body servant of Tweed, ruled this neighborhood with an iron hand. The Tammany chieftain had made him "Negro leader" of the district. It was said that "he was the man who must be seen by Democrats who coveted the colored vote and are willing to use practical methods of getting them."

"ROLL JORDAN"

Notorious among the joints in Hank Anderson's district was the *Black and Tan*. Here, before a narrow bar serving vile whiskey, gathered Negroes along with a few Malays, Chinese, and American Indians. Occasionally a white man was seen. The women were of

---

[1] Gustavus Myers, *The History of Tammany Hall* (New York, published by the author 1901) 263.

all shades and races. The accent and the bright colored bandannas of many of the Negro women suggested that they were of southern origin. The bar's backroom, lighted by kerosene lamps and decorated with gaudy sporting pictures, served as a gambling den. A steep stairway led into an improvised ballroom in the low-ceilinged basement. Here the patrons danced to the music of a Negro band composed of a piano player, a violinist, a flutist, and a banjo player. Between the dances, the white-aproned waiter would shout:

> Come, gents, give yer orders—treat yer partners in dis yer dance—keep yer jint well-oiled, take beer or suthin' an be quick about it.

Across the street from the boisterous *Black and Tan* there was, in a narrow two-story building, a night mission conducted by H.B. Gibbud. It was here that spirituals were first heard in New York by a chronicler. One of the mission's more frequent visitors was a small Negro girl known only as "Roll Jordan," who was reputed to be a mean fighter when drunk. At such times she would stalk into the mission and sing in a loud shrill voice:

> Dar am no hippercrites
> In de heaben ob my Lord,
> Oh how I longs ter go!
> Judgment, Judgment,
> Judgment day am a rollin' along,
> Oh how I longs ter go!

This verse, it is said, always electrified her hearers, indicating as it did her drunken state and her complete willingness to become the terror she could so easily be. She regarded any display of reluctance to sing along with her as a challenge to combat. All present would join in the chorus and swing out for dear life:

> Roll, Jordan, roll,
> Roll, Jordan, roll,
> I wants ter go to heaven when I dies
> Ter hear old Jordan roll.

There is no doubt that southern spirituals had some place in the Negro churches in New York from the earliest period, but the singing of them appears to have escaped the ears of the recorders of the times. One reason for this might be that New York Negroes of that day hated everything that reminded them of the South and slavery. Such songs of course did not have the dignity of being an "art form" then but were regarded as a vulgar type of singing.

NEGRO "400"

Not every Negro of this period was wretchedly poor, nor lived dismally in the slums. The larger group of Negroes was employed principally as waiters, coachmen, bootblacks, and hairdressers. Nevertheless there were many who acquired a measure of wealth and lived in the better neighborhoods. Some of the more thrifty and more industrious made money as real estate speculators and head-waiters. A few made profitable entrances into small businesses and the professions. On June 5, 1887, the New York *Sun* published an article under the title, "Some Rich Colored Men." It said that the "Afro-American" residents of New York City had an aggregate wealth of more than three million dollars; about two million dollars of this in cash and on deposit in the various savings banks. It listed among the most conspicuous taxpayers Philip A. White, a druggist; Mrs Mary Vandyke, a philanthropic widow; and P. W. Ray and Susan McKinney,[2] physicians. The Gloucester Estate, administered by Dr J. N. Gloucester, was valued at $35,000. Sixteen years later, on January 18, 1903, the *Sun* carried an illustrated feature entitled "New York's Rich Negroes." This time it reported that there were more than three hundred families who could afford to buy houses from forty thousand dollars to one hundred thousand dollars in value, and live on the scale of white people who spend from ten to twenty-five thousand dollars a year. The *Sun*'s survey was made after whites had stoned the homes of Negroes living in Brooklyn, following the appearance of the first large automobile owned by a Negro family. That this family had also bought property in the best residential section was perhaps added cause for resentment.

Unnoticed by the white world, a Negro upper class which lived in the manner of typical middle-class white families had come into being. There was this difference, however. Discrimination against

---

[2] In 1870 Susan McKinney became the first Negro female graduate from a medical college (women's) in this country.

Negroes generally limited their activities. Yet these Negroes filled their homes with oaken and black mahogany furniture, so popular at this time, and drew their servants from the Scandinavian and German immigrant groups. Here and there an English butler was to be found. A careful inquiry revealed few Negroes or Irish employed by these Negroes. Their complaint against employing them as servants was that they failed to show proper deference to Negro employers. Sons of such families attended college abroad, chiefly to escape the prejudice in the American institutions. A great many went to Howard University, the Negro institution established in Washington after the Civil War, while others went to liberal Oberlin. A few attended Harvard and Yale. The girls went to fashionable northern colleges for women, the few which admitted Negroes, and returned home with the same social ambitions and tastes as young white girls of similar training.

The colored families of this class studiously kept their family and social affairs out of the sight of the rest of the world. They sought to be as inconspicuous as possible, especially as far as white people were concerned, for they had a deep sensitivity to being reminded that they were despised because of their color. Barred from fashionable restaurants like Delmonico's and Sherry's, they spent most of their money on fine homes, expensive foods, and lavish parties. Unwelcome in reputable places of amusement conducted by whites, they did not choose to frequent the saloons, the restaurants, and the clubs of the Negro neighborhoods, which were in West Fifty-third Street, where the Negro sports, the theatrical people, and the "bohemians" spent their time and money.

Social distinctions developed among New York Negroes that were as rigid as those of the white world, as is seen in the case of the Society of the Sons of New York, an ultra-exclusive social organization which was founded in the Eighties. The society was formed some ten years after the "solid respectable element" of the white community had set the pattern by fixing that mystical "400" as the number of guests to be invited to the famous Centennial Hall in 1876. The Sons of New York drew its membership from the "Four Hundred" of "Afro-American" society and admitted only colored men born in New York. Southerners could become associate members, but could take no part in the deliberations of the group. Negro social leaders, American to the core, were accused by Negroes not within the pale of "Society" of being only "lamp-black whites" or carbon copies of white society. The white aristocracy, as Mrs J. Van Rennselaer King complained, was composed of successful butchers, farmers, miners, grocers, and merchants who had sprung from obscurity. In its way, Negro society was equally distinguished; it was made up of prosperous head waiters, real estate speculators, politicians, cooks, and professionals. White and black alike, New York's society folks aspired and thrilled to the world of "rustle and perfume, the glitter and show, the pomp and circumstance."

In an illuminating comment, a spokesman for the Society of the Sons of New York said its membership had been carefully selected with a view to admitting only men who satisfied "the most delicate taste of gentleman-like tone and behavior." While the society did not wish to appear snobbish, he said, it did seek to exclude all "vulgarity and every trace of ungentleman-like deficiency" and sought "only the cream of colored society." This Ward McAllister of Negro New York's polite world then handed down the following dictum:

> If the possession of money is also a requisite for admission to its sumptuously appointed clubhouse in Fifty-third Street, the requirement is the same that applies to all fashionable clubs and to the society of fashion generally. Poverty and fashion cannot travel together, for fashion is expensive. All elegant and luxurious society is based on wealth, or at least wealth is essential to it. A man may have all the virtues in the calendar, but unless he is rich also, he cannot drive in his own carriage and travel in his own yacht and his own private car. Unless he is pretty well supplied with money he cannot buy his clothes from a Fifth Avenue tailor and import costly wardrobes from Paris in order that the beauty of his wife and daughter may shine resplendent at the balls of the gay season. The colored club simply recognizes this self-evident truth. It is not for all; it does not pretend to be for all; it is for the chosen and fortunate few.[3]

---

[3] New York *Sun*, September 1, 1893.

BLACK WORKERS

An era of great wealth and gaiety was ushered in with the Eighties which lasted until the close of the century. Profits were reported to be abundant and many seemed to have become millionaires overnight. But the Negroes did not share in the abundance, nor had the wealth of the common people grown proportionately. While the New Rich were guilty of "conspicuous waste," their employees were underpaid and as a consequence slums and crime abounded. When outcries came from impoverished labor, moral blue-noses, and the public generally, the modern barons declared that their extravagances were designed to create employment and that the proceeds were to be devoted to charities. Such a view was plausible enough, but this money never did seem to filter through to the masses of people.

This situation soon had its reflection in acute labor unrest. The growing problem was heightened by the new influx of immigrants, which began during the Civil War when an Immigration Act to aid further new heavy industries and manufacturers allowed contract labor to be imported freely. This immigration reached its peak during the Eighties, intensifying the unemployment of the native American laboring class and of the Negroes in particular. To better their conditions many black men, like so many white men, sought membership in trade union organizations, but Negroes were met with strong barriers by the established white unions.

Meetings of the National Labor Union, state and local conventions of Negro workingmen, had been held as early as 1868 and 1869. Much of their proceedings remain in obscurity, but from available records it appears that they aimed at political, economic, and educational reforms without racial discriminations. Out of them grew the first national convention of Negro Labor in the United States, which met in Union League Hall at Washington, D.C., January 13, 1869. The credentials committee reported 161 accredited delegations from the various states, including New York. Several resolutions on political reform, equal citizenship rights and free land were introduced. The delegates split on the question of the relations of white and Negro labor; the matter was finally tabled and the convention adjourned. A convention of Negro workers was held in New York, November 11, 1869, for the purpose of sending representatives to the National Negro Labor Congress when it should convene again the following month. The fields represented suggest the widespread realization of the need for organization.[4] By 1870 Negro Labor of New York, encouraged by the Workingmen's Assembly, had formed three organizations—the Saloon Men's Protective and Benevolent Union, the Colored Waiters' Association, and the First Combined Labor Institute.

The National Negro Labor Congress held its next meeting in Washington, D.C., in December of the same year (1869), as planned. This time the question of fraternizing with white labor was frankly met, and a delegation to the white National Labor Union, which was to meet the following month in Philadelphia, was elected. It included Isaac Myers, James Weare, Ignatius Gross, Squire Fisher, and Robert N. Butler, a New Yorker. The result of this appearance at the white convention caused the appointment of a committee, which included Butler, to organize the Negro workingmen of Pennsylvania. The National Labor Union, while desirous of uniting Negro and white labor, was careful not to raise the question of racial discrimination. It attempted to create a congress of white and Negro delegates, representing Negro and white unions. Even this attempt to back into the house of solidarity met with opposition, which finally broke out in racial discord and made cooperation between the races impossible after 1870.

The final break came when a proposal was made to divide the National Labor Union into industrial and political divisions and to form the National Labor Reform Party. Isaac Myers, president of the Negro Labor Congress, protested that all reforms should come from the Republican Party, but the resolution was carried by a large majority. No Negro delegates appeared again at the National Labor Union; and in 1872, when the Negro organization assembled in New Orleans, it repudiated the white National

---

[4] The delegates represented the following occupational groups: fifty engineers, four hundred waiters, seven basketmakers, thirty-two tobacco twisters, fifty barbers, twenty-two cabinetmakers and carpenters, fourteen masons and bricklayers, fifteen smelters and refiners, two rollers, six moulders, five hundred longshoremen, and twenty-four printers.

Labor Union and declared loyalty to the Republican Party. After this act the Negro organization ended its activities and passed into oblivion.

KNIGHTS OF LABOR

A more advanced policy towards Negroes was shown by the Noble Order of the Knights of Labor, which came to the fore in 1880, after it had thrown off the secrecy in which it had worked since its founding in 1869. It took up the task of organizing Negroes, women, and unskilled labor. It offered a wide program of education, mutual aid, cooperative workshops and consumer cooperation. The ambition of the order was to organize all workers, skilled and unskilled, without regard to nationality, sex, or color. The resolution which it passed in 1885 was indicative of its enlightened policy concerning Negroes: it asked for the appointment of Negro organizers for each of the southern states. The estimate of the organization's secretary, John W. Hayes, as quoted by the *Black Worker,* is that more than sixty thousand Negroes were members of the order by 1888.

In 1881 the Federation of Organized Trades and Labor Unions of the United States and Canada was formed; but in 1886 this group withdrew from the Knights of Labor, declared its independence and its interest in only skilled craft workers, and formed the American Federation of Labor. Its policy naturally militated against the unskilled laborer and especially Negroes who were then 97 per cent unskilled.[5] There were also clauses in the constitution of many unions admitting only "white men." Consequently the great masses of Negroes were automatically excluded from the labor movement. Though the Federation came out abstractly against color discrimination by stating that it "looks with disfavor upon trade unions having provisions which excluded persons on account of race or color," traditionally the American Federation of Labor has been the bulwark of racial prejudice in the American labor movement.

---

[5] Sterling D. Spero and Abram L. Harris, *The Black Worker: the Negro and the Labor Movement* (New York, Columbia University Press 1931) 41-42.

UNION OF WHITE MEN

The leadership of the A. F. of L. was not long in realizing that this policy stood in the way of its expansion. Presented with the choice of remaining a militant body true to its ideals or compromising for the sake of an increased white membership, it chose the latter course with little soul-searching. When the problem was brought before the 1900 Convention, Gompers said: "To insist . . . upon a delegation . . . of colored workers being accorded representation in a central body would have meant the dissolution of that organization." This was the beginning of a historic retreat; two years later (1902), the Federation provided for the issuance of separate charters to Central Labor. Unions, local unions, and Federal Labor Unions, composed exclusively of Negro workers.

Under the plea of autonomy the various national unions introduced different types and methods of segregation. Negroes were chiefly organized in auxiliary locals usually in subordination to the nearest white local. They could not transfer to white locals even if there were no Negro unions in the vicinity. They were declared ineligible for skilled work, could not hold office, and could be represented in conferences and conventions only by whites. Many unions limited their membership by putting up prohibitive initiation fees and allowing new members to come in only on the recommendation of their friends already within the ranks. These factors took an obvious toll of the number of Negroes to enter the labor movement. By 1905 only five per cent of the total labor union membership were Negroes, though there were two million organized workers at this time.[6]

The progress of a broad working-class movement was thus halted by the growth of craft unionism and the decline of Negro workers in industry. Underscoring this was the additional factor of mutual antagonisms between the white and black laborers. As early as 1863 Negro strikebreakers and white longshoremen out on strike fought bitterly in New York and other eastern cities. On the Negro's side a great barrier to broad unionization was the growth of middle-class ideals in Negroes, a product of preachers with

---

[6] Mary White Ovington, *Half a Man: the Status of the Negro in New York* (New York, Longmans, Green 1911) 236.

more missionary zeal than economic understanding and of educated Negroes with their individualistic slant on life. It may well have been the prejudice and discrimination against them that reinforced their middle-class thinking, so that they regarded their choice as the only way out of an economic dilemma. In any case, this intangible but altogether formidable barrier has perpetuated itself to this day in Negro life. Though white labor looked upon the Negro as a "competitive menace," a contemporary labor historian has correctly observed: "Divergent as were the interests and political outlook of the Negro and white wage earners, these interests were not so irreconcilable that statesmanship might not have harmonized them."[7]

NEGRO INVENTORS

New York Negroes were a definite part of the social and economic pattern. They were not, as so often said, only wards of the rich. Besides their industrial labors, they were, in fact, conscious contributors to the new prosperity, for many of them enriched the country by invention. The bewildering array of technical inventions, which altered human life within a brief span, found Negroes in the vanguard of this development. But the machine age, which did so much to bring about divisions in the ranks of labor, put men out of work and caused protest from sections of the laboring population, also brought whites new reasons to bolster their hatred of Negroes.

Before 1865 only three patents are known to have been granted Negroes, and these were to free men of color. Henry Blair, of Maryland, was granted two patents, in 1834 and in 1836, for perfecting a mechanical corn husker; James Forten, of Philadelphia, made a device for handling sails; and Norbert Rillieux, an engineer of Louisiana, invented a vacuum pan in 1846, which revolutionized sugar refining. There were isolated instances of masters applying for patents on the inventions of their slaves, but a slave's case was a complicated one, as he had no standing before the law and could not legally apply for a patent; and his master, inasmuch as he was not the inventor, could not be the assignee of the slave, since the master could not legally make the required oath.[8] Not

---

[7] Spero and Harris, *The Black Worker* 30.

[8] Henry E. Baker, "The Negro as an Inventor" in *Twentieth Century Negro Literature,* ed. D. W. Culp (Naperville, Ill., Nichols & Co. 1902) 399-413.

satisfied with this ruling of the Commissioner of Patents, an appeal was made to the Secretary of the Interior by one Stewart, a slave master, in the middle of the last century. The matter was referred to Jeremiah S. Black, the U. S. Attorney General (1857-1860). A pioneer verdict was reached when Black nailed the question in place with this statement: "A machine invented by a slave, though it be new and useful, cannot, in the present state of the law, be patented." [9] Not until emancipation in 1865 did all Negroes secure the right to be granted patents. Thirty-five years later there were fully four hundred patents granted to them.

Most of the early inventions of Negroes were agricultural implements and culinary utensils, a reflection of their occupations. As they began to enter other fields, patents were obtained on mechanical devices, clothing, railroad machinery, and, later still, patents for electrical equipment. On February 6, 1872, T. J. Byrd was granted a patent for an improvement on horse-rein holders; today, with the horse almost obsolete, R. H. Pryor has patented a radical-type auto engine; Elbert Robinson has perfected a process for hardening steel, and Paul E. Johnson has invented a therapeutic lamp. A considerable variety of inventions emerged from the hands of black men, reflecting, too, the many-sidedness of their activities; for example, a machine for embossing photos, an ice-cream mold, a carpet beater, a foot-powered hammer, a dustpan and a pencil sharpener. In 1867 H. Lee patented an animal trap; in 1865 Sarah E. Good perfected a folding cabinet bed; and in 1886 R. F. Flemming Jr obtained a patent on a guitar.

THE "BLACK EDISON"

When the third-rail was invented and electricity replaced steam on the elevated railways in this city, the white men, who lost their jobs as steam locomotive engineers because of the innovation, heaped all manner of abuse on the whole Negro race because its inventor was a Negro.[10] After its installation, Negroes were not safe on the streets of New York. They were frequently attacked by persons aware only that a new-fangled electrical device invented

---

[9] *Official Opinions of the Attorneys General, United States, 1857-1860*, ed. J. Huxley Ashton (Washington, D.C., W. H. and O. H. Morrison 1866) IX 171-172.
[10] *Cosmopolitan Magazine* XVIII No. 6 (April 1895) 761-762.

by some "damn nigger" had taken away their jobs. Violence sub-
sided only when the company finally rehired the old engineers
and taught them the new job of motormen. The inventor, Granville T. Woods, a native of Ohio, arrived in New York in 1880
and soon after invented a system by which telegraphing was made
possible between trains in motion, technically known as "induc-
tion telegraph." During the next thirty years, until he died in
New York City in 1910, he perfected twenty-five inventions. He
was employed by Thomas Edison, and while working at his laboratory at a yearly salary of ten thousand dollars, The American Bell
Telephone Company purchased his electric telephone transmitter.

Vastly important to northern manufacturing were the inventions of Jan E. Matzeliger and Elijah McCoy, both Negroes. McCoy
was a pioneer in the lubrication of machinery and had fifty-seven
patents to his credit. He first applied the principle of supply-
ing oil to machines in intermittent drops from a cup to avoid
the necessity of stopping the machine to oil it. McCoy's lubricat-
ing cup was standard equipment for all up-to-date machinery forty
years ago. Matzeliger's invention was even more far-reaching. Soon
after the Civil War he perfected a machine for attaching soles to
shoes. It was the first appliance of its kind capable of performing
all the steps required to hold a shoe on its last, pull the leather
down around the heel, guide and drive the nails into place, and
discharge the complete shoe from the machine. The patent for this
invention was bought by the United Shoe Company of Boston,
after an initial bid of $1,500 had been turned down. It formed the
basis of an enterprise that consolidated forty subsidiary companies
and gave to the United States world supremacy in the shoe industry. Matzeliger died of tuberculosis in a public ward in September
1889, at the early age of thirty-seven. He left a few shares of his
stock to a white church in Lynn, Massachusetts, the North Con-
gregational, which had befriended him during his lean days. When
the church found itself in financial straits some years later, it sold
the stock for $10,860.[11]

---

[11] One of the principal beneficiaries of his invention, the already rich Colonel
Gordon McKay, left four million dollars to Harvard University when he died in 1903,
which under the provisions of his will would amount to about twenty million dollars when paid. He also founded the McKay Institute for Colored Boys at Kingston, R.I.
Dictionary of American Biography (New York, Charles Scribner & Sons 1933) XII 73-74.

One of the most important of the New York inventors was Louis Howard Latimer, who invented a carbon filament for the Maxim Electric Lamp and superintended the installation of the electric lighting systems in New York City, Philadelphia, some Canadian cities, and London, England. He became associated with Thomas Edison in 1896, and as a member of "the Edison pioneers," made drawings for the first Bell telephone from a design by Alexander Graham Bell. He was the chief draftsman for the General Electric and the Westinghouse companies before his death in this city, December 11, 1928. In the meantime other New Yorkers were active. A.B. Steele perfected a device to open and close the rear door of an automobile from the driver's seat, and E. F. Johnson invented a window ventilator which acts as a filter for dust and air.

Most of these men, who are but a few of the Negro pioneers in science and invention, received royalties for their inventions, though many, like inventors everywhere, were victimized by unscrupulous men. Granville T. Woods, for instance, spent all his earnings in litigations to establish ownership of his patents.

The U. S. Patent Office, when it was preparing to participate in the Paris Exposition of 1900, communicated with every patent attorney, requesting whatever data they may have had concerning Negro inventions, as the Patent Office did not keep a special file of Negro inventors. Many brows wrinkled at this request. Negro inventors? Lips pursed. They knew ebony-hued longshoremen, lean toilers of the fields, and listless black boys of the town; Negro inventors were unknown, but definitely. Henry E. Baker, a Patent Office examiner who received the replies, reports the amazement of most of the attorneys: "Negro inventors—ridiculous!" cried some; "I never heard of a Negro inventor," wrote an Alabaman; "There'll never be a Negro inventor," replied a Georgian. The *Negro Year Book* (1937-38) reports that more than four thousand patents are held by Negroes.

SOCIAL EMERGENCE

BLACK BOHEMIA, 1890-1900—Towards the close of the nineteenth century the activities of New York Negroes began to take new shape and direction and to emerge in the form it assumes today. This occurred largely in a section called "Black Bohemia," [2] a neighborhood imprisoned behind the striped shadows of the El on West Fifty-Third Street. The concentration of Negroes in this area had followed a general shift of the black population. At the turn of the century there was another movement northward to "San Juan Hill" (West Sixty-First, Sixty-Second, and Sixty-Third Streets). Most of the well-to-do Negroes lived in Brooklyn; their exodus from Manhattan was caused principally by the Draft Riots in 1863. A considerable number of them owned homes, with the result that Brooklyn was the center of upper-class social life.[3]

Manhattan's Black Bohemia differed radically from the Brooklyn and the lower Manhattan sections, because it embodied the newer and more daring phases of Negro life.[4] For it was in this neighborhood that most of the clubs frequented by both the sporting and theatrical people were located.[5]

---

[1] "2nd Draft" was written at the top of the page. The chapter covers the period 1890-1900, but the dateline was crossed out.—Ed.

[2] New York *Sun,* June 5, 1887.

[3] The following was crossed out: "characterized by a jealous respectability which still marks the older settled sections of that borough."—Ed.

[4] Crossed out: "It constituted a part of the famous old 'Tenderloin' and retained a number of the old vices that were present when whites were the principal residents. Chief among these vices were gambling and prostitution."—Ed.

[5] Crossed out: "One of the clubs of this district was Ike Hines's, an exclusively professional place on the main floor of a three-story building. There were two large rooms: a carpeted parlor and a square back room into which the parlor opened. Small tables and chairs were neatly arranged about the room. The windows were draped with lace curtains and the walls were literally covered with photographs or lithographs of every Negro in America who had ever 'done anything.' There were pictures of Frederick Douglass and of Peter Jackson, the pugilist, and of all the lesser lights of the prize ring, all the famous jockeys and the stage celebrities, down to the newest song-and-dance team. In the back room was a piano, tables which hugged the wall, and a bare floor with its center left vacant for singers, dancers, and other theater people who wished to reward eager patrons with tastes of their talents."—Ed.

Many[6] of the men who frequented this area earned large sums of money, easily and spasmodically.[7] One of the popular figures of the area was the jockey, Isaac Murphy, the "Black Archer," whose appearances in New York always caused a great stir. Hailed as America's greatest rider, he won the Kentucky Derby three times—in 1884, 1890, and 1891—a feat that was not duplicated until some forty years later by Earle Sande, a white jockey.

Though many of the Negro jockeys threw away incredible sums of money, many were merely small-town boys, heady with success, seeking amusement in a big city; and Black Bohemia was the Negro metropolis in that day. Most of these riders were from the South, where horse racing began, and where Negroes of the servant class were the first stableboys, trainers, and jockeys. In time they developed into horsemen with few white peers in America. When the first Kentucky Derby was run in 1875 there were thirteen Negro jockeys mounted out of a field of fourteen starters. From that year to 1902 no less than seven Negroes won this classic eleven times.[8] At one time or another the races at Coney Island and Saratoga brought these personalities to the city. Ike Hines's was the headquarters for such ranking performers as Pike Barnes, Andy Hamilton, Jimmie Winkfield, Willie Simms, Johnny Stoval, Willie Walker, "Tiny" Williams, the Clayton brothers, "Soup" Perkins, "Monk" Overton, Linc Jones, Bob Ison, Emanuel Morris, Felix Carr, and Jimmie Lee.

Lee drew special attention from the racing fans. He was credited with making a clean sweep of the entire card of six races at the Churchill Downs in Louisville, June 5, 1907. His chief rival for the admiration of Ike Hines's customers was Willie Simms, who

---

[6] Preceding section heading crossed out: *Black Jockeys*—Ed.

[7] Crossed out: "consequently a great deal of money was spent there. One of the reputedly big spenders was a dapper brownskin fellow, whose name has been lost in the passage of time. It was said that he earned twelve thousand dollars a year and spent 'about thirty times that rate' in this club. After an important horse race it was his custom to fete the crowd that thronged this place with champagne at the cost of five dollars a quart! He may have been any one of the jockeys of that period. In the heyday of racing the winner of the Futurity, the Suburban, the Realization, the Brooklyn Handicap, the Metropolitan Handicap, or the Saratoga Cup was almost as widely known as a twentieth century prize fight champion. Certainly no American jockey was ever more popular than [Isaac Murphy]."—Ed.

[8] Kentucky Derby winners: Lewis (1875), Walker (1877), Murphy (1884-90-91), Clayton (1892), Perkins (1895), Simms (1896-98), Winkfield (1901-02).

won the Kentucky Derby in 1897 and again in 1898, and was credited with being the first American jockey to shorten his stirrups and ride the monkey-on-a-stick (monkey crouch) style, which has since been universally adopted.[9]

When the center of racing moved from the South to the East, the Negro was elbowed out. The sport had become a national pastime and was now big business. Bookmakers had an important role in the sport's development. The last Negro winner of the Kentucky Derby was Jimmie Winkfield, who won it in 1902.

No longer were jockeys among the big spenders at Ike Hines's. The decline in the number of Southern breeders contributed in a large measure to the dearth of Negro turf performers after 1900. The majority of successful stables were now owned by Northerners, and the East dominated the sport.[10] Today the Negro jockey has almost entirely disappeared from the American track.[11] When jockeys began to earn more than ten thousand dollars a year, riding became a white man's job.

"COLORED BASEBALL"

Many of the personalities who frequented Black Bohemia were drawn from the field of baseball, though they could hardly compete with the jockeys as spenders. This sport did not produce figures as colorful as the jockeys, but there was a great deal of enthusiasm over the Cuban Giants, an unusual New York unit which played fast, snappy baseball. They were always good story material for sports writers because they[12] introduced baseball comedy.[13]

---

[9] Crossed out: "Riding abroad under the color of Dwyer and Tammany boss Croker, he was the first 'new English' jockey to win a race on an English track."—Ed.

[10] Crossed out: " 'A nigger knows a horse and a mule,' was a forgotten tradition of the turf."—Ed.

[11] Crossed out: "Not the least of the reasons for his passing is economic."—Ed.

[12] Crossed out: "(they) brought something original to the professional diamond."—Ed.

[13] A long section describing the team's comedy acts, including comic pantomime, was crossed out. Part of a sentence is illegible; the remainder reads: "After a good play the whole team would cut monkeyshines, which made the grandstands and the bleachers roar with delight. This innovation never made any headway among the white professional clubs. Most of the white players who attempted it appeared embarrassed and foolish. Baseball in the white world remained a serious business. In later years, however, the Washington Senators had a splendid pantomimist in Nick Altrock."—Ed.

When in 1867 the National Association for Baseball Players was organized in Philadelphia a resolution was passed barring Negro clubs from the association. This was the chief factor in the eventual organization of Negro professional teams. The first Negro team was organized in 1885 in New York at Babylon, L. I., by Frank P. Thompson, headwaiter at the fashionable Argyle Hotel. He enterprisingly assembled a team to entertain the guests and incidentally to supplement his income. Thompson selected players from among his waiters. They were former ballplayers who could find no employment with white clubs and had turned to waiting on tables for a livelihood.

Walter Cook, a white promoter, seeing a future for Negro baseball, became its backer and renamed the club the *Cuban Giants* to circumvent the particular prejudice against Negro players in the South and West. Cook worked out a salary scale, which does not vary much from what Negro players earned in 1939. Pitchers and catchers were paid $18 a week, infielders $16, and outfielders $12; all traveling expenses were paid by Cook. By 1887 there were seven Negro clubs playing professionally and they formed themselves into a league. Two years later the first championship games between the East and West were played. In 1887-88 all leagues either drew the color-line or inserted a clause in their constitutions limiting the number of Negro players. This provision was rigidly interpreted and brought about the total exclusion of Negroes from the sport.

In the spring of 1901, John J. McGraw, who later became manager of the New York Giants, was in Hot Springs, Ark., training the Baltimore Orioles. He was attracted by Charles Grant's skillful playing of second base with the Columbia Giants, a Negro team from Chicago. McGraw thought he saw in him a player who would bolster his lineup, and incidentally be a new drawing card. With the color line so rigidly enforced, he conceived the idea of smuggling Grant into the major league as an Indian. When Grant arrived in Chicago with the Baltimore team there were many anxious moments before he made his appearance on the field. The Negro women of that city, unable to contain themselves, proudly appeared at the ball park and presented Grant with a bouquet of flowers. McGraw was immediately notified to release the Negro.[14]

Grant's stature as a personality was enhanced by this incident and he became one of the leading figures of Black Bohemia; his frequent trips to play in this city took on the proportions of triumphal tours. In the meantime the Negro clubs had grown so powerful that the Philadelphia Giants, the Negro champions of 1907, challenged the champions of the white leagues of that year. Their contention that no league or team could claim the world's championship unless it had defeated all worthy opponents was regarded favorably by many northern newspapers. But the white leagues declined, pointing out innocently that there was a possibility of the Negroes winning and that this would prove "distasteful" to many of the white fans. In time arguments raged in the clubs and saloons of Black Bohemia as to the relative merits of Negro and white players. Since few, if any, records of individual performances of Negro players were kept, a little volume, *Official Guide of Colored Baseball* (1907) by Sol White, a noted Negro player, proved the only source of settling such disputes. White's evaluations, regarded as baseball "Bible," listed the great Negro diamond stars of the era.[15]

BLACK BOXERS

While the baseball players were performing in a segregated league, the Negro pugilists were flourishing in open competition with white men. New York Negroes were particularly peeved though over John L. Sullivan's refusal to meet Peter Jackson, the Australian champion, thereby being the first champion to draw the color line in the prize ring. Negroes conceded that boxing had offered the Negro his fairest opportunity in sports, for reliance on individual effort was brought into play more fully in prize fighting than in most sports, but they never forgave Sullivan for not giving Jackson a crack at the title.

---

[14] Adrian C. (Pop) Anson, captain of the Chicago National League team, with his great personal popularity and power, did more than any one man to keep the Negro out of organized baseball.

[15] James Booker, Clarence Williams, Arthur Thomas, Tom Washington, George Stovy, Dan McClellan, William Sheldon, Andrew (Rube) Foster, William Malone, Emmett Bowman, George Williams, Sol White, Frank Grant and William Monroe.

Negroes had been a factor in the prize ring since 1809 when Tom Molineaux was the acknowledged heavyweight champion of the country. For the prize fighter had an advantage even over the jockey, who might be handicapped by hopeless mounts. But the Negro prize fighter more often than not ran up against the antagonism of the crowd.[16] Nevertheless, the twenty years from 1889 to 1909 were the Golden Age of Negro pugilism.

GEORGE DIXON

Few of the boxers in this period were actually residents of New York, but all of them found their way to Black Bohemia at some time or another. One of the most popular of the fighting visitors was George Dixon, the first American Negro to win a world's championship. He came to New York in 1886 from Nova Scotia and won the bantamweight title in 1891 by defeating the British champion, Nunc Wallace, exactly one hundred years after the first Negro on record had entered the prize ring.[17] Spirited discussion was provided by the sports writers of the time who said that Dixon had all the essentials of a great fighter: a fighting head and as deft a left as the prize ring had ever seen. In timing and judging distance he was well nigh perfect. It was said of the little boxer that he never lost his head in time of stress, and in "ring poker" he was a master in hiding his hurts. The "Little Chocolate" battled through a brilliant career until 1906 when he died of tuberculosis in a New York hospital.

JOE WALCOTT

The fighting boys of this period achieved great success as powerful punchers. Joe Walcott, for example, far-famed as a terrible puncher, won the welterweight title in 1901. He shipped from Barbados, British West Indies, as a cabin boy at the age of fifteen and arrived in Boston in 1887 where he engaged almost immediately in amateur fights. Later he came to New York where engagements

---

[16] Crossed out: "It was only when these men performed among members of their race that they were not faced with an atmosphere of crackling hostility. This was so real a handicap that only the stout-hearted overcame it."—Ed.

[17] Pierce Egan, the famous English boxing historian, found that a group of Negro fighters, known as the "Tar Babies," appeared in the ring as early as 1791.

were more lucrative. It was Walcott's unusual physical development that made his ring career such a distinct success. He had an unusually short neck, his head seemingly being set right down on his shoulders. This enabled him to duck blows easily. Though almost a pigmy in height he was called the "Caveman of the Ring." Walcott is listed as a welterweight, but he fought men in all classes, for in those days none was squeamish about such details as weight. The squat boxer won the welterweight title, December 18, 1901, from Rube Fern in Toronto, Canada. Some years after his retirement, a reporter asked him what he thought of the present day Negro boxers: "They treated us the same way back there as they do colored boxers today. We had to beat a white man half to death to get a decision."

JOE GANS

One of the extraordinary Negro fighters of this period was Joe Gans, whose many battles in the ring provided as many tales in Black Bohemia. Particularly was he beloved by the sports of that section because he was a heavy drinker and gambler and a curious mixture of poet and pugilist. His prowess as a skilled ringman was established in his battles with Battling Nelson, the famous "Iron Man." In one of these affairs, he fought Nelson forty-one rounds in the blistering sun at Goldfield, Nevada, September 3, 1906, and won on a foul. This fight, promoted by Tex Rickard with a record purse of $34,000, was the beginning of "big money" in pugilism. Much of this stake was "blown in" in the clubs of Black Bohemia. In his last meeting with Nelson at Colma, California, September 9, 1908, the Gans of uncanny skill, wonderful defense, clever footwork, and terrific punching power was no more, and he was knocked out after twenty-one rounds. Drinking and tuberculosis had taken their toll and he died two years later at Phoenix, Arizona, after, in the now famous words of his mother, "bringing home the bacon" for a number of thrilling years.

Gans was known in gambling circles as a plunger and wild spender, but his gentlemanly characteristics earned him the title of the "Brown Gentleman." He had a curious love of poetry and is known to have stopped in the middle of his training to recite a line whose beauty had struck him. His sparring mates were hired with the understanding that they would patiently listen to his flights into poetry. Jim Tully provided the "Old Master's" epitaph: "This superb lightweight had brains, poise and the soul of a dreamer."

JACK JOHNSON

Towards the close of this pugilistic era, Jack Johnson won the world's heavyweight championship from Tommy Burns in fourteen rounds, December 26, 1908, after chasing him to Australia. One of the strangest manifestations of prejudice in this period was the elevation of a "white hope" in the boxing game, after Johnson had won the heavyweight crown. "Li'l Artha," as the Negro was called, was not alone in feeling the lash of prejudice. The whole Negro race was a victim of its manifestations and Black Bohemia did plenty of grumbling. This was certainly so when Johnson retained his title by knocking out Jim Jeffries at Reno, Nevada, July 4, 1910. The majority of the thousands of spectators at this fight frankly howled for Jeffries to "kill the nigger." Johnson did more than physically meet Jeffries; psychologically he had to fight the majority of the white population of the United States, for Jeffries had been hailed as its "white hope."

A large section of the press and many of the literary fellows industriously fomented the sentiment that the security of white civilization and "white supremacy" depended upon the defeat of the Negro. Acting the role of both prophet and comforter, an inspired writer contended that Jeffries was bound to win, because, while he had Runnymede and Agincourt behind him, the Negro had nothing but the jungle. And he added that merely a look in the eye would be sufficient to wilt Johnson.

MONOLOGUE TO 20,000

Past thirty-five years of age, poor Jeff was goaded into coming out of a well-deserved retirement for an awful beating at Reno. Johnson gave the ex-boilermaker one of the most "artistic" lacings a fighter had ever received in the ring. "The greatest battle of the century," wrote Jack London, "was a monologue delivered to 20,000 spectators by a smiling Negro." Johnson toyed with Jeff, while joshing with his aides and the crowd. "From the opening round to the closing," said London, "he never ceased from his witty sallies, his exchange of repartee with his opponent's seconds and with the audience." [18] The next morning the New York *World* observed "That Mr Johnson should so lightly and carelessly punch the head off of Mr Jim Jeffries must have come as a shock to every devoted believer in the supremacy of the Anglo-Saxon race. The sinister fact is not that Mr Johnson won but that he won so easily and that his once terrific opponent manifested so small a capacity for taking punishment."

While the New York *Herald* wondered "as to the effect of Johnson's victory on the colored population," Negroes were attacked by whites all over the Nation when news of Johnson's victory was heard. In New York City thousands of white men attacked Negroes who, the *Herald* reported, "were badly beaten." The *Herald* felt called upon to give the story a headline: "Half Dozen Dead As Crowds Attack Negroes; Reign of Terror Here." Mob passion reached such a height that Congress passed a law prohibiting the interstate exhibition of moving pictures of prize fights. Tex Rickard, who promoted the fight, swore never to stage another interracial heavyweight championship and he kept his word. Johnson finally lost his title to an acknowledged second-rater, Jess Willard, in Havana, Cuba, in 1915.

Perhaps it was Jack Johnson's sense of humor that carried him over many of the rough spots in his stormy career. Inside of the ring the man with the "golden smile" was a marvel in many respects; outside of the ropes he did not seem to possess the same talent and ability to manage his affairs. His conduct [19] brought him disfavor, even persecution. But he was no more than a product of that boisterous and rowdy period. What probably angered the white community more than Johnson's winning the title was his marriage to a white woman. Black Bohemia and later Harlem were particularly vocal on this point. While Negroes criticized Johnson their reasons were not the same as those which he received from the white world, for Negroes felt that his conduct was unbecoming a great champion.[20] Immediately following Johnson's marriage virtu-

---

[18] New York *Herald*, July 5, 1910.

[19] "Bizarre behavior" was crossed out and "conduct" substituted.—Ed.

[20] "Was unbecoming a great champion" was substituted for "brought disgrace to the race."—Ed.

ally identical bills against intermarriage of the races were initiated in Wisconsin, Iowa, Kansas, Colorado, Minnesota, New Jersey, Michigan, and New York. Bills were introduced in Congress, the penalties varying from imprisonment to enforced surgical operation. In New York efforts were made to legalize segregation by ordinance, and boxing contests between Negro and white people were prohibited by executive action. Attempts at caste legislation were met by strong protest, and Assemblyman A. J. Levy saw the need to introduce a civil rights bill in the legislature "to strengthen the present provisions."

SAM LANGFORD

The saga of Jack Johnson and of prizefighting might have been different if the Negro champion himself had not drawn the color line too—against another Negro, Sam Langford, who was probably one of the cleverest fighters in the history of the ring. While Johnson met willingly all white aspirants to his title, he steadfastly refused to risk his crown against the squat little boxer called the "Boston Tar Baby."

Johnson had a reason. He had fought Langford once—before he became champion—and one fight with Langford, even a winning one, was one to remember.[21] Johnson, on his way up the ladder, met Langford, then a welterweight, at Chelsea, Mass., April 26, 1906. In the second round the "Boston Tar Baby," outweighed by fifty pounds, landed a quick left hook on Johnson's jaw and sent him to the floor. Johnson got to his feet after a slow count of nine. Prominent sporting men holding watches at the ringside declared that the future champion was down for a long count.[22] Johnson held on for the rest of the round and fought Langford at long range for the thirteen ensuing stanzas to get the decision—but he never met Langford again.[23]

Johnson was not the only fighter who evaded Langford. The leading white boxers of the decade flatly refused to meet him unless

---

[21] "Was one to remember" was substituted for "usually lasted an opponent a lifetime."—Ed.

[22] From "Johnson's Record," New York *Sun,* July 5, 1910. "Long Count'" was substituted for "full sixteen records."—Ed.

[23] "Met" was substituted for "made the mistake of entering the ring with."—Ed.

he signed a "gentlemen's agreement" assuring the outcome. Few fighters in the history of the ring engaged in more "fixed" bouts than did this talented pugilist, of whom W. O. McGeehan said: "In his prime, Sam could have beaten any human, black or white."

Langford, who became one of the free-spending leading lights of Black Bohemia, was a natural fighter. The son of a fighting logger in Weymouth Falls, Nova Scotia, and brother of the local Negro preacher who taught him the manly art of self-defense, young Sam ran away from home at twelve and began fighting for a living almost immediately. In his earliest recorded professional fight, at Boston, January 13, 1902, he defeated two white men—Jack Mc-Vickar and William McDonald—the same night. This double bout took place exactly one month before Sam's sixteenth birthday!

Although Langford never won a title (the gentlemen's agreement always prevented this) he fought the best contenders in all classes. He first won fame by defeating the aging Joe Gans as a lightweight in Boston, December 8, 1903. Ten months later he fought his famous "grudge" bout with Joe Walcott. Friends of Walcott had steamed him into the fight by telling him that Sam was trying to steal his girl and the pair battled to a draw after fifteen rounds at Manchester, N. H. (Sept 5, 1904). Joe kept his girl incidentally, because Sam had never met her nor shown even a remote interest in the unidentified young lady.

Like most Negro fighters of the times, Langford was woefully exploited by his white manager. Looking back over his career in 1935, the blinded and impoverished ex-pugilist told a reporter: [24]

> I once fought three fifteen round bouts in a week and got less than $100. My manager (a white man named Joe Woodman) always counted my money first. He was one of them 'I'll-take-care-of-you' brothers. Folks always ask me, I made so much money why I don't save it. You heard of the time I fought Jack Johnson? . . . . Well, I got $250 for that fight, minus training expenses and my manager's bit. . . .

Describing his fighting tactics, Sam said: "I never hit a man's elbow nor his head. I hit 'em in the body and then I hit 'em on the point of the chin and I sent 'em home early if they wasn't good boys...I had 500 fights and every one was a pleasure."

---

[24] A. J. Liebling, New York *World Telegram*, February 6, 1935.

MAJOR TAYLOR

A name that blazed across New York billboards and newspapers in this period was "Major" Taylor, who added new glories to the accomplishments of Negroes in sports, but who was rarely seen in Black Bohemia because he was deeply religious. Taylor won the bicycle sprint championship of America in 1898. This was a sport of considerable popularity in the 1890s, with many enthusiastic Negro participants. The "Colored King" began racing in 1894 under the guidance of William A. Brady, who was then also the manager of James J. Corbett, the prize fighter. Brady piloted Taylor into many lucrative races and the Negro cyclist in time held nearly every championship in this country.

Taylor was never a popular hero for he brought into his profession more honesty than required on the race tracks and this was regarded as gross impertinence by the white men who controlled the tracks and betting rings. His firm stand against split purses and shady matches brought him much hatred and abuse. "What money I win, I keep," he once declared. "I only split with the hotel keeper who lodges me and the railroad man who transports me." Taylor attributed much of his success to his own peculiar style of riding, for he adopted the extension handlebars for his sprint races and perfected a racing stance that called for no unnecessary motion of head or body. Taylor retired in 1910, comparatively wealthy and famous, after defeating all the top-notch performers in matched races. The only great white riders he never met were Bald, Gardiner, and Kiser. They drew the color line.

THEATER PEOPLE

Black Bohemia's most popular club was *The Marshall,* at West Fifty-third Street, a place that became famous as the headquarters of Negro talent. There gathered the actors, the musicians, the composers, the writers, the singers, dancers and vaudevillians. There one went to get a closeup of the theatrical stars—Williams and Walker, Cole and Johnson, Ernest Hogan, Will Marion Cook, Jim Europe, and Aida Overton, for Negroes had made a beginning and some headway on the stage. Two of the most frequent visitors were the writers, Paul Laurence Dunbar and James Weldon Johnson. These personalities naturally drew many of those who loved to dwell in the sunshine of greatness. The first modern jazz band ever heard in New York, or perhaps anywhere, was organized at *The Marshall*. It was a playing-singing-dancing orchestra, making the first dominant use of banjos, saxaphones, clarinets and tap drums in combination, and was called the Memphis Students.[25]

The whites who were out sightseeing or slumming also visited *The Marshal,* but many of them who came were themselves performers who acted Negro roles[26] and visited this place to secure firsthand imitations.[27] "There was one [Negro] man," wrote James Weldon Johnson, "who, whenever he responded to a request to 'do something,' never essayed anything below a reading from Shakespeare. How well he read I do not know, but he greatly impressed me; and I can say that at least he had a voice which strangely stirred those who heard it. Here was a man who made people laugh at the size of his mouth, while he carried in his heart a burning ambition to be a tragedian; and so after all he did play a part in a tragedy."[28]

Perhaps the chief influence that Black Bohemia had was upon the people in the theater. In the many professional clubs of the 1890s[29] an atmosphere of congeniality[30] pervaded, which gave birth and nourishment to new artistic ideas. Without these clubs it is doubtful that any collective advance would have been made by Negroes in the theater.

MINSTRELSY

The earliest appearance of Negroes in the theater was semiprofessional, when *Othello* and *Richard III* were being performed

---

[25] James Weldon Johnson, "The Making of Harlem" in *Survey Graphic* No. 6 (March 1925) vi 635.

[26] "Acted Negro roles" substituted for "delineated 'darky characters.' "—Ed.

[27] Crossed out: "from the Negro entertainer."—Ed.

[28] Although *op. cit.* was given as a footnote, this quotation could not be found in the Johnson article referred to in footnote 25.—Ed.

[29] Crossed out: "Negro theatrical talent created for itself."—Ed.

[30] Crossed out: "and guildship."—Ed.

in the African Grove as early as 1821. The first professional appearance of the Negro was on the minstrel stage about the middle of
the last century. Though Negro minstrelsy is a form of popular
entertainment which seems to have disappeared from the New York
theaters, it was really America's first completely original contribution to the theater. The pattern was originally set by the dancing
and singing slaves of the old South. But whites first exploited its
commercial possibilities.[31]

Minstrelsy[32] was not long in becoming the chief popular entertainment of the country. Some of the minstrels toured Europe, but
with less success than in America. During the early part of the nineteenth century Haverly's Mastodon Minstrels, a group of white
Americans bearing the boastful legend "40, Count them, 40," arrived in Germany to "play" the Berlin music halls, proudly expecting to repeat their American triumphs. But they had not counted on
the Teutonic lack of humor because they were threatened with
arrest for impersonating Negroes.

Though early minstrelsy had its basis in the imitations of Negro
plantation entertainers, it became a caricature of Negro life when

---

[31] "The pattern was originally set by the dancing and singing slaves of the old
South. But whites first exploited its commercial possibilities" was substituted for
"Negro minstrelsy had its origin among the slaves of the old South, who danced
and sang to the accompaniment of banjo and bones."—Ed.

[32] A preceding paragraph was crossed out: "White actors very early saw the
commercial possibilities of Negro minstrelsy. As far back as the 1820s black-faced
acts by white performers were touring the country. One of the most famous of
these pioneer 'singles' was Dan Rice's 'Jump Jim Crow.' In the summer of 1830,
Rice, then an obscure performer, was wandering through the streets of Cincinnati
when he heard a ragged Negro singing 'Jump Jim Crow.' The idea struck him that
he would make a hit with both the song and the impersonation. He tried it in the
fall of that year at Pittsburgh with success. In Washington, during the same year,
Rice made the act a 'double,' his partner being Joseph Jefferson, the noted actor,
then abbout four years old. Rice brought in Jefferson in a sack slung over his
shoulder and, stepping to the footlights, sang: 'Ladies and gentlemen, I'd have you
for to know that I've got a little darky here that jumps Jim Crow,' and with
this he emptied little Jefferson from the sack, in rags, blackface, and all,
as a diminutive Jim Crow (*Atlantic Monthly*, November 1867). The first blackface
minstrel troupe to appear in a regular theater was a quartet of white men known
as the Virginia Minstrels headed by Dan Emmett, the Yankee, who wrote 'Dixie.'
This troupe gave its first performance in New York City in February 1843. Similar
companies sprang up in the larger northern cities and minstrelsy was not long in
becoming the chief popular entertainment."—Ed.

it mounted the stage. The eternal battle of Mr Tambo and Mr Bones against the Interlocutor, as produced by whites for whites, had a great deal to do with the creating of a Negro stereotype which showed the Negro as addicted to big words, gaudy apparel and chicken stealing. In its early years white minstrelsy was often proslavery. When the Negro came into the field "the mould was too set to be radically changed," and he, too, was forced to don the burnt cork. Minstrelsy in time lost its realism and became a travesty.[33]

Until the Civil War most of the professional minstrels were white men, Dan Emmett, "Jim Crow" Rice, and Billy Whitlock being its chief exponents. The greatest of the early Negro comedians were Billy Kersands, Sam Lucas (Milady) and James Bland, the composer of *Carry Me Back to Ole Virginny*. Kersands was the most famous of all the genuine Negro minstrels. It was he, according to James Weldon Johnson, who introduced the Virginia "essence," which is still one of the fundamental steps in Negro dancing. Sam Lucas, the "Grand Old Man" of the Negro stage, was the most versatile of this trio.[34] His career extended from soon after the Civil War to 1915, when he appeared as Uncle Tom in the first screen version of *Uncle Tom's Cabin*.[35]

Lucas had a curious passion for diamonds. Many legends sprang up about his collection.[36] The fact that they were utilitarian as well as decorative had much to do with the growth of these tales. The famous producer, Gustave Frohman, finding himself in a tight spot

[33] Sterling A. Brown, *Negro Poetry and Drama* [Bronze Booklet No. 7] (Washington, D.C., The Associates in Negro Folk Education 1937) 104-106.

[34] Crossed out: "He was born in Washington, Ohio, in 1840. He was well educated, cultured, and neat in his dress, and described as the type of man who looked well in a frock coat. Lucas was an active figure in the theater from the early days of minstrelsy down to modern Negro musical comedy. As late as 1910 he played a leading part in Cole and Johnson's *Red Moon*."—Ed.

[35] Crossed out: "He, himself, made the plunge into the river to save Little Eva, a fact that his friends felt brought on his death, January 10, 1916, in New York City."—Ed.

[36] Crossed out: "which was the envy and admiration of his colleagues in Black Bohemia."—Ed.

more than once, made frequent use of them during his many years on the road with shows.[37]

By 1885 the vogue of Negro blackfaced actors was definitely on its way. At Saratoga the Negro waiters gave a minstrel show which was recorded in the manner of that day by the *London Saturday Review:* "When the curtains were drawn aside, discovering a row of sable performers, it was perceived, to the great and abiding joy of the spectators, that the musicians were all of a uniform darkness of hue, and that they, genuine Negroes as they were, had 'blackened up,' the more closely to resemble the professional Negro minstrel."

The nineties produced a crop of talented Negro performers, who though they took frequently to the roads always returned to New York for new bookings. A[38] departure from strict minstrelsy occurred in 1891, when Sam T. Jack, a white man, started it with the *Creole Show.* Jack, a burlesque owner and theater manager, presented[39] the first Negro show featuring Negro girls.[40] The

---

[37] Crossed out: "In 1876 Frohman had launched the Stoddard Comedy Company, and, by hook and by crook, the company had worked its way through Texas, Arkansas, and Tennessee up to Richmond, Kentucky. Biographers of Mr. Frohman relate:

At Richmond, Gustave had an inspiration. Then, as always, 'Uncle Tom's Cabin' was the great life-saver of the harassed and needy theatrical organization. . . .
'Why not have a real Negro play Uncle Tom?' said Gustave.
So he wired Charles as follows:
'Get me an Eva and send her down with Sam Lucas. Be sure to tell Sam to bring his diamonds . . .'
Gustave knew that these jewels, like Louise Dillon's seal-skin sack, meant a meal ticket for the company and transportation in an emergency.

Gustave Frohman's visions of big business melted away at Wilmington, Ohio. With a last gasp of despair the Stoddard Comedy folded up and the ill-starred tour ended. Some of Lucas' diamonds were pawned by Frohman to get the company back to Cincinnati.

BURNT CORK ROLE

The Negro's full entry on the American comedy stage took place toward the end of the 1860s. A Negro unit, Lew Johnson's Plantation Minstrels, was organized and toured the country during the early part of that decade. Then followed such popular companies as Callender's Minstrels and the Georgia Minstrels, who moved across the country in Lew Johnson's wake with confident stride. These Negro troupes accepted almost whole the performance pattern that had been worked out and laid down by the white minstrels during the preceding twenty-five years, even to the blacking of their faces."—Ed.

[38] "A departure" was substituted for "'It was during this period that the first departure" . . .—Ed.

[39] "presented" substituted for "conceived the idea of putting on"—Ed.

[40] "Negro girls" substituted for "sixteen beautiful girls."
Crossed out: "together with a cast of skilled male performers."—Ed.

Creoles opened in Chicago in 1891.[41] Subsequently it appeared in New York City at the old Standard Theatre in Greeley Square.[42]

WILLIAMS AND WALKER

Jack's success led to the presentation on Broadway of musical comedies written and produced by Negroes. Cole and Johnson, Williams and Walker, and Ernest Hogan were the leaders in this type of entertainment. They gained their early training with Worth's Museum and similar stock companies, subsequently branching out to exploit their own talents. This second phase of the Negro in the theatre saw the rise of such personalities as Bert Williams, George Williams, George Walker, Aida Overton, and Mme. Sissieretta Jones, the "Black Patti." But the minstrel tradition dogged their steps to stardom, and the blackfaced comedian with his antics remained an integral part of their offerings.

MAN OF LAUGHTER

Bert Williams, the most distinguished comedian of his time, studied for the legitimate stage under the great pantomimist, Pietro; and though sidetracked, he achieved something approaching phenomenal success in the burnt-cork role. Though born and reared in the West Indies, he differed from the early minstrels in that he brought something of the American Negro's genuine humor and philosophy to the stage. His was a cartoon in make-up only. He made his reputation as a member of the team of Williams and Walker, which came to New York singing one of the catchiest songs of the day, "Dora Dean." They had written this number themselves after a sight of Miss Dora Dean, one of the famed beauties of the *Creole Show*. They reached New York in 1896 and together underwent all the hardships of a colored vaudeville team of the period. Assisted by two girls, Williams and Walker did much to make the cakewalk popular. Cakewalk pictures of the quartet were reproduced in colors and widely distributed as advertisements by a big cigarette concern.

---

[41] Crossed out: "and continued there the whole season of the World's Fair, 1893, playing at Sam T. Jack's Opera House."—Ed.

[42] Crossed out: "they were a sensation for five or six seasons."—Ed.

Nourished in Black Bohemia, the popularity of the cakewalk soon sprang up in the carpeted salons of the rich and became such a fad that the pair challenged William K. Vanderbilt to a dance duel. Dressed a point or two above the height of fashion, Williams and Walker, as a publicity stunt, called at the financier's home and left him the following letter: [43]

> In view of the fact that you have made a success as a cake-walker, having appeared in a semi-public exhibition and having posed as an expert in that capacity, we the undersigned world renowned cake-walkers, believing that the attention of the public has been distracted from us on account of the tremendous hit which you have made, hereby challenge you to compete with us in a cake-walking match, which will decide which of us deserve the title of champion cake-walker of the world.
>
> As a guarantee of good faith we have this day deposited at the office of the New York *World* the sum of $50. If you purpose proving to the Public that you really are an expert cake-walker we shall be pleased to have you cover that amount and name the day on which it will be convenient for you to try odds against us.

In 1900 the two comedians brought out their own show, the *Sons of Ham*. But *In Dahomey,* which opened two years later, was their big success.[44] In the spring of 1903 the production was taken to London, where it ran for seven months at the Shaftesbury Theatre. The last touch of approval was placed on it on June 23, a few weeks later, when the company appeared by royal command at Buckingham Palace, in celebration of the ninth birthday of the Prince of Wales, now the Duke of Windsor. The Williams and Walker company was easily the most popular Negro theatrical combination of that day. In addition to its stars there were Jesse Shipp, Alex Rogers, Will Marion Cook, and Aida Overton, the wife of George Walker. The last show that Williams and Walker produced was *Bandana*

---

[43] James Weldon Johnson, *Black Manhattan* (New York, Alfred A. Knopf 1940) 105.

[44] This sentence replaced one crossed out: "Two years later they produced *In Dahomey,* and made Negro theatrical history by opening it at Times Square, then New York's theatrical center."—Ed.

Land in 1907. During its run George Walker's health broke and that "sleek, smiling dandy" never again pranced on a stage.[45]

Egbert Austin Williams, who is regarded as the greatest Negro comedian of all time, was said to have been the grandson of Svend Eric, a white Danish consul to Antigua who had married one of the native beauties. As a Negro immigrant, Williams found it necessary to remark on one occasion that "It's no disgrace to be colored, but it's so inconvenient." And it may be for this reason that he began his theatrical career as a Hawaiian in San Francisco. It was here that he met George Walker in 1889, and on the wave of blackface popularity they shrewdly appeared as "Two Real Coons," at a salary of fourteen dollars a week for the act. Before he died, Williams was credited with earning an annual salary of fifty thousand dollars. Williams was, however, impatient with his blackfaced role and said, "If I were free to do as I liked, I would give both sides of the shiftless darky—the pathos as well as the fun." Booker T. Washington regarded him an "asset to the Negro race," because of his sympathetic delineation of Negro characters.[46]

---

[45] The next paragraph was crossed out: "In 1909, Bert Williams, who played the slow-witted, shuffling half of the team, toured the provinces alone in *Mr. Lode of Kole*. It had little success and was the last Negro show in which he appeared. The next year he was engaged for *Ziegfeld Follies* and remained a member of the cast for ten seasons. In 1920 he was the star in *Broadway Brevities*, and in 1922 the star in the *Pink Slip*, which, after a try-out, was rewritten and called *Under the Bamboo Tree*. He was ill when he went out with this last show; and after it had been on the road a few weeks, he collapsed and had to be brought back to New York. He died, March 11, 1922, not quite forty-seven years old. Bert Williams' singing of a plaintive Negro song was unrivaled, and his rendition of "Nobody" remains a perfection for that type of droll comedy. In Negro circles Williams is regarded as the greatest Negro comedian of all time."—Ed.

[46] The following section headed *Sissieretta Jones* was crossed out:

"Many women were successful on the stage and in the concert hall during this period. Beginning early in Negro musical history (1851), Elizabeth Taylor Greenfield, known as the 'Black Swan,' attracted attention by singing for the Buffalo (New York) Mutual Association, and later by her tours of New England, the Middle Western States, and Europe.

"The first Negro singer with both the natural voice and the necessary training and cultivation to appear on the concert stage was Mme Marie Selika, who was popular both in America and Europe.

"The most popular of all the women singers was Mme Sissieretta Jones, called the 'Black Patti.' In September of 1854, she sang for President Harrison at the White House. After a successful tour of Europe, she returned to New York where the management of Voelekel and Nolan presented her in an all-Negro show. Bob Cole was engaged to write it and the *Black Patti Troubadours* was produced and played for a number of years. Before her retirement Sissieretta Jones was signed by Abbey, Schoeffel, and Grau, managers of the Metropolitan Opera House, to sing the dark roles in *Aida* and *L'Africaine;* unhappily, the plan fell through. This age was, however, the beginning of a cycle of great Negro concert artists."—Ed.

MINSTRELSY'S END

Though the *Creole Show* was the first to depart from the minstrel pattern, a greater step was taken by Bob Cole's *A Trip to Coontown,* which was the first production to be organized, produced and managed entirely by Negroes. Previously, two gifted collaborators, Will Marion Cook, composer, and Paul Laurence Dunbar, the poet, presented *Clorindy—The Origin of the Cakewalk,* a novelty which had tremendous popularity on Broadway in 1898. By 1909 the Negro had produced such hits as *Jes Lak White Folks,*[47] the *Shoefly Regiment,* and *Rufus Rastus,* featuring such additional theatrical folk as S. H. Dudley, Bob Cole, James Weldon Johnson and his brother, J. Rosamond Johnson. The untimely death of Bob Cole and George Walker, and the entry of Bert Williams on the white stage, all of which occurred within a brief period, brought the development of the Negro theater to an abrupt close. The interval between this and another revival was, however, of brief duration.

---

[47] Crossed out: "the *Policy Players.*"—Ed.

CHAPTER XI

THE TALENTED TENTH

New York, 1900-1910.—The year 1900 marked the beginning of a
new epoch for New York Negroes. The status of the Negro as a
citizen had been steadily declining and was in some respects worse
than at the close of the Civil War. The new amendments to the
Constitution which had been passed in his behalf had been almost
completely nullified in the southern states where he was disfranchised, Jim-Crowed, and denied the equal protection of the laws.
The New York press reported that some two thousand Negroes
had been lynched in the United States up to this time.

As early as 1889 the realization of their danger had prodded
Negro leaders into action and they took steps that year to gather
forces for a new struggle. A promising move in this direction was
made when one hundred and forty-one delegates from twenty-
one states met at Chicago, January 15, 1890, and organized the
Afro-American Council. A man who had achieved considerable
prestige as a leader, J. C. Price, head of Livingstone College, North
Carolina, was elected president, and a New Yorker, T. Thomas
Fortune, secretary. The following year Fortune succeeded Price
as president when the council met at Knoxville, Tenn. But the
organization was silent until 1898 when fresh outrages caused
Bishop Alexander Walters, of New York, to urge Fortune to reas-
semble the council. Still it was found impossible to arouse the
spirit necessary for real growth, nor were the leaders able to raise
sufficient funds to create a permanent machine, and so after a
somewhat indifferent existence the Afro-American Council faded
and died. However, by 1900 a new committee had to be formed
to protest against new and more violent assaults on Negroes.

RACE RIOT

The riot of 1900, New York's fourth great riot involving Negroes, started on the night of August 12, 1900, when a Negro named Arthur Harris left his "girl," May Enoch, on the corner of Eighth Avenue and Forty-first Street while he went to buy a cigar. He returned to find her struggling in the grasp of a white man who was later identified as Robert J. Thorpe, a police officer in plain clothes. Harris immediately went to her rescue. The white man struck him down with a club and Harris retaliated with a penknife, wounding the white man fatally in the abdomen.

The funeral of the officer was attended by a large contingent of the police force who were incensed by his death, in addition to the usual throng drawn by morbid curiosity. In the meantime Harris had disappeared. During the day of the funeral the temper of the crowd to wreak vengeance upon some Negro grew strong. Thorpe's death had stirred the smoldering ill-feeling between the races, and as the day closed, rumors of trouble circulated quickly. Knowing only too well the consequences of any manifestations of it, Negroes locked their doors and kept off the streets.

The storm burst on the evening of August 15, the day of the funeral. A Ninth Avenue crowd began by roughly handling Spencer Walters, a Negro who was passing near the home of Thorpe's sister. Another Negro, Richard Williams, came to Walter's aid, discharging a revolver as he advanced. In a short time thousands of white people were pouring into the streets and attacking every Negro regardless of age or sex. Nearly every house in the locality of Thirty-fourth to Forty-second Streets, between Eighth and Ninth Avenue, was occupied by Negroes. "The mob seemed to know this and they made for these houses," said the New York *Sun*. "Every time a Negro put his head out of a window, a shower of stones, clubs and other missiles would sail towards the Negro. The head would disappear and then would come an answering volley from the roof." At the sight of a passing streetcar which bore Negro passengers, the lawless crowd blocked the tracks, piled on, and dragged Negroes off over the laps of other passengers. A stream of bleeding Negroes was soon pouring into the police stations and hospitals. A saloon at Thirty-first Street and Sixth Avenue, conducted by Joe Walcott, Negro pugilist, was mobbed, sacked, and its occupants beaten. The rioters were heard to scream for the heads of Williams and Walker,[1] the popular Negro vaudeville team which was known to frequent this place.

White eyewitnesses accused the police of doing little to prevent the assault on Negroes and declared the mob was only checked when it attempted to invade the fashionable Broadway hotels in search of Negro employees. When Negroes appealed for aid, according to the New York *Times*, they received a smash over the head with a nightstick for a reply. Negroes who ran to policemen for protection, even begging to be locked up for safety, were thrown back to the rabble.

That evening fifteen patrol wagons loaded with Negroes were taken to the police station. The next morning when the prisoners were arraigned before Magistrate Cornell, he said: "I don't see why you have no white men here . . . I'd like to see some of the people who really started this riot in court."

AFFAIR WHITE-WASHED

Demands for an investigation met with a series of excuses and delays on the part of both the city officials and the police authorities. The Negro citizens then took steps to force action. A meeting was promptly called at St Mark's Church in West Fifty-third Street and the Citizens' Protective League was organized. The Rev William H. Brooks, pastor of St Mark's, was elected president; James E. Garner, a successful businessman, treasurer; and T. Thomas Fortune, owner and editor of the New York *Age,* was made chairman of the executive committee.

A mass meeting was held in Carnegie Hall, September 12, and funds were raised to carry on a vigorous campaign. The organization retained Israel Ludlow, who brought claims against the City Comptroller's office totaling $250,000, one of which was on behalf of Paul Laurence Dunbar, the Negro poet.[2] An aroused Negro public brought the league's membership up to five thousand within a few weeks. In a letter to Mayor Van Wyck, the organization demanded the conviction and removal of all officers who had at-

---

[1] See p. 161—Ed.
[2] See p. 161—Ed.

tacked Negroes during the riot. The mayor replied that the whole matter was in the hands of the Police Board. A police department investigation was finally held. Negro citizens who testified that they had been beaten by the police were themselves treated as accused persons. One after another, the policemen swore that the witnesses who testified against them had lied. The investigation turned out to be a sham and whitewash. The affair had its last official gasp when a grand jury investigation of the riots produced no indictments.

Arthur Harris, the slayer of Policeman Thorpe, was captured in Washington, D. C., and returned to New York where he was convicted, October 29, 1900, of second-degree murder. Negroes were afterward admonished from pulpit and press to "get a permit to carry a revolver. You are not supposed to be a walking arsenal but don't get caught again. Have your houses made ready to afford protection from the fury of the mob."

THE AFRO-AMERICAN

T. Thomas Fortune continued to be active on the local scene. A writer of considerable ability, he was regarded by his contemporaries as the dean of Negro journalists. He began his career as editor of the New York *Globe* in 1880. For a while he had been an assistant to Amos Cummings on the Evening *Sun*. Later he was a contributor to the New York *Sun* under Charles A. Dana. Fortune was by far one of the most powerful and influential Negro editors of his time; his editorials in the New York *Age* drew repeated comments from the white dailies. Theodore Roosevelt, when police commissioner, was quoted as saying, "Tom Fortune, for God's sake, keep that dirty pen of yours off me." When Roosevelt became President, it was Fortune whom he sent to investigate conditions in the Hawaiian Islands and the Phillippines. As friend and advisor to Booker T. Washington, he assisted the educator in the preparation of his autobiographies. Because of the disagreeable connotation of the word "nigger," he excluded "Negro" from his vocabulary and is credited with being the originator of the term "Afro-American." He was also editor of Marcus Garvey's *Negro Times,* before his death in 1923.

BOOKER T. WASHINGTON

In September 1895 Booker T. Washington, who had been for some years a national rising figure, made a memorable speech at the opening of the Cotton States Exposition in Atlanta, Ga. In this speech Washington said: "In all things purely social we can be as separate as the five fingers and yet one as the hand in all things essential to mutual progress."

He scoffed at Negroes holding seats in the government so soon after emancipation and declared: "The agitation of questions of social equality is the extremest folly." On the question of southern invasion by foreign labor he said: "To those of the white race who look to the coming of those of foreign birth and strange tongue and habit for the prosperity of the South, were I permitted I would repeat what I say to my own race, 'Cast down your buckets where you are.'" He then pleaded for the employment of Negroes "who have without strikes and labor wars tilled your fields, cleared your forests, builded your railroads and cities, brought forth treasures from the bowels of the earth, and helped make possible this magnificent representation of the progress of the South."

The South in general construed the speech as Negro abdication from claims to equal citizenship rights. For its conciliatory aspects indicated the black race's willingness to accept the status of contented and industrious peasants. The northern financial and industrial leaders saw in his speech, now that the war was over, the achievement of the desired harmony and peace they so needed to develop and prosper. At one stroke Washington had gained the support and approval of the influential white people of both North and South. Thenceforth he was acclaimed by them as the economic emancipator of the Negro, the first of a succession of leaders imposed on Negroes by whites.

Washington's life story reads like the Horatio Alger novels so popular during his day. According to his autobiography, *Up From Slavery,* he was born a slave amidst squalor and poverty and as a child slept "on a bundle of filthy rags laid on the dirt floor." Knowing nothing of his father and set free at emancipation a ragged, illiterate, penniless boy, possessing only the name Booker, he rose to make the name of his own choice famous throughout

the world. Born in a log cabin where even a table was a luxury,
he lived to dine at the table of a President of the United States
and to take tea with Queen Victoria of England.

"KITCHEN CABINET"

His leadership of Negroes rested partly upon the counsel he
gave them on their economic welfare. When Washington delivered
his Atlanta address, the skilled Negro worker was being eliminated
from industry by white workingmen, supported by what Negroes
described as "lily-white" trade unions. To meet the competition of
white workers and at the same time to raise the Negro's economic
standards and win the respect of the white man, Washington la-
bored to make Negroes into efficient workers through industrial
education. He encouraged them to become independent through
the establishment of Negro business and trade. Tuskegee Institute,
of which he was founder, was the symbol of this. Moreover, his
influence as an educator so extended into the ramifications of life,
that he dictated the rise and fall of many Negroes occupying polit-
cal and private positions controlled by whites. The number of Negro political job-holders was so generally increased under Washington that there were few Negroes who dared criticize him in
public or let it be known that they were not in sympathy with
his work, for he held the key to most of the patronage distributed
to Negroes by the dominant class. His role as "headman" of the
extra-legal or liaison group of Negroes known as the "Black Cabinet" or the "Kitchen Cabinet," which functioned as advisor to the
national administration, whether it was Republican or Democratic,
cemented Washington's strategic position in American life. The
idea among whites of a "Kitchen Cabinet" persists to this day
though it has been elevated to the "Black Brain Trust."

W.E.B. DUBOIS

While Washington was rising to fame as the author of this conciliatory formula and his preachments on thrift and humility,
W.E.B. DuBois, who represented the educated Negro elite, came forth
with the thesis "that the Negro race like all races is going to be
saved by its exceptional men." This group he called the "talented

tenth." In presenting a program to develop these leaders DuBois said:

"The best and most capable of their [Negro] youth must be schooled in the colleges and universities of the land. . . . I insist that the object of all true education is not to make men carpenters, it is to make carpenters men, each equally important; the first is to give the group and community in which he works liberally trained teachers and leaders to teach him and his family what life means; the second is to give him sufficient intelligence and technical skill to make him an efficient worker; the first object demands the Negro colleges and college bred men, not a quantity of such colleges but a few excellent in quality; not too many college bred men, but enough to leaven the lump, to inspire the masses, to raise the talented tenth to leadership; the second object demands a good system of common schools, well taught, conveniently located and properly equipped."

Scoring what was described as Washington's "Atlanta Compromise," DuBois contended that the southern leader distinctly asked black people to give up at least for the present, three things: first, political rights; second, insistence on civil rights; third, higher education for Negro youth. DuBois then asked what had the Negro received in return for this "tender of the palm branch," and listed the following as having occurred in the post-Civil War period:

1. The disfranchisement of the Negro.
2. The legal creation of a distinct status of civil inferiority for the Negro.
3. The steady withdrawal of aid from institutions for the higher training for the Negro.

DuBois formulated many of his views in 1903 in his *Souls of Black Folk,* which was a collection of essays, one of which, entitled "Of Mr Washington and Others," was a critique of the Tuskegee educator's philosophy. The author of the *Souls of Black Folk* had no similarity to the author of *Up From Slavery* in background or training, except that he was also a Negro. DuBois was born two years after the close of the Civil War in a New England town, Great Barrington, Mass. Here he received his elementary schooling. He attended Fisk University, Harvard, and the University of Berlin.

NIAGARA MOVEMENT

A split of the race into two contending camps which came about at this time was to last for more than twenty years. The followers of Booker T. Washington were afterwards derisively labeled "handkerchief-head niggers," "white-folks' niggers," and "Uncle Tom niggers." Under DuBois' leadership a conference was held July 11-13, 1903, at Buffalo, New York. Twenty-nine representatives were present from thirteen states and the District of Columbia. Three states of the old South were represented—Georgia, Tennessee, and Virginia. A national organization was formed and called the Niagara Movement. It approved the following objectives: (a) freedom of speech and criticism; (b) an unfettered and unsubsidized press; (c) manhood suffrage; (d) the abolition of all caste distinctions based simply on color and race; (e) the recognition of the principles of human brotherhood as a practical present creed; (f) the recognition of a highest and best human training as the monopoly of no class or race; (g) a belief in the dignity of labour; (h) united effort to realize these ideals under wise and courageous leadership. In brief, its purpose was to abolish all distinctions based on race, class, or color.

A meeting was held the following year at Harper's Ferry, the scene of John Brown's raid. The movement, hampered as it was by a lack of funds and by a membership confined to one race, died an early death. It did, however, set the stage for the formation of the National Association for the Advancement of Colored People.

WHITE LIBERALS

In the summer of 1903 the country was shocked by race riots at Springfield, Illinois, the birthplace of Abraham Lincoln. A mob, including many of the town's "best citizens," raged for two days, killing and wounding scores of Negroes and driving thousands of them from the city. Articles on the outburst appeared in leading publications throughout the country. One of these, "Race War in the North," by William English Walling, which appeared in the *Independent,* moved Mary White Ovington, a white woman, to form a "large and powerful body of citizens" to revive the "spirit of [the] abolitionists." Perhaps she was, like others, stimulated by the reform movement which swept over the country in the years between the close of the Spanish-American War and the entry of the United States into the World War.

"So I wrote Mr Walling," relates Miss Ovington, ". . . and we met in New York in the first week of the year 1909." With them was Dr Henry Moscowitz, then prominent in the administration of John Purroy Mitchell, Mayor of New York. No minutes of the meeting were taken, but the trio decided to issue a call for a national conference on the Negro question on the celebration of the centennial of Lincoln's birth. The call was subsequently drafted and issued by Oswald Garrison Villard,[3] then publisher of the New York *Evening Post*.[4]

In May 1910, after a temporary organization had been formed, a conference was held in New York, at which the Negro radicals of the Niagara Movement and the white liberals of abolition tradition merged to form the National Association for the Advancement of Colored People. Its platform, essentially the same as the Niagara Movement, was declared to be "extremely radical." The same year the association called DuBois to the post of director of publicity and research. He resigned his professorship at Atlanta University and came to New York, and the publication of the monthly magazine the *Crisis* was begun. This organ, which has been doing pioneer work for more than twenty years and which reached a peak circulation of a million in 1919, has had considerable influence in American life. Up to the time he resigned his editorship, June 1934, DuBois did more than any other one man to pave the way for what is regarded in Negro circles as the "New Negro," meaning the type of Negro who demands his full rights as a citizen.

N. A. A. C. P.

Founded in 1909 as an interracial organization, the National Association for the Advancement of Colored People had by 1939

---

[3] The grandson of William Lloyd Garrison, the abolitionist.

[4] Among the white people who signed the call were Charles Edward Russell, Jane Addams, Samuel Bowles, John Dewey, Mary E. McDowell, John Haynes Holmes, Florence Kelley, Lillian D. Wald, John E. Milholland, Rabbi Stephen S. Wise and William Dean Howells. The Negroes included W.E.B. Du Bois, Bishop Alexander Walters, Ida Wells Barnett, and the Rev. Francis J. Grimke.

grown to 350 branches in nearly every state in the Union, 113 youth groups in twenty-four states, and 43 college groups in eleven states. Its national headquarters is located in New York City at 69 Fifth Avenue. The association is interested in civil liberties. It demands that the Negro receive decent and equal treatment in all public places and that he be accorded all his constitutional rights, including full suffrage. It has conducted a continuous war on lynching by writing, lecturing, and mass demonstrations. It fought for the passage of the anti-lynching bills and through its efforts several United States Supreme Court decisions were won.

Until recently, when the association took up the fight of discriminations against Negroes employed by the PWA and WPA and recipients of direct relief, the problems of the Negro as a worker were in the main not a concern of the association. The position of the N.A.A.C.P. in this respect was strikingly illustrated in its campaign against the confirmation of Judge Parker's nomination as a Justice of the Supreme Court of the United States some years ago.[5] It opposed Parker because of his unsympathetic attitude toward the Negro's political aspirations as expressed in certain remarks made ten years earlier in one of his campaign speeches in North Carolina, in which he declared that Negroes were unfit to participate in politics. Organized labor, on the other hand, opposed him because of his approval of the "yellow dog" contract. Though the judge's economic views were of direct concern to thousands of wage-earning Negroes, the N.A.A.C.P. bent all of its great energy toward defeating Parker on the racial issue. However, this incident served to show the techniques used by the association in its many fights. As in this case, it draws all interested forces to the firing lines, whatever their particular quarrel with a case at issue.

The association has worked not infrequently in the interest of the Negro's relations to labor organizations. It has fought attempts of plumbers, electricians, railway workers, and other organized groups to keep Negroes out of their unions or to force them out of the occupations which those unions attempt to control. In every case the association has fought for the Negro's admission into the

[5] Spero and Harris, *The Black Worker* 464.

union on the grounds of civil liberties; the principle of labor solidarity was left to other agencies.

The organization had much success in its legal defense of Negroes, largely because of the voluntary services of such noted white lawyers as Moorfield Storey, Louis Marshall, Clarence Darrow, Charles A. Studin, Arthur Garfield Hays, Arthur B. Spingarn, and Morris Ernst; and such Negro attorneys as Charles Houston, William Hastie, and James A. Cobb. Its activities in these years were directed principally by W.E.B. DuBois, James Weldon Johnson, William Pickens, and Daisy Lampkin. In 1933 Walter White, after Du Bois' resignation, became its executive director and Roy Wilkins editor of the *Crisis.*

"NOT ALMS BUT OPPORTUNITY"

The restricted field of the association's activities made it apparent that other organizations were necessary to carry on fights on a broader level. Shortly after its formation another important national organization to work for the improvement of the Negro's status was established—the National Urban League. Its main purpose was to work for the industrial, social, and health improvement of the Negro people, especially those living in urban centers.[6] In addition to these activities, the Urban League collected through extensive research a great deal of valuable data and statistics in those fields in which they were interested. With its national office in New York and two strong New York branches, the league grew rapidly and today has affiliated branches in the principal cities of all sections of the country. Each branch office is manned by a trained secretary and a staff of social workers. Like the N.A.A.C.P., the Urban League is an organization in which both races cooperate.

The Urban League, as an administrator of white philanthropy, made direct efforts to lift trade union racial barriers, not on any trade principle but to provide greater economic opportunity for the Negro worker, because they believed that if the Negro could get into the unions he would be able to follow trades which were

---

[6] Among those who took part in its founding were Mrs. Ruth Standish Baldwin, Edwin R. A. Seligman, Miss Elizabeth Walton, L. Hollingsworth Wood; and the Negroes, George E. Haynes, Fred R. Moore, and Eugene Kinckle Jones, the league's present executive secretary.

barred to him. The lifting of trade union barriers was but one method by which the Urban League sought its ends. It aimed to foster kindly attitudes toward the Negro. Its main appeal was to the employers and the wealthy white upper-classes and occasionally to the trade union leaders. It made little effort to reach the white or black rank and file. Its principle financial backing was received from the white upper classes.

In 1922 the National Urban League founded a monthly magazine, the *Opportunity, a Journal of Negro Life,* to publicize the movement. One of the most characteristic features of this publication was its seemingly studious avoidance of controversial subjects. Whenever these were introduced, they were either in the form of experts from other papers and magazines or articles signed by individuals, for which the editors assumed no responsibility. *Opportunity* was seldom challenging or categorical in tone or attitude. But it covered the fields of literature, art, drama, social welfare, and the general social and economic life of the Negro. Today the magazine bears an eclectic stamp of liberalism, tolerance, and "fair play." Its present editor, Elmer A. Carter,[7] has continued the tradition of its first editor, Charles S. Johnson, who characterized the aim of the magazine as an "attempt to make available to white people information on the Negro that would tend to clear up many of the mooted questions about the Negro."

---

[7] Appointed in 1939 a member of the New York State Unemployment Insurance Appeal Board.

BOOK FOUR

(1910 – 1940)

CHAPTER XII

NEW FACES

HARLEM, 1910-1914.—The trek of Negroes to Harlem began in 1900, but the neighborhood only started to take shape as a Negro community in 1910. This pilgrimage of the blacks, made in gradual stages, took centuries and was generally timed to the expansion of the city. Occasionally the overflow of Negroes had moved across the East River to Brooklyn. Most white neighborhoods were not entered without skirmishes. The bloodiest of these occurred in the "Tenderloin" and "San Juan Hill" districts, where Negroes were involved in almost daily battles with the immigrant Irish. But the resistance to blacks moving into Harlem assumed a decidedly subtle form.

The first white man to set foot in Harlem was the adventurous Dutch trader, Hendrick de Forest, who braved the wrath of hostile Indians and settled there in 1637. He was followed at long intervals by others. The little outpost was named "Haarlem Village" and life took on much the same aspect as a Holland town. Not until 1658 was there any general movement toward settling this section. To promote the development, Governor Stuyvesant offered the "Company's Negroes" to help build a wagon road from New Amsterdam to Haarlem, on an Indian path known today as Broadway. The Dutch governor said, in an expansive statement (strangely prophetic), that this was all being done "for the greater recreation and amusement of this city." By 1660 New Amsterdam, as a trading center, had become the metropolis of New Netherland and the little Haarlem outpost grew in importance as its playground, for a pleasant plantation life had been established there.

The territory of Haarlem, considered then "well out in the country," included roughly the area extending from what is now

179

74th Street to 128th Street, bounded on the east by the Harlem River and on the west by the Hudson. The community was neatly laid out and during its rule under the Dutch it contained a church, a sawmill, and a magistrate's court. The introduction of the patroonships in the province had brought new pioneers from all parts of Europe. So, even from the start, the population of Harlem was composed of diverse races and speeches; not only were there Dutchmen and Walloons, but also Huguenots, Germans, and Englishmen. The scarcity of hands to work the land and build dwellings consequently caused Negroes to be brought to this area. From that time until the Revolutionary War, when the Battle of Harlem Heights was fought, life here was prosaically quiet.

CATO ALEXANDER

In the early years of the nineteenth century, this section, with its elaborate estates and quiet aloofness, was spoken of as "a community which knew nothing of sensational issues." Alexander Hamilton was one of the first aristocrats to take up residence in Harlem when he built the Grange, a beautiful colonial structure which still stands at 141st Street on Hamilton Place, directly in back of the Negro church, St James' Presbyterian. The distinguished Colonel Roger Morris also built a house in this fashionable suburb with a view in command of the Harlem River.

Land speculators looked upon this rural locality as "a far off country" too remote without adequate transportation to be available for city lots and, no doubt, too aristocratic for republican popularity; though the Knickerbockers shrewdly invested in Haarlem land, laying the foundation for one of the great American fortunes. Later, the few scattered and less-affluent dwellers began to use stagecoaches to travel downtown. Hostelries, separated at convenient distances, dotted the roads, and at these man and beast could procure refreshments. At one time, a Negro, Cato Alexander, operated one of these waystations near the summer home of the Beekman family. His inn had a diminutive sitting room with a bar, sanded floors and coarse white walls covered with odd engravings. For years it was a much-frequented resort for sightseers visiting New York. Its hospitality was described as "unbiased by any

modern abolition doctrines." Mr Alexander was, it appears, a remarkable host.[1]

"BROWNSTONE FRONTS AND SARATOGA TRUNKS"

In 1853 the Third Avenue horse-railroad received a charter to
operate a line to Harlem. The horse-drawn car took an hour and
twenty minutes from lower Manhattan to Harlem—provided, travelers complained, "no horse balked or fell dead across the tracks."
The Harlem Navigation Line, operating boats on the Hudson
River, was the more practical means of conveyance, making the
journey from Peck Slip to Harlem in an hour, and thus retained
its importance as the commuting businessman's "special."

One of the stations on the stagecoach line was situated at 125th
Street on Third Avenue, where the only public school in Harlem
was located. The entrance of the first Negro child into this school
caused great consternation. There were few Negro families in Harlem during the middle of the last century and when it was learned
that the new pupil was the twelve-year-old daughter of the cook
of a Mr Brunner, the residents were particularly indignant and
severe objections followed.

Harlem figured but little in the city's annals from 1860 to 1910.
A chronicler spoke of it as "a quiet country town shut off by a
long ride or sail from its ruling center in 1860." During the 1880s
the lower section was known as "Goatville," because of the domestic goats of the Irish squatters who lived in shacks in what is
now Central Park. But with the erection of the elevated railway
in the 1890s Harlem's development was accelerated. It became an
area of fine drives and expensive apartment houses, with streets
laid out in gridiron fashion. Now it was the stronghold of the
uppermiddle class and was referred to as a neighborhood of
"brownstone fronts and Saratoga trunks." Lenox and Eighth Avenues were used for the showing of fine horses and polo was actually being played on the Polo Grounds. Before the construction of
the Harlem River Speedway in 1898, that part of Seventh Avenue
which lies between Central Park to the Polo Grounds was a favorite track of many wealthy horsemen of the city. Here, any after-

---

[1] As a matter of fact, his inn was a station of the Underground Railroad and he
an active conductor.

noon, the finest trotting stock of New York could be seen, driven by such owners as Commodore Vanderbilt, Colonel Rhinlander Kip, and Russell Sage. Oscar Hammerstein climaxed the development of the section by erecting the Harlem Opera House on West 125th Street.

A "SEGREGATED CORNER"

Until 1910 the center of Negro life was in Black Bohemia, an area which included the westside area between Twenty-seventh and Fifty-third Streets. While life in this neighborhood was perhaps a little more colorful than in other districts, the section was no more than a glorified slum, typical of the "segregated corners" where Negroes lived. The streets snugly lined with crowded boarding and lodging houses were choked with vehicles and pedestrians. Wagon drivers had to wait with their teams for an opportunity to wedge their ways through.

The average Negro workingman earned at this time about seven dollars a week.[2] A "tiny four-room apartment" rented for twenty-five dollars a month. Brothels had nosed into the community, and landlords sought the sporting class as tenants, for these people demanded fewer improvements than respectable workers and obviously paid more rent. So unhappy was the housing problem that Negro comedians lampooned it in songs like: "Rufus Rasus Johnson Brow, What you gwine do when de rent comes roun'?"

The tenement child bore the brunt of this poverty. An investigator discovered that Negro babies died principally from "improper infant feeding," since a disproportionate share of the income was used to pay rent.[3] In a typical year, 1908, two Negro babies in every seven under the age of one year died; the infant mortality among white babies for the same period was less than half that of the Negro. The Negro births for Manhattan and the Bronx were

---

[2] Records of New York State employment agencies from 1906 to 1909 showed that out of a total of 682 males, 513 or 75.2 per cent received wages under $6.00 and $8.00 per week; while only 4.1 per cent received $9 or more per week. Among Negro women the wage levels were even more striking. Out of a total of 2,138 females, 1,971 or 92.2 per cent received less than $6 per week and of these, 1,137 or 53.2 per cent received less than $5 per week. Of those receiving $6 or more per week, only 8 out of 3,138 or .04 per cent received as much as $9 or more per week. George Edmund Haynes, *The Negro at Work in New York City, A Study in Economic Progress* (New York, Columbia University, Longmans, Green and Co. 1912).

[3] Ovington, *Half a Man* 56.

1,459, and the deaths under one year of age, 424, an infant mortality rate of 290 per thousand.[4]

An unusual factor helped to point up the problems of this neighborhood. There was a ratio of 123 Negro women to 100 Negro men in New York. The women were mostly domestics and earned from sixteen to twenty-five dollars a month. They lodged either with their employers or crowded into the tenements. When they had a day off from work they played havoc with their neighbors' sons, even with their neighbors' husbands, for the lack of men made marriage impossible for "about a fifth of New York's colored girls." Some of these women supported unemployed men. "If there would also be an economic incentive for male Negroes," observed Mary White Ovington, "the city's civilization would be battered."

Employment agencies ruthlessly preyed upon Negro girls by decoying them to the city with the lure of "traveling expenses" and they were held in debt until the cost of the journey had been repaid many times over. Helplessly in the power of these agencies, many girls were driven into prostitution. The unsuccessful search for congenial and adequately paid work was the chief reason for a "proportionately larger black slave than white slave traffic." [5]

"INVASION OF HARLEM"

The westside section of Manhattan increased its Negro population from three hundred to almost five thousand families between 1903 to 1911. Six blocks contained this human landslide. In 1903 Philip A. Payton, a Negro real estate operator, shrewdly persuaded the white owners of a few houses in the Harlem area—on West 134th Street, east of Lenox Avenue—to rent their long vacant apartments to Negroes. He succeeded in doing this by dangling the bait of high rents which he assured the owners Negroes would pay, as they desired to flee the "Tenderloin" slums. Little did Payton or the white property owners envision the direct outcome—the enormous transplantation of Negroes from downtown to Harlem. The first timid steps gave no sign that this movement would assume the proportions of an exodus.

---

[4] *Ibid.*
[5] Ovington, *Half a Man* 154-155.

The little Negro colony of 134th Street expanded, moved west and then across Lenox Avenue. The white residents became alarmed and took steps to check the advance of blacks. They formed holding companies to buy property in the neighborhood of the Negro houses, to encircle them, and thus to halt their spread. Properties were purchased through the Hudson Realty Company and Negro tenants were evicted. The New York *World* discussed editorially the attempts to drive the colored population out of the neighborhood and conceded that the Negro was "entitled to pitch his tent wherever he sees fit," but added that wherever he did, "calamitous depreciation" was the result. Although, as the *World* put it, the assimilative ideal was premature and Harlem had suffered "to an almost incalculable extent," still, the comment finished, "the average Negro is ... law-abiding and proves a good-paying tenant."

CONFLICT

This rather liberal view went unheeded by white owners of Harlem property. A white real estate corporation, Shaw & Company, of 1 West 125th Street, circularized for "an incorporated real estate company to get rid of colored people." Negroes countered with similar companies, not as wealthy to be sure, but with sufficient zeal and funds to make serious inroads. One of these was the Afro-American Realty Company, capitalized at five hundred thousand dollars and formed to buy and lease houses to be rented to Negro tenants. This counter-stroke held the opposition in check for several years. Negroes with money began to feel it was a "race duty" to buy Harlem property, dispossess whites, and install members of their own race. The Negro press and pulpit carried on such a campaign to encourage and stimulate the buying and leasing of Harlem property.

Negroes filtered west across Seventh Avenue. And the whites resisted with renewed vigor. This time the plans of the white people were more deeply laid and harder to defeat, for as formulated, they assumed the nature of a conspiracy. The white property owners cunningly brought pressure on financial institutions not to lend money or to renew mortgages on properties occupied by blacks.[6] The Harlem Property Owners' Improvement Association was formed "for the purpose of preventing Negroes from coming into Harlem to live." The New York *Indicator,* a real estate publication, spoke of the "invasion" of Harlem and contended that the presence of Negroes depreciated real estate values there and in other parts of the city. "This in itself," concluded the article, "is an indication that their presence is undesirable among us, and that they should not only be disfranchised, but also segregated in some colony in the outskirts of the city, where their transportation and other problems will not inflict injustice and disgust on worthy citizens."

WHITES FLEE

The Afro-American Realty Company with its small amount of capital was soon defunct, but several individual Negroes carried on. Philip A. Payton and J. C. Thomas, a prosperous undertaker, bought two five-story apartment houses, dispossessed the whites, and rented them to Negro tenants. Nail and Parker, a real estate firm, bought a row of five apartment houses and did likewise. St Philip's Protestant Episcopal Church, one of the oldest and richest Negro congregations in New York, bought a row of thirteen apartment houses on 135th Street, between Lenox and Seventh Avenues, at a cost of $620,000, evicted all the white tenants and rented them to Negroes.

The situation had resolved itself into a struggle. Negroes not only continued to move into apartments outside the segregated zone east of Lenox Avenue, but began to purchase the fine private dwellings west of Seventh Avenue and those bordering on St Nicholas Park. The whites regarded this new entrance as an "invasion" of their social rights and despairing at stemming the tide of blacks, fled as from a deluge. In what is architecturally one of the better neighborhoods in New York, house after house and block after block were deserted. This occurred after the white prop-

---

[6] The plans to bankrupt Negro and those white property owners who rented to Negroes had considerable success and reached far beyond the situation with which they were formed to deal, for the precedent established then has since been one of the greatest handicaps to the Negro owner.

erty owners had held their houses for some time, stubbornly refusing to sell or rent to Negroes. Eventually they were forced to sell at prices that were far below the property's assessed value. For example, the Equitable Life Assurance Society sold some eighty brick houses on West 138th Street, each of which contained fourteen rooms, two baths, French doors, and hardwood floors, for an average price of two thousand dollars each, in a section which later became fashionable as "Striver's Row," the stronghold of the Negro upper class.

The mass movement of Negroes from the South to the North and the large-scale immigration from the West Indies ballooned Harlem real estate to fantastic prices, a swell that almost made the community's business people dizzy. The Rev A. Clayton Powell, Sr, reported the purchase of a limestone front private house, with mahogany woodwork, on West 136th Street, between Seventh and Eighth Avenues, for $6,000, which was resold six years later for $15,000. By the 1920s conservative estimates placed the total Negro ownership of Harlem property at two hundred million dollars.

NEGRO SCARE RACKET

In the years immediately following their first entrance, Negro real estate operators made considerable money and in time rivaled white owners as grasping landlords, though many of them, deceived by the phenomenal increases in values after the whites had retreated, thought their wealth permanent.

Some Negroes, as well as the many white property owners, acquired large sums of money by the "Negro scare" racket. This was a scheme in which Negro tenants, anxious for better living quarters, were moved into white neighborhoods by unscrupulous men, who then waited for the alarmed white residents, who desired to prevent Negroes from entering the area, to bid for their property at outrageous prices. Suburban areas were particularly plagued by these men. One Negro operator made the scheme very profitable. He threatened to open a beach for Negroes in Nassau County on one occasion and, on another, he announced the opening of a "Negro cult." The bottom fell out of this racket with the advent of the Depression.

PIG FOOT MARY

Illustrative of the manner in which individuals, with almost no initial capital, managed to become moderately wealthy in this period is the story of Pig Foot Mary, a huge Amazon who arrived in New York early in the fall of 1901. Mary, whose real name, Lillian Harris, was known to few people, separated herself from a hapless brood in the Mississippi delta and ran away to make her own way in the world, eventually drifting into this city penniless. Within a week after her arrival she had earned five dollars as a domestic. Mary spent three dollars of the amount for a dilapidated baby carriage and a large wash boiler and invested the other two in pigs' feet. Then she wheedled the proprietor of "Rudolph's," a popular saloon near Sixty-first Street on Amsterdam Avenue, into allowing her to boil the delicacy atop his cookstove. Mounting the steaming boiler of pigs' feet on the baby carriage, she wheeled all her worldly wealth through the swinging doors of the saloon and set up business at the curb in front.

The pigs' feet business soon showed a profit, and hog-maws, chitterlings, and corn on the cob were added to the menu. Pig Foot Mary, now a licensed peddler, presided over a specially constructed portable steam-table, which she had designed herself. Pleasant-faced, deep-voiced, her enormous proportions neatly swathed in starched checked gingham, she was at her stall from early morning until late at night. Her personal needs were few; she owned two cotton dresses and lived in a small furnished room. Her bank account mounted, for Mary was saving money against her old age. She often explained that she intended to have enough to buy a place for herself in an old folk's home for respectable colored people. Nothing else interested her.

After more than sixteen years at her Amsterdam Avenue stand, Pig Foot Mary was forced to trail her migrant customers to Harlem. This time she rented a tiny booth, an appendage to a newspaper and shoe shine parlor, at Lenox Avenue and 135th Street. In less than three weeks she married the stand's owner, John Dean. As Mrs. Dean, Pig Foot Mary's concern about her old age lessened and she allowed herself to be persuaded to invest her savings in Harlem properties. Her first venture was the purchase of a $44,000 Seventh

Avenue apartment-house building, which six years later she sold to a Negro undertaker, Adolph Howell, for $72,000. Her subsequent dealings in real estate were equally successful, and at one time her total holdings were valued at $375,000.

Regarded as one of the community's shrewdest business women, Pig Foot Mary could neither read nor write. When requesting that her agents remit rental moneys, it was the habit of the Pig Foot Queen to end the correspondence with the command to "send it and send it damn quick." Occasionally her secretary sought to economize on the use of expletives. But Pig Foot Mary had learned to identify her favorite phrase, even transcribed to the written page, and when this last line did not conform to her established mental picture she never failed to demand loudly that all missing "damns" be meticulously inserted. She died in California in 1928 at the age of fifty-eight.[7]

BLACK BELT TO BLACK BELT

A less spectacular phase in the development of Harlem was the Negro migration from the southern "Black Belt," bringing thousands to Harlem.

The outbreak of the World War caused a shortage of labor. The withdrawal of many white men from industrial pursuits for military service after the United States entry into the conflict, together with pressure for increased production, encouraged this migration into the large cities. Negro labor suddenly became a necessity. This unprecedented shortage resulted in a mad scramble to draw on the South's great reservoir of black labor. Labor agents scoured the southern states and they brought back consignments of blacks to be shoveled into the mouth of starved industry. An eyewitness related that he saw a crowd of Negroes estimated at 2,500 being sent off from a southern city in one day. They were packed in day coaches, with all their baggage and other impedimenta, on a train which was run in three sections.

In an effort to relieve this shortage of labor in the North, the Department of Labor aided and encouraged the migration of Negroes through its employment service. But the movement north-

[7] Interview with Mrs Ella Evans, July 31, 1939.

ward grew to such tremendous proportions that this department withdrew its assistance when its attention was drawn to the "possible effect" of the labor drainage on the South.

Deserted by the Labor Department, many northern employers undertook to act by themselves. In 1915 New England tobacco planters rushed to New York and gathered up hundreds of Negro girls for work in the fields. Importuned for help, the National Urban League supplied many Connecticut farmers with southern blacks. In January of 1916 a conference of tobacco growers of that state met and decided that the Urban League should continue to procure laborers. But in their journey from the South to Connecticut (by way of New York), many of the Negro migrants remained in this city. It is said that in the summer of 1916 the Pennsylvania and Erie Railroads "promiscuously picked up trainloads of Negroes (from southern areas), on the promise of a long, free ride to the North." *Opportunity,* magazine of the Urban League, found that "the Pennsylvania and Erie Railroads were the first to import Negroes in large numbers."

Negro newspapers took up the cry. "Go North, where there is more humanity, some justice and fairness." In many sections of the South the sale of northern Negro newspapers was forbidden. The South did not limit itself to this, it passed laws to check migration, but the movement continued. Negroes traveled by train and by boats; their travels were marked with joyousness and prayers of thanksgiving. It is reported that a party of 147 Negroes when leaving Hattiesburg, Mississippi, "held solemn ceremonies while crossing the Ohio River. They knelt down and prayed; the men stopped their watches and, amid tears of joy, sang the familiar songs of deliverance." On the eastern seaboard, New York City was a center of this movement. No less than seventy thousand southern Negroes arrived in New York City at this time and a large portion of this number remained here, although Albany, Poughkeepsie, Buffalo, and smaller cities received a share. The reason for this movement is found principally in the abuses of the tenant farm system. Also, the desire of southern Negroes to escape from a pattern of life in which competing groups of the white race wielded ruthless power to preserve racial inequalities was also a large factor. Legends of urban freedom were alluring to them. Most important was the lure of high wages. Between 1914 and 1917 more than four hundred thousand southern Negroes moved North. New York received a large share of this exodus.

BLACK IMMIGRATION

As early as the middle of the last century, foreign-born Negroes were settling in New York; they came from Cuba, the Virgin Islands, the West Indies, the Philippines, and even from faraway West Africa. In 1850 a total of 4,067 Negro immigrants arrived in this country; in 1870 the figure had grown to 9,494; and in 1889, to 14,017. By the close of 1899 there were more than fifty thousand foreign-born blacks in the United States. However, voluntary Negro immigration is chiefly a twentieth century occurrence. It was particularly important in the development of Negro New York, because it brought a worldliness to Harlem early in its career.

The Bureau of Immigration blanketed all the newcomers under the easy label "African, black." They were in fact many colored—quadroon, mulatto, and black—with numerous caste and class differences.[8] Their modes of living, eating, dressing, and the like, ran all the way from European, through island peasant, to native African.

HAITIANS

Many of Harlem's French-speaking Negro immigrants came from the Negro Republic of Haiti. They mingled freely with the native-born black New Yorkers and resented equally the prevailing prejudice against colored people. Through them an awareness of the problems of Haiti became the concern of many Harlemites.

The Haitians in New York were generally engaged in importing, industry, trades and the professions. Some made an effort to interest American Negroes in Haiti and its commercial possibilities. It was significant that few Haitian immigrants were to be found in domestic service. Chief among their places of employment were fur shops, electrical concerns, clothing factories and dressmaking establishments.

---

[8] The United States is one of the few nations that analyzes its international migration on the basis of race.

FRENCH COLONIALS

From the French Colonial Island of Guadeloupe and Martinique came a second group of French speaking Negroes. Many of them arrived in New York between 1919 and 1929. They were proud of being Frenchmen. They boasted of their racial heritage and established the custom of an annual dance on Bastille Day. They kept the reputed taste of the French people for good foods and fine wines.

Many of them found employment as domestics and as factory workers. The factory workers were particularly active in the fur workers' unions.

PUERTO RICANS

Although housed within Harlem's boundaries, the large Spanish-speaking population of New York cultivated little contact with native-born Harlem Negroes. Often they lived in the same tenements with Negroes and frequented the same places of amusement, but rarely did they intermarry. The Spanish-speaking Negro, black as he might be, resented being mistaken for an American Negro. He held to the Latin meaning of the word "Negro." To him it meant full blooded black. The colored immigrant understood quickly that most white Americans regarded anyone who spoke a foreign tongue, particularly Spanish, as being white, and therefore the immigrant called himself "white."

BRITISH WEST INDIANS

From the British West Indies came the largest body of Negro immigrants. They had left a land where Negroes were in the majority, to find themselves on arrival in New York a part of a minority group within a black minority. They chafed under segregation, Jim-Crowism, and discrimination, and news of lynchings appalled them. In their homeland these things were practically unknown. They showed resentment of any manifestation of discourtesy from whites. And such designations as "George," "Sam," and "boy," which are the white American's frequent manner of addressing Negro menials, were so emphatically resented by the West Indians that many employers refused to hire them on that account, complaining that West Indians did not make good servants. Because of their refusal to accept insults from passengers quietly, the Pullman Company discouraged the employment of West Indian Negroes as porters. Perhaps for this reason it was often said that when a West Indian got "ten cents above a beggar" he opened a business, which might run from a tailor shop to a Wall Street stock firm.

The ambition of the West Indian was to become financially independent. Of all the Postal Savings Banks of the country, the Harlem branches had the largest number of depositors, of which the majority were West Indians.[9] Among the business enterprises there was the West Indian-directed Antillean Realty Company, which was capitalized at $750,000 to operate in Harlem real estate. Many of these enterprises were community affairs, in which public sales of stock were held and peddled on an appeal to "race loyalty."

Those with a middle-class outlook frankly said that it was only for financial advantage that they had come to the United States. As a rule they entered the fairly lucrative professions of medicine, dentistry and law. Eventually they became one-third of that group.

Often the newly arrived West Indian Negro's clash with the American color line developed in him an exaggeratedly pro-British attitude. If there were discriminations or insults from white Americans the British Consul could be visited and a complaint registered. British citizenship meant in theory, therefore, even more freedom and greater equality in New York City. When the West Indian finally became naturalized, it was often a "citizenship with reservation," for one foot remained on British soil.

Thus friction arose between American Negroes and the West Indian immigrants. Friction which only faded in the face of common racial enemies. Much of this was the result of the strenuous competition for jobs. American Negroes along with white Americans generally had cultivated a prejudice against foreigners. Unwittingly victims of exploitation, the immigrants were falsely charged with a willingness to work for low wages. Still, the American Negroes' strongest criticism of the newcomers was that they robbed the entire Negro population of a potent weapon in its strug-

[9] Ira De A. Reid, *The Negro Immigrant* (New York, Columbia University Press 1939) 119.

gle for equal rights by not becoming naturalized, thereby depleting the power of the ballot.

HARLEM PREJUDICE

And it was out of the American Negro's resentment against the West Indian that such derisive phrases as "monkey-chaser," "ringtail," and "king Mon" sprang. An accusation persisted that the West Indian came here to "teach, open a church or start trouble." His strong English accent was distorted by the native born Negro into a comic dialect. Numerous ditties were sung reflecting much of the native-born's attitude toward the West Indian immigrant, and reflecting also something of the prevalent misinformation about the habits, customs, and institutions of these foreign-born people:

> When I get on the other side,
> I'll buy myself a Lizzie,
> Climb up in a cocoanut tree,
> And knock those monkeys dizzy.

> When you eat split peas and rice
> You think your eatin' somethin'
> But man you ain't taste nothing yet
> Till you eat monkey hips and dumplin.

> When a monkey-chaser dies,
> Don't need no undertaker,
> Just trow him in de Harlem River
> He'll float back to Jamaica.

> When I get on the other side,
> I'll buy myself a mango,
> Grab myself a monkey gal
> And do the monkey tango.[10]

The islander's tropical clothes were ridiculed. Frequently his white suit and cane brought him a shower of stones from Harlem street urchins.

BLACK LANDSMANSCHAFT

The black immigrant began to seek ways of combating the hostilities that confronted him. He formed clubs and organizations to provide fraternity for his fellow immigrants. He made an aggressive drive for leadership within the black community. In many instances his organizations resembled Jewish *Landsmanschaft* so-

[10] Edgar Dowel, Spencer Williams, and Clarence Williams, "The West Indies Blues," quoted in Reid, *The Negro Immigrant* 114-115.

194 THE NEGRO IN NEW YORK

cieties, groups formed to maintain contact and to preserve traditions of immigrants from the same town or region.[11] They usually remained independent and did not cooperate with other similar groups. The chief bar to unity was the existence of little known antagonisms between West Indians from the different islands. Each island is an independent unit with its own tradition, culture, and history. But both white and Negro Americans mistakenly grouped all their people under the inclusive heading, "West Indian," thus implying a sameness of background and interest. Competing with these regional societies were a few fraternal orders, which took in all West Indians regardless of origin. Undoubtedly, those who joined the Ancient Order of Free Gardeners or the Ancient Order of Mechanics were drawn from the more Americanized elements who preferred these lodges because of the absence of distinction based on color-caste or island origin.

All these organizations aided in making adjustments, but the immigrant's integration came principally through the churches.

TRINIDAD CALYPSO

Much of West Indian culture filtered into Harlem life. A number of tropical foods began to find their way to the tables of American Negroes. Imported yams, West Indian pumpkins, eddoes, mangoes, paw-paws, ginger root, avocadoes, and plantains were sold in Harlem's markets. So popular did the use of West Indian pepper sauce become that it displaced American-prepared red peppers on the shelves of many of the Harlem chain-stores.

West Indian music, too, found vogue with American Negroes. In 1915 phonographs throughout Harlem hummed the whimsical folk tale of "Sly Mongoose," a chicken-stealing animal of Trinidad. From Trinidad also came the fashion of the Calypso, which was a rhyming, vocal commentary on local and world events sung particularly during carnivals.

[11] Each island is represented by at least one group, usually a mutual aid or benevolent society, in which the island customs are retained and where an interest is taken in homeland affairs. Charity contributions are made. This fact is revealed by the presence of more than thirty organizations, like the St Vincent Benevolent Society, Windward Islands Progressive League, Sons and Daughters of Barbados, Dominica Benevolent Society, Montserrat Progressive Society, St Lucia United Association, Antillean League, British Jamaicans' Benevolent Association, Grenada Mutual Association, Trinidad Benevolent Association, Sons and Daughters of Nevis, and Sons and Daughters of St Christopher Society.

CHAPTER XIII

THE "WHITE MAN'S WAR"

HARLEM, 1914-1918.—Where a previous generation of Negroes had all but given up the ghost, the pre-war generation under the preachings of the radicals found new hope.[1] The streets of Harlem were the scenes of nightly outdoor forums. Socialism was frankly advanced as the instrument of emancipation. Dozens of street orators hammered away at Negroes scoring the accepted cautious attitude of American black men. Such terminology as "class war," "imperialist ambitions," and "proletariat" were easily bandied about.

Harlem, no less than any other American community, exhibited little enthusiasm for war. For months war had been the topic of discussion in all sections of the Negro population. And while these discussions increased in frequency and intensity, the opinion seemed to prevail that "this is a white man's war—the Germans ain't done nothin' to me and I ain't doin' nothin' to them." Some felt that the matter did not touch their lives and when an attempt was made to place the problem squarely on their doorstep, they were apt to cast it aside with characteristic good humor.

The attempts of organized Allied propaganda to solicit American sympathy for the plight of the Belgians met only with indifferent shrugs from Negroes, who knew too well of Belgian atrocities in the Congo. The New York *Age*, in January, February, and March of 1917, republished reminders of that tragic episode in the black man's history. The *Crisis* of May 1917 carried a cartoon of a mutilated Congo native addressing the English King thus: "We could be of greater service to you now if your cousin had spared

[1] In 1917 New York Negroes elected their first Assemblyman, Edward A. Johnson, Republican, from Twenty-third A. D.

us our hands." The Negro press consistently derided President Wilson's speeches on world sanity and justice and the rights of a democracy, and pointed to the glaring lack of these virtues within the United States. The New York *Sun* (February 11, 1917) published the following letter from a Negro reader:

> The first blood shed for American Independence was by Crispus Attuck, a black man in Boston. But a question comes in my mind now, should a black man shoulder a gun and go to war and fight for this country which denies him the rights of citizenship, under a flag which offers him no protection, strips him of his manhood by enacting laws which keep him from the ballot box, disfranchised, segregated, discriminated against, lynched, burned at the stake, Jim-Crowed and disarmed. If he fights and fight he must, for what does he fight?

Nevertheless, after the declaration of war, the drums beat with as much fury in Harlem as they did anywhere else.

The declared purpose of the United States' entrance into the World War, as enunciated by the national administration, was to uphold and extend democratic ideals. The striving of small nations and subject minorities would be assisted, autocratic rule would be abolished, and the benefits of "self-determination" made available. Though the Negro people responded to the call of the nation, they were somewhat skeptical of the lofty principles of democracy proclaimed by the government and the Allies. British imperialism ruling millions of their African blood brothers was no less savage, they argued, than the German conquerors of the Cameroons and German East Africa. Nor could the United States itself have a virtuous stake in this struggle as long as social, political, and economic rights were denied its black citizens.

"CLOSE RANKS"

When the United States joined the Allied forces in April 1917, amid appeals for democracy, Negro leaders regarded it as an opportunity to drive the Negro problem into the public scene and to renew the claim for the Negro's rights as an American citizen.

What had been an undercurrent of protest before the declaration of hostilities now broke out in open demands. The manner in which the Negro leaders sought to accomplish their purpose was, on the one hand, to pledge loyalty to the country and, on the other, to demand democracy for the Negro masses. An editorial in the New York *Age* (February 17, 1917) best illustrates this:

> We hold that because the Negro has a case in court upon which his life depends and which he cannot afford in any way to jeopardize, he should not let go of his rights by default, neither shall he weaken his claim to any of those rights by a non-performance of duty. To keep his case in court clean and to win, the Negro must continue to claim every right of citizenship and always be ready to perform any duty.

Men of the political and intellectual stature of W.E.B. DuBois, Robert R. Moton, Kelly Miller, James Weldon Johnson, and Fred R. Moore, editor and publisher of the New York *Age,* all subscribed to this view. The *Crisis* said: "Out of the outstanding jealousies of all Europe, the Polish people will probably come to their own, and another oppressed race (the Negro) will have a chance for development after a high noon of despair." By May 1917, the *Crisis* felt that as a result of the war freedom for Russia and suffrage for English women had been achieved, and this led to the opinion that black men would eventually win their freedom through America's fight against Germany. To this Colonel Charles Young, a West Point graduate and ranking Negro officer in the United States, added: "Two wrongs never make a right. . . . Let us do nothing to divide our people in this hour of our country's trials." In a letter to President Wilson, Robert R. Moton, principal of Tuskegee Institute and successor to Booker T. Washington, wrote:

> Notwithstanding the difficulties which my race faces in many parts of this country, some of which I called to your attention in my previous letter, I am writing to assure you that you and the nation can count absolutely on the loyalty of the mass of the Negroes to our country and its people North and South, and as in previous wars, you will find the Negro people rallying almost to a man to our flag.

New York's Negro churchmen gave voice to precisely the same view. A typical expression was uttered by the Rev A. Clayton Powell, Sr, pastor of the influential Abyssinian Baptist Church, who took up the issue in sermons to his congregation. "This is the psychological moment," he said, "to say to the American white government from every pulpit and platform and through every newspaper, 'Yes, we are loyal and patriotic.'" But, he reminded the administration, "we do not believe in fighting for the protection of commerce on the high seas until the powers that be give us at least some verbal assurance that the property and lives of the members of our race are going to be protected from Maine to Mississippi." His conclusion was a faithful reflection of Negro thinking. "It is infinitely more disgraceful and outrageous to hang and burn colored men and boys and women without a trial in times of peace than it is for Germans in times of war to blow up ships loaded with mules and molasses."[2]

> We of the colored race have no ordinary interest in the outcome. That which the German power represents today spells death to the aspirations of Negroes and all darker races for equality, freedom and democracy. Let us not hesitate. Let us, while this war lasts, forget our special grievances and close our ranks shoulder to shoulder with our own white fellow citizens and the allied nations that are fighting for democracy. We make no ordinary sacrifice, but we make it gladly and willingly with our eyes lifted to the hills.[3]

In a short time a list of demands, manifesting the uniform desires of Negroes throughout the Nation, was promulgated and appeared in the *Crisis,* almost taking the form of an ultimatum to the government:

1. The right to serve our country on the battlefields and to receive training for such service.

2. The right of our own men to lead troops of their own race in battle, and to receive officers' training in preparation for such leadership.

3. The immediate stoppage of lynching.

4. The right to vote for both men and women.

5. Universal and free common school training.

6. The abolition of Jim-Crow cars.

7. The repeal of segregation ordinances.

8. Equal civil rights in all public institutions and movements.

---

[2] Adam Clayton Powell, Sr., *Against the Tide: an Autobiography* (New York, Richard R. Smith 1938) x, 327 p.

[3] Editorial in *Crisis,* XVI No. 3 (July 1918) 111.

The final say came from DuBois in his "Close Ranks" editorial. Equitable though these demands were they caused considerable debate throughout the Nation, particularly in the South, where the United States Senator from Mississippi, James K. Vardaman, declared: "Universal military service means that millions of Negroes who will come under this measure will be armed. I know of no greater menace to the South than this."

SILENT PROTEST PARADE

In the midst of these events there were two riots. The East St Louis (Ill) race riot, which took place, July 2, 1917, was one of the bloodiest of the twentieth century. An immediate cause of the violence was the migration of Negroes from the South into the northern industrial centers where, it was asserted, blacks took the jobs of whites at much lower wages. The trade union leaders of that city, particularly, aided in fomenting hostility against the Negroes. W.E.B. DuBois and Martha Gruening, a white woman who investigated the attack for the N.A.A.C.P., reported that during the riot the whites drove six thousand Negroes from their homes, two hundred of whom were murdered by shooting, burning, and hanging.

Harlem was aroused and on July 28, 1917, fifteen thousand Negroes silently marched down Fifth Avenue to the roll of muffled drums.[4] Little children clad in white led the demonstration, then came the women also in white, followed by men in black. This was the "Silent Protest Parade." [5] Blacks marched in silence and whites watched in silence. The newspapers report there were no jeers, no jests, nor even indulgent smiles on the faces of the onlookers who lined the sidewalks; and many were seen to brush tears from their eyes. The Negro onlookers permitted themselves no outbursts or cheers. Some of the banners read: "Mother, Do Lynchers Go to Heaven?", "Mr President, Why Not Make America Safe for Democracy?", "Treat Us So That We May Love Our Country," "Patriotism and Loyalty Presuppose Protection and Liberty." A banner, censored by the police, depicted a Negro woman kneeling before President Wilson appealing to him to "Bring De-

---

[4] New York *American*, July 29, 1917.

[5] The demonstration was organized by such Negro leaders as W.E.B. DuBois, James Weldon Johnson, John E. Nail, Rev Hutchens C. Bishop, Rev F. A. Cullen, and Rev Charles Martin.

mocracy to America Before You Carry It to Europe." [6] During the
parade, circulars entitled "Why We March" were distributed by
Negro boy scouts. They read:

> We march because the growing consciousness and solidarity
> of race, coupled with sorrow and discrimination, have made us
> one, a union that may never be dissolved in spite of the shallow-
> brained agitators, scheming pundits, and political tricksters who
> receive a fleeting popularity and the uncertain financial support of
> a people who ought to consider themselves as one.
> "We march because we want our children to live in a better
> land and enjoy fairer conditions than have been our lot.[7]

"HELL FIGHTERS"

The nationwide persecution of Negroes did not cause any lag
when the call for volunteers was issued. But Negroes soon discovered they were not to be accorded the same treatment as whites.
DuBois observed that black men were "allowed to volunter only
as servants in the Navy and as common laborers in the Army outside of the regular four Negro regiments."

Quite different was the application of conscription. More than
two million Negroes were registered under the Selective Service
Law, and more than three hundred thousand were drafted. In
New York State more than six thousand Negroes were called. To
the number drafted throughout the country may be added an additional 37,723, representing the Negro regulars and National Guard
units. This comprised a total of 380,000, of whom about two hundred thousand saw service in France. They were not incorporated
in white regiments, but were organized as separate Negro out-
fits. Because of the latter fact, the American high command was
charged with segregation.

Of the two hundred thousand Negro soldiers who saw service
in France, only fifty thousand were used as combat troops. The
Negro fighting units constituted the 92nd and 93rd Divisions. To
the 92nd was attached the 367th U. S. Infantry, popularly known
as the "Buffaloes," while the 15th Regiment (the New York National Guard) was part of the 93rd. Both of these regiments were

---

[6] Johnson, *Black Manhattan* 236.
[7] New York *Age*, August 17, 1917.

from New York, the former consisting of drafted men, while the latter was the old 15th Regiment, renamed the 369th U. S. Infantry.

Six years before the United States entered the war, the Equity Congress, a Harlem civic organization, had procured an election promise from William Sulzer, the Democratic candidate for governor, to form a Negro regiment in the State militia. When Sulzer became governor he kept his promise and signed the bill for a Negro regiment on June 2, 1913. But the law was not put into effect until June 16, 1916, when Republican Governor Charles S. Whitman instructed Colonel William Hayward, a white officer of the National Guard, to organize a regiment. It was a left-handed victory, for no headquarters or equipment was supplied and the men were forced to drill in an abandoned dance hall. In spite of this, some six hundred Negroes paraded down Fifth Avenue in celebration of the event. Since they had no guns they marched with broomsticks. At the head of this procession was Bert Williams, the famous comedian, astride a white horse. Many whites laughed at these "darkies playing soldiers." But it was this same regiment that became known as the "Hell Fighters" and was decorated by the French Government for bravery.

Not until war was declared did the Federal Government recognize the regiment as a National Guard unit. Four months later it was called to arms, placed under the command of Colonel William Hayward,[8] and sent to Spartanburg, South Carolina, where other units of the New York Guard were encamped. Here they suffered all the indignities of Jim Crow. The proprietor of a local hotel ordered a Negro soldier to remove his hat when he entered the lobby and kicked him into the street when he refused to do so. A riot was averted only by the restraining influence of Jim Europe, famous and popular leader of the 15th Regiment band. On another occasion fifty men marched on the city to "avenge" two missing buddies and only the efforts of Colonel Hayward prevented bloodshed.[9] The regiment was thereafter removed to Camp Mills, Long Island, where they were quartered with white troops

---

[8] A Negro, Colonel Benjamin O. Davis, took command of the 369th (old 15th) Infantry, New York National Guard, in 1939.

[9] Interview, October 3, 1939, with Lieutenant-Colonel Charles W. Fillmore, Negro captain of the 15th Regiment during the war.

from Alabama and Mississippi. Here again indignities were suffered and trouble broke out the first night over discrimination shown in the canteen. The next day, November 12, 1917, the regiment embarked for France. It was one of the first units of the National Guard of the whole country to go overseas.

The Negro press kept a careful account of the activities of this regiment and reported the problems it had to encounter in France. It was attached to the Eighth Corps of the Fourth French Army as a combat regiment, and carrying its state colors fought with the French throughout the war. It was the only American unit to do this. The unit was under shell fire 191 days and held one trench for 91 days without relief. At the declaration of the armistice, it was the first of all the Allied forces to set foot on enemy territory as the advance guard of the French army of occupation.[10]

"THE BATTLE OF HENRY JOHNSON"

The first American privates to receive the *Croix de Guerre* were the Negroes, Henry Johnson and Needham Roberts, of the Fifteenth.[11]

Early in the morning of May 14, 1918, these two men together with others were surprised by a German raiding party while in an observation dugout. They fought their way out in what was described by the New York *World* as "The Battle of Henry Johnson." The approach of the enemy had been detected by the sound of wire clippers cutting the barbwire defenses. The Negroes immediately signaled the enemy's presence by rockets. The Germans replied with a volley of grenades which wrecked the tiny post, imprisoning three sleeping men and wounding Johnson and Roberts. Johnson seized his rifle and started to shoot. Roberts, critically wounded, propped himself up against the door of the damaged dugout and hurled grenades at the onrushing enemy. In the darkness few reached their mark. When Johnson had exhausted his supply of bullets, he used the butt of his rifle in the hand-to-hand engagement that followed. Roberts was seized, but as he was about to be carried off, Johnson sprang up and plunged his bolo knife

[10] Arthur W. Little, *From Harlem to the Rhine: the Story of New York's Colored Volunteers* (New York, Covici Friede 1936) xviii, 382 p.

[11] Little, *From Harlem to the Rhine* 192-201.

into the skull of the man who had captured his buddy. One of the men whom Johnson had clubbed regained consciousness and shot at Johnson who fell. Feigning a mortal wound, Johnson waited until the German came close to him and disembowled the man with his knife. Demoralized, the enemy patrol, estimated at twenty-four men, retreated under a rain of grenades from Johnson.

COUNTER PROPAGANDA

All during the war, Negroes, both here and abroad, were subjected to a barrage of German propaganda. The New York *Tribune* published accounts of the activities of German conspirators working among Negroes. Captain George B. Lester, of the Military Intelligence Bureau, revealed attempts made to win Negroes to the cause of Germany by telling them that in Germany blacks were equal to the whites and that if Germany won, the rights of the colored people the world over would be equal to those of the whites. The 15th Regiment was the particular object of German propaganda. On its arrival at the front, the men were bombarded, not with shells, but with leaflets:

> *TO THE COLORED SOLDIERS OF THE AMERICAN ARMY*
> Hello, boys, what are you doing over here? Fighting the Germans? Why? Have they ever done you any harm? Of course some white folks and the lying English-American papers told you that the Germans ought to be wiped out for the sake of humanity and democracy.
> What is Democracy? Personal freedom, all citizens enjoying the same rights as the white people do in America, the land of Freedom and Democracy, or are you rather not treated over there as a second-class citizen? Can you get a seat in a theatre where white people sit? Can you get a seat or a berth in a railroad car, or can you even ride in the South in the same street-car with white people? And how about the law? Is lynching and the most horrible crimes connected therewith a lawful proceeding in a democratic country? . . . .[12]

TRANSPLANTING

It was not until after the war that the full measure of the injustices suffered by the Negro troops came to light, and this, only

---

[12] Emmett J. Scott, *Scott's Official History of the American Negro in the World War* (n. p. 1919) 139.

after DuBois had visited Europe in 1919. Though President Wilson had declared on several occasions that he was determined to see that the Negro received proper treatment and though administration leaders had mouthed vague promises of a similar nature, the Negro troops appeared to have suffered all forms of discrimination, humiliation, and even slander. Nevertheless, the official attitude as expressed by Secretary of War Baker in a letter (November 30, 1917) to Emmett J. Scott, special Negro assistant in the War Department (1917-18), was: "We are bending all our energies to the building up of an army to defeat the enemy of democracy and freedom, and the army we are building contains both white and colored men. We are expecting that they will all do their duty, and when they have done it they will be alike entitled to the gratitude of their country." [13]

Subsequent to this statement, a document, *Secret Information Concerning Black American Troops,* fell into the hands of Negroes and was published in the *Crisis,* despite an attempt to suppress the issue.[14] Though it was written on French War Department stationery and was signed by two French officers, it was said to have emanated from General Pershing's headquarters, August 7, 1918. Emmett J. Scott recognizes its existence in his official history of the Negro troops. It was intended for dissemination among the civil population as well as the French troops. When the French Ministry heard of its distribution, says DuBois, it ordered all copies to be collected and burned. The document said in part:

> It is important for French officers who have been called upon to exercise command over American troops, or to live in close contact with them, to have an exact idea of the position occupied by Negroes in the United States . . . Negroes would create for the white race in the Republic a menace of degeneracy were it not that an impassable gulf has been made between them . . . Indulgence and familiarity are matters of grievous concern to the Americans. They consider them an affront to their national policy . . .[15]

---

[13] Scott, *Scott's Official History* 61

[14] Interview with W.E.B. DuBois, August 14, 1939.

[15] Documents of the War, collected by W.E.B. DuBois in *Crisis* XVIII No. 1 (May 1919) 16-18.

In its conclusion, it instructed French officers not to indulge in any intimacy with black officers: "We must not eat with them, must not shake hands or seek to talk or meet with them outside of the requirements of military service." After admonishing that "familiarity on the part of white women with black men is furthermore a source of profound regret," it ordered that a point be made not to "spoil" Negroes.[16]

The same issue of the *Crisis* (May 1919) carried several other documentary items, evidence of conditions faced by Negro troops in the World War. For example, it reported that "the Mayor of Bar-sur-Aube" had issued the following order on June 26, 1918: "According to the orders given by American military authorities, it is strongly recommended that no French women receive visits from colored soldiers or talk with them on the streets." That these conditions had repercussions in the Negro ranks is apparent, as on Thanksgiving evening, November 23, 1918, the Negro regiment, whose casualties numbered eleven hundred and whose bravery in combat in the great offensive at Champagne had, only a month before, earned for it the *Croix de Guerre,* stood in a field near Metz and silently displayed its resentment against the insincerities of its homeland. The music boomed and the soldiers, the warriors from Harlem, some three thousand of them and a scattered half dozen of white officers, were asked to sing, "My Country 'Tis of Thee." Instead, the Negroes stood quietly with grim and sober faces and from all that assemblage the only voices heard were those of six white men.

President Wilson had already sent Dr Robert R. Moton to France to talk with the Negro troops. While there Dr Moton is reported to have said to the Negroes that he had "asked the President his views as to the practical application of democracy toward the colored man in the United States . . . [and] I was very much pleased with his reply; but gentlemen, I cannot quote the President." Even Emmett J. Scott, the Negro assistant in the War Department, was criticized by the *Crisis,* which, after declaring that "the state of affairs in regard to Negro troops . . . is astounding!", asked him if he was aware of the treatment accorded the black soldiers. It was also pointed out that no Negro women were among the nurses sent to France. A public reply to the following questions, which were never answered, was asked of Scott: [17]

1. Did you know the treatment which black troops were receiving in France?
2. If you did not know, why did you not find out?
3. If you did know, what did you do about it?

RETURN TO STATUS QUO

Early in 1919 three thousand Negro veterans of the 369th Regiment, led by white Colonel William Hayward, returned to New York. A million New Yorkers lined the streets to watch the men parade. The steel-helmeted soldiers passed beneath the Victory Arch in Washington Square and swung up Fifth Avenue in their long journey back to Harlem, where more than one hundred thousand Negroes gathered along the line of march. Jim Europe's band, which had won international fame for its introduction of jazz abroad, was one of the dramatic features of this event. At the same time the administration leaders began a campaign to convince the returning Negro soldiers that they could not expect any great change in the Negro's traditional position in America. Newton Baker was particularly vocal on this point.

The effect of such a policy was immediately apparent, as Negroes became victims of new outrages throughout the country. A magazine, the *Veteran,* took up the cause of the Negro veterans so militantly that agents of the Department of Justice swooped down on its office and attempted to close it. The problem of unemployment became particularly acute among the Negro veterans. George E. Haynes, head of the Negro Division of the Department of Labor, said in a magazine article: "The United States Employment Service is glad to do what it can to place these men [Negro] at work but it is limited by the apparent unwillingness of employers to wipe out the color line in the slightest degree. The fact is that in certain industries employers are taking advantage of the end of the war to make a blanket dismissal not only of those colored employees who were taken on during the War but also of those who

---

helped them to solve their labor scarcity problems created by the stoppage of immigration two years before the United States entered the War." [18]

Blind intolerance against all who dissented from the established order followed the close of the war. The Federal Government took the lead by vigorously hunting down racial aliens. In New York State the legislature expelled five of its members in January 1920, because they were members of the Socialist Party. Many people agreed with the public officials that free expression of opinion was dangerous to American institutions, while a great many more preferred to ignore the social and economic injustices which had caused these protests. The Ku Klux Klan, which had been revived in 1916 with a branch in New York City, flourished with five million members, and the Republican and Democratic Parties, in the face of so strong an organization, ignored the issue.

Anti-Negro feeling was brought to a head during the early days of the war by a film called *The Birth of a Nation,* based on the novel *The Clansman* by Thomas Dixon. The picture, supposedly historic but actually a grossly inaccurate and distorted portrayal of the Reconstruction Period, made a sensational appeal to race prejudice. It was shown to packed houses in New York and throughout the Nation, reviving old hostilities, which on occasion broke into open warfare. Another decade of racial and class hatred, of open lawlessness, had set in and Negroes were again prominent among the victimized. At the same time, much was said and believed about the danger of communist agitation among Negroes, who were viewed as ready material for "subversive" ideas. Once again white New Yorkers were aggressively arrayed on either side of the Negro question.

---

[18] George E. Haynes, "Wanted: a Fair and Square Chance," *Southern Workman* (Feb. 1919) 60-64.

The above is given as the source, but the quotation could not be found in the article.—Ed.

POST-WAR ERA

HARLEM, 1918-1925—Harlem was being excited by the Back-to-Africa propaganda of Marcus Garvey after the war. On the wild currents of post-war national and racial hatreds, he poured a brand of "Black Zionism" as a solution of the Negro Problem, demanding in no uncertain terms "self determination" for blacks in a sort of world Black Belt. He preached a doctrine of an all-Black World, ruled by blacks for blacks. With this visionary program, he stirred some two million Negroes to a fierce race-consciousness which is still a compelling force in Negro life.

FIRST OF THE HARLEM MESSIAHS

Marcus Garvey, whom W.E.B. DuBois described as a "little, fat, black man; ugly, but with intelligent eyes and a big head," was a full-blooded black man and a grandson of an African slave. Born in Jamaica, B.W.I., in 1887, he had grown up under the triple caste system of white, mulatto, and black, of the West Indian islands. Even as a boy, this caste system aroused his resentment against not only whites but mulattoes as well. At about the age of twenty-one he left Jamaica and traveled in South America, and then went to England where he resided for several years. A printer by trade, his journeys became an odyssey in search of a place of escape from color prejudice and a quest for an opportunity to earn a livelihood. In England he became intimate with an Egyptian Negro political writer, Duse Muhamed Effendi, who was editing a small revolutionary newspaper in London and who had

---

[1] "2nd Draft" was written at the top of the page. *The Post-War Era* was substituted for *The Premature Fascist* as the chapter title. The dateline—*Harlem,* 1918-1925—was crossed out and also the opening of the first sentence: "Years before the names of Hitler and Mussolini splashed across the headlines of the world. . . .—Ed.

a wide knowledge of European affairs. It was probably here that the dream of a Black Empire ruled by black men came to Garvey. Determined to lift the black masses, he returned to Jamaica in 1914, where he organized and led successfully a printer's strike in Kingston. Soon afterwards he began organizing the Universal Negro Improvement Association. In search of a plan, he read Booker T. Washington's *Up From Slavery* and then wrote to this American leader. He subsequently received an encouraging offer to come to the United States, but before Garvey left Jamaica Washington died.

Garvey arrived in New York March 23, 1916. Harlem first met the man, June 12, 1917, after, as he says, he had traveled through thirty-eight states, studying the conditions of Negroes. On that date he addressed a mass meeting called by a radical named Hubert Harrison at Bethel A.M.E. Church, for the purpose of organizing a Liberty League. According to an eyewitness, his torrential eloquence, heightened by a magnetic personality and an intuitive knowledge of crowd psychology, carried the audience along with him. His speech included an endorsement of Harrison's movement.

Doubtless, it was the enthusiasm displayed by that audience which determined Garvey to start his own movement, as he was not the man to tag along with somebody else's program. Very few recruits rallied to his program in the beginning.

One day, a lone, disgruntled follower, protesting that he'd been duped by the organizer, dashed excitedly into Garvey's dingy little office at 56 West 135th Street and shot the little leader, grazing his forehead. Garvey rushed hysterically into the street with the blood of a martyr streaming down his face. The incident was given much space in the local press, and he was a made man.

BACK-TO-AFRICA

Riding hard on this publicity he gathered about him a dissatisfied fringe from the radical movement, among whom were William H. Ferris, Hubert Harrison, W. A. Domingo, and organized and incorporated the Universal Negro Improvement Association in the United States, with New York as its headquarters. His first appeal was to the West Indian section of the population, not only to the British, but also to the Spanish and the French. Many of the foreign-born flocked to him and were known as "Garveyites." He established the *Negro World,* a weekly, and included in it a Spanish and later a French section, and subsequently the *Negro Times.* He built Liberty Hall, a great zinc-roofed shed on 138th Street between Lenox and Seventh Avenues, capable of holding five or six thousand people. There the association held its first convention in 1920, during the whole month of August, with delegates from the various states, the West Indies, and Africa.

At the outset the movement attempted an economic solution of the race problem through the establishment of "Universal Negro" shops, factories, and financial institutions. In effect, they sought to establish a "black economy" within the white capitalist world. But the idea soon expanded to a nationalistic scheme for the redemption of Africa and the establishment of a Negro merchant marine, known as the Black Star Line. The aims and objects of the U.N.I.A. were now:

(a) To bring together the Negroes of the world into one solid and indissoluble body.

(b) Relieve Africa of Anglo-Saxon oppression and domination.

(c) Build Africa industrially and commercially, establish schools and other educational institutions.

(d) Build churches to administer to the spiritual uplift of the people.

(e) Promote and encourage agriculture so that Africa within the next few years may be the commercial and agricultural center of the world.

"It is only a question of a few more years when Africa will be completely colonized by Negroes, as Europe is by the white race," Garvey assured his followers. Money poured in from the residue of a wartime prosperity. "No one knows when the hour of Africa's Redemption cometh. It is in the wind. It is coming. One day, like a storm, it will be here." And more money poured in.

Units of the organization sprang up in all parts of the world. People were carried on a tidal wave of "race-consciousness" and Africanism. The movement grew quickly, and by August 1921, the organization reported a membership of more than four million persons, the largest following any Negro in America had yet had. In his last speech in Liberty Hall, Garvey claimed a membership of six million persons in nine hundred branches throughout the world. Anti-Garvey leaders said there was "plenty yeast" in those figures, but then Garvey was a truant from truth. An official who has since left the organization puts the figure at two million "active, paying members" and six million world-wide followers.[2]

Elevating himself to the "Provisional President of Africa," a title which at least suggested republicanism, Garvey proceeded to create the "Court of Ethiopia" patterned after the British monarchy. On his most trusted aides, he conferred titles of Dukes, Duchesses, Ladies-in-Waiting, Knight Commanders of the Distinguished Order of Ethiopia, and Knight Commanders of the Sublime Order of the Nile. There were gorgeous uniforms of black and green, trimmed with gold braid; and handbooks on court etiquette "made for the Government of the Universal Negro Improvement Association, Inc, and African Communities' League, Inc, of the World." According to its dictum, "No lady below the age of eighteen shall be presented at the 'Court Reception' and no gentlemen below the age of twenty-one." All recommendations for "social recognition" had to be made through the local divisions to the office of High-Commissioner-General, who was required to edit a list of "social eligibles."

An African Legion, in which Garvey took especial pride, was established with a full line of commissioned officers, a quartermaster staff, and a commissariat for each brigade. The rank of an officer was determined by the number of sphinxes and gold buttons he wore. Black Cross nurses and African Motor Corps were also organized. Classes were held for girls and boys in race pride, Negro history, etiquette, ritual of the U.N.I.A., and military tactics. Garvey's parades, with his followers resplendent in full regalia, became a high spot in Harlem life and threatened to steal the show from the marching clubs of the Negro Elks. In short, a movement with no detail forgotten was in full blast, even to the manufacture of brown and black doll babies, which are still immensely popular in Harlem.

But Garvey's most potent instrument for wielding influence was his weekly newspaper the *Negro World,* which sold for five

---

[2] Interview, August 6, 1939, with George A. Weston, former President-General, U.N.I.A. (1926).

cents a copy in New York and ten cents elsewhere and had a nation-wide circulation. Its twelve to sixteen pages were devoted largely to "the philosophy and opinions" of Marcus Garvey. Edged between his long polemic articles were essays, editorials, and advertising of the U.N.I.A. projects, patent medicines, beauty preparations, plus an occasional small cigarette advertisement. His editorials referred to the history of Negroes, reminding them of Africa's past splendor. It popularized the slave struggles for freedom and recounted tales of the heroism of such leaders of slave revolts as Denmark Vesey, Gabriel, and Nat Turner. Exploits of the long dead Zulu and Hottentot warriors who fought against British rule were not forgotten, nor were the histories of the Moorish and Ethiopian empires. Toussaint L'Ouverture's leadership of the Haitian Rebellion was stock copy.

A BLACK CHRIST

The man became a world figure, and his movements and utterances were watched by European powers with possessions in Africa. The U.N.I.A. grew in the United States, spread to the Caribbean, and to far-off West Africa. The movement almost assumed the character of a religion and its members became zealots. Meetings at Liberty Hall were conducted with an elaborate ritual and liturgy. The moment for the entry of "His Excellency, the Right Honorable Marcus Garvey, Provisional President of Africa, Secretary-General of the Universal Negro Improvement Association," was approached in solemn silence. The African Legion and the Black Cross nurses flanked the long aisle and came to attention as the band and audience joined in the hymn, "Long Live Our President." Only then did Garvey, surrounded by his Royal Guard of honor, stride majestically through the double line and mount the rostrum.

On August 31, 1924, in an impressive ceremony, a "special form of Divine Service" was held for the purpose of "canonization" of the Lord Jesus Christ as the "Black Man of Sorrows" and the Blessed Virgin Mary as a "Black Woman." The services were performed by His Grace, Archbishop George Alexander McGuire, Primate of the African Orthodox Church who had been elevated to the rank of Chaplain General of the movement. With one stroke, Garvey carried his all-black world to its logical conclusion—only those who were "100% Negroid" could hold office in the organization. He admonished whites and blacks accordingly:

> It is the duty of the virtuous and morally pure of both the white and black races to thoughtfully and actively protect the future of the two peoples, by vigorously opposing the destructive propaganda and vile efforts of the miscegenationists of the white race and their associates, the hybrids of the Negro race.[3]

The movement was not without actual violence to wayward followers. In the 1922 convention of the U.N.I.A., James W. H. Eason, the American leader, was tried and found guilty of "acts unbecoming a high officer of the High Executive Council," and was removed from office. Smarting under his disgrace, Eason started another organization known as the "New" U.N.I.A. in open challenge to Garvey. New Orleans became its headquarters and many of Garvey's disgruntled followers joined its ranks. One evening as Eason made his way to an anti-Garvey meeting, he was ambushed and assassinated. His assailant was never apprehended, but it was frankly said at the time that Garvey had engineered his murder.

DARK LAUGHTER

In the early days of the Garvey movement, its leader was proudly hailed as a "West Indian," but as his influence began to decline and as his American enemies became more vocal, he was referred to as a "Jamaican Jackass." Perhaps no men fought Garvey more bitterly than W.E.B. DuBois, editor of the *Crisis,* and A. Phillip Randolph and Chandler Owen, editors of the radical *Messenger.* Their attacks gradually assumed an anti-West Indian aspect. It is characteristic that this attitude should find expression in ridicule and jest among the masses of native-born Harlemites, and particularly is it characteristic that Negroes would express it in song. Thus, "The West Indian Blues" emerged from the collective pen of the American Negroes, Edgar Dowell, Spencer Williams, and Clarence Williams, popular songwriters of the day. The words attempt to recapture the West Indians' dialect, but are in fact a mixture of West Indian parlance and southern dialect.

---

[3] *Philosophy and Opinions of Marcus Garvey,* ed. Amy Jacques-Garvey (New York, Universal Publishing House 1923) x, 102.
Exact quotation not located.—Ed.

WEST INDIAN BLUES

Got my grip and trunk all packed,
Steamship I'm gwine to take her,
So good-bye old New York Town,
I'se gwine to Jamaica.
When I git on de odder side,
I'll hang aroun' de waters,
I'll make my livin' sure's you born,
A-divin' after qua'ters.

Chorus: Gwine home won't be long,
Gwine home sure's you born,
I'm gwine home won't be long 'cause
I've got no time to lose.
Gwine home I can't wait, gwine home
Mon, I'm late, I'm gwine home
I can't wait, 'cause I've got the
West Indies Blues,
Got the West Indies Blues, Got the
West Indies Blues.

Done give up de bestes' job,
A runnin' elevator,
I told my boss "Mon" I'd be back
Sometime soon or later.
When I git back to dis great land,
You better watch me Harvey,
'Cause 'm gonna be a great big "Mon"
Like my frien' Marcus Garvey.[4]

KU KLUX KLAN SUPPORT

Garvey's downfall began in 1923. Yet with his amazing energy
and daring and his dictatorial personality, he might have carried
on longer. He had stirred the imagination of Negroes, as no man
had yet done, and had drawn tens of thousands of followers to
his banner. He raised more money in a few years than any other
Negro organization had even dreamed of. He naturally attracted
many followers, among whom were many crafty knaves who saw
in the movement an opportunity to enrich themselves. It was upon
the latter group that Garvey laid the blame for his failure and,

---

[4] "The West Indies Blues" in Reid, *The Negro Immigrant*, 114.

indeed, his organization did disintegrate when defections began in the ranks.

The little leader's attack on every Negro rights organization in the country had earned for him many enemies. So articulate an opponent as A. Phillip Randolph conceded the movement had stirred Negroes to the realization of a need for organization and had demonstrated the ability of Negroes to organize under Negro leadership. While it stimulated pride in Negro history and thus helped to break down the remnants of "slave psychology which throttles and strangles Negro initiative and self-assertiveness," he attacked the movement as an ally of the anti-Negro groups. He cited the fact that genuine Negro leaders were beaten, driven out, and even murdered, when they attempted to hold rallies in many cities, while Garvey was applauded and given right of way in the same cities. The Ku Klux Klan and the Anglo-Saxon clubs, headed by E.S. Cox and John Powell, respectively, openly supported Garvey and these men spoke several times from his platform at Liberty Hall. "The only convenient friend the Negro or laborer has in America," said Garvey, "is the white capitalist." And in reply to a deluge of criticism for having Ku Kluxers appear in Liberty Hall, he said:

> I regard the Klan, the Anglo-Saxon clubs, and the White America Societies, as far as the Negro is concerned, as better friends of the race than all the groups of hypocritical whites put together. . . . You may call me a Klansman if you will, but, potentially, every white man is a Klansman, as far as the Negro in competition with whites socially, economically and politically is concerned, and there is no use lying about it.

DENOUNCE MULATTOES

One of Garvey's vital blunders was his attempt to use the mulatto or "high yellow" Negroes as a buffer class between whites and blacks. The whites of the United States, unlike the whites of the West Indies, make almost no distinction between mulattoes and blacks, nor do Negroes. While there are certain social lines among American Negroes based upon color, yet they have always maintained a solid front on the rights of the race. Garvey proceeded on the assumption that there were three distinct races in the United States: the white, the mulatto, and the black, a classification which exists in the West Indies. In an "Exposé of the Caste System among Negroes," [5] Garvey accused the N.A.A.C.P. of a policy of dividing the race into two groups. One group, he said, was regarded by it as superior because it was "near-white" and the other inferior because it was "black," a vestige of the slave period. Garvey said he had discovered in New York, Boston, Washington, and Detroit the presence of a "Blue Vein Society," composed of "near-white" Negroes, and a "Colonial Club," a West Indian group, which erected the same standards for admission. These groups gave annual balls, monthly *soirees* and pink teas, at which no less than a quadroon was admitted. He denounced mulattoes even more sharply than he did whites. For a time this type of propaganda was successful in driving a wedge between the blacks and the mixed-bloods, a policy which served to arouse a latent pride in the darker Negroes.

The basic cause of Garvey's failure was, however, his amazingly meager design for colonizing the territory of imperialist nations. His program was in reality only a restatement of the American Colonization Society's plan of deportation which had been advanced three different times in the history of the country, and which on every occasion had caused strong protest from Negroes. The central idea of Garvey's scheme was absolute abdication of the Negro's place and rights in American life. But the vast majority of Garvey's followers had no idea of going to Africa. They followed Garvey because his doctrines gave a sorely driven race a new and abundant dignity, enough to squander.

BLACK ZIONISM

The *Messenger,* an influential monthly magazine, recognized the movement for what it was and drew an interesting parallel between "Black Zionism" and Jewish Zionism. In the same article it contrasted Garvey's program with that of the Sinn Feinists and other nationalistic movements, and conceded that these "isms" were possibly a "purifying cultural idealism." But it stated that they held out no hope for the "proletariat" and that it was at best "a will-o'-wisp iridescent dream which could only be born in the head of an irresponsible enthusiast." The whole scheme of a black em-

[5] The *Negro World,* August 31, 1923.

pire "in the raging sea of imperialism," wrote Randolph, "would make it impossible to maintain power; nor would it bring liberation to Africa, for Negro exploiters and tyrants are as bad as white ones." [6] Soon after the publication of this article, Randolph received a threatening letter together with a human hand, a black one, wrapped in a package, with a command that Randolph stop attacking Garvey and join the U.N.I.A., "the only real Negro organization in the country."

TRIAL OF GARVEY

Early in 1923 the Federal Government investigated the Black Star Line, and Garvey was indicted and tried for using the mails to defraud. It was very clear from the beginning that the authorities had no real desire to punish Garvey, but the insistent demands of Negroes, principally George W. Harris,[7] an alderman and editor of the New York *News,* William Pickens, and his former followers, W.A. Domingo, and Edgar Grey, brought action. Arthur Brisbane, the Hearst columnist, protested Garvey's arrest for alleged fraud, declaring that to jail Garvey would be equivalent to "jailing a rainbow."

The trial began May 28, 1923, before Judge Julian Mack, and lasted more than a month. Garvey had as his counsel Cornelius W. McDougald, who was later appointed as a United States Assistant District Attorney. Dissatisfied with McDougald's method of defense, Garvey discharged him soon after the trial opened. He conducted his own case, hiring a Jewish attorney, Armin Cohn, as advisor, despite the fact that he had been castigating the Jewish people as exploiters of the Negro people. The chief allegations against Garvey were that he intended fraud; and that he had no intention of securing a ship; that his first wife, Amy Jacques-Garvey, controlled the treasury, giving account to no one; and that he ordered his treasurer to sign "whole rows" of blank checks for which Garvey gave no accounting. The Government witnesses said there was a total deficit in the Black Star Line of more than five hundred thousand dollars, and that at stockholders' meetings anyone who drifted in could vote.

[6] *Messenger* Magazine, January 1922.
[7] Republican, elected in 1920 as the first Negro to sit on the Board of Aldermen (N.Y.).

The vastness of Garvey's operations was revealed by the government's estimate that there were more than forty thousand stockholders. Thomas A. Merilees, an accountant for the Department of Justice, said that Garvey's bookkeeping had been of the loosest kind, and that he had to build up the accounts from "returned checks as there had been no vouchers of any sort." Merilees fixed the liability of the line at more than seven hundred thousand dollars, with a total bank balance of $31.12, and said that this did not represent the total loss "as the first year's takings had not been written in at all." Moreover, only 156,056 shares of stock valued at $765,130 had been accounted for. The strongest point against Garvey was that on February 22, 1921, he had asserted in a speech which was published in the *Negro World* that the Black Star Line had $750,000 in realizable assets, capable of paying dividends of from ten to forty per cent; whereas, the line was over two hundred thousand dollars in debt and had only six thousand dollars in the bank at that time.

The Black Star Line had in fact three ships: the *Yarmouth,* which was bought from the North American Steamship Company for $165,000 and rechristened the *Frederick Douglass;* the *Kanawha,* a former H.H. Rogers yacht, purchased at sixty thousand dollars and renamed the *Antonio Maceo;* and the *Shadyside,* a discarded Hudson River steamer, bought for $35,000. Garvey had purchased these ships for the pilgrimage of his followers to Africa and to establish trade relationships among the Negro peoples of the world. He had hoped that through the Black Star Line, the African Negroes could ship their produce and raw materials to America, where the U.N.I.A. would establish factories in the industrial centers of the country. The raw materials would then be manufactured into commodities for a Negro world market. This, he said, would provide employment for Negroes everywhere.

Garvey's shipping project may have had an unhappy career, but the sailing of his first ship, the *Yarmouth,* was spectacular. Thousands of Harlemites gathered at the pier, cheering and waving flags, as the ship slipped out of port. Loaded with a cargo of whiskey from the Green River Distillery Company which was to be delivered in Cuba, the *Yarmouth* broke down outside of New York's harbor. None of his ships was seaworthy. Driven by his critics, he had purchased vessels when they were at a premium, as many ships were needed at the time to bring American troops back from Europe. But soon afterwards the demand for ships fell off and they became a drug on the market. The Federal Government burned its own ships by the hundreds. The Black Star Line fleet, such as it was, was now worth only the scrap iron in its construction. The *Yarmouth* was finally sold at auction for $1,100.

There were a number of other concerns from which Garvey drew large sums. These were the African Communities League, Redemption of Africa Fund, the Liberty Loan, and the Liberian Construction Loan. Garvey's first wife estimated that between 1918 and 1921, only three years, Garvey took in a sum close to ten million dollars. An index to the number of contributors might be gained from the fact that the largest individual contribution was one thousand dollars, a gift of Casper Holstein, a prosperous Negro policy banker. Henry Lincoln Johnson, attorney for Elie Garcia, one of Garvey's co-defendants and his Auditor-General, shrewdly analyzed the scheme in his defense speech:

> Gentlemen, you can't have any idea what it means to be a Negro in a day like this—the ignominy of it! If every Negro could have put every dime, every penny into the sea, and if he might get in exchange the knowledge that he was somebody, that he meant something in the world, he would gladly do it. The black man does not live who does not hope that his children may be established in a settled business; who does not pray that this hideous curtain of hell and hate may some day be lifted from his children. I hope it for my children. So does every black man for his.
>
> The failure of the Black Star Line was a loss in money but it was a gain in soul. If all the people who ran ships and lost were to be put in prison there would be no room in Atlanta for them—the Shipping Board would be there. If the Shipping Board failed with all the wealth of the United States, the Rockefellers, and the Morgans, and the services of some of the greatest experts in the world behind it, why should more be demanded of poor inexperienced Negroes who were honestly seeking a way out of the dilemma of race prejudice? If the Black Star Line had pleaded guilty for playing the fool, I'd agree with the government; but I fail absolutely to see where the charge of fraud comes in.

After long search, the government was unable to find any funds hidden by Garvey. He testified that all the money he had in the world was some forty dollars and 289 shares of his own worthless stock. The case against Garvey was admittedly weak, but what served most to convict him was the conduct of his own case and the temptation to strut before a crowded courtroom. He brushed aside his lawyer and handled his case himself. He himself examined and cross-examined the witnesses (including himself); he himself harangued the judge and jury; and he (by himself) was finally convicted and sentenced to five years' imprisonment, a one-thousand dollar fine, and the court costs. The case against his co-defendants was dismissed. But this was not to be the end of the dreamer of a Black Empire.

SUPPPORTS WHITE CANDIDATE

Released on bail, pending his appeal, Garvey rallied his followers in a mighty demonstration at Carnegie Hall, and they quickly subscribed more than one hundred thousand dollars. He then formed Black Cross Navigation Company, which was incorporated in the State of New Jersey, April 19, 1924, and bought a ship, the *General Goethals,* from the Panama American Steamship Company. This vessel, of 5,300 tons, was in good condition and the price paid for it was said to be $170,000, although there is no record of the purchase. The company advertised 31-day round trips to Central America for $400, first class, the only kind of passage offered. Renamed the *Booker T. Washington,* it sailed from New York for the West Indies with passengers and United States mail, January 18, 1925, but never returned, having been impounded for debt.

After his tangle with the law, Garvey reversed his position by urging all his followers to take an interest in American politics. He encouraged his West Indian followers to become naturalized, so that they could vote. Claiming that the New York Republicans had persecuted him, Garvey formed the Universal Negro Political Union and issued a list of nationwide candidates for whom his followers were to vote. He supported Coolidge for President, and Tammany Hall locally; he backed a white Democrat, Royal H. Weller, for Congress, against a Negro Republican, Dr E.P. Roberts.

Alfred E. Smith and Mayor John F. Hylan spoke at Liberty Hall during the fall campaign of 1924.

In the meantime the final collapse of the Garvey movement came when Garvey lost his appeal, and entered Atlanta Penitentiary, February 8, 1925. President Coolidge pardoned him and he was deported, November 26, 1927, to Jamaica, B.W.I., as an "undesirable alien." This brought to a close the tragi-comic story of a premature "Fascist" who aspired to be a dictator. He afterwards said of his conviction: "When they wanted to get me, they had a Jewish judge to try me, and a Jewish prosecutor (Mattucks). I would have been freed but two Jews on the jury held out against me ten hours and succeeded in convicting me, whereupon the Jewish judge gave me the maximum penalty." [8]

BLACKS FOR BLACKS

Marcus Garvey left behind him a residue of profound race consciousness which he had aroused in Negroes. In a sense, this had redounded to his credit. So conservative an observer as the Rev A. Clayton Powell, Sr, has given a fairly accurate estimate of Garvey and his movement:

> The coming of Marcus Garvey to Harlem in 1916 was more significant to the Negro than the World War, the southern exodus and the fluctuation of property values up-and down-town. Garvey, with his Black United States, Black President and Vice-President, Black Cabinet, Black Congress, Black Army with Black Generals, Black Cross Nurses, Black Negro World, Black Star Line and a Black Religion with a Black God, had awakened a race-consciousness that made Harlem felt around the world. The cotton picker of Alabama, bending over his basket, and the poor ignorant Negro of the Mississippi Delta, crushed beneath a load of prejudice, lifted their heads and said, 'Let's go to Harlem to see this Black Moses.'
>
> Harlem became the symbol of liberty and the Promised Land to Negroes everywhere. During the reign of Garvey there were two places in America—the Federation of the forty-eight states and Harlem, and two million Negroes thought that Harlem was both of them. I am not writing a brief for Marcus Garvey, but it is recording the truth, and perhaps for the first

---

[8] Philadelphia *Tribune*, September 27, 1928.

time, to say that he is the only man that ever made Negroes
who are not black ashamed of their color.[9]

In 1937 Garvey declared Mussolini and Hitler had stolen his
idea, as "we were the first Fascists, when we had one hundred
thousand disciplined men and women and were training children."[10] He is more than anyone responsible for the beginnings of
anti-Semitism among the Negroes.

HUBERT HARRISON

Perhaps the first and certainly one of the most informed of the
Negro radical leaders was Hubert Harrison, who became a member of the Socialist Party long before the wave of radicalism dashed
upon the shores of Harlem. As a labor leader, he had taken an
active part in strikes in New Jersey silk mills in association with
Elizabeth Gurley Flynn, Morris Hillquit, and Bill Haywood. He
later became an instructor at Stelton, N.J., and a lecturer for the
Board of Education (N.Y.). Disappointed with his socialist friends,
he withdrew from that party and came to Harlem, where he
founded the *Voice,* a magazine which maintained much of his so-
cialistic philosophy but bore heavily on the race question. His
volume, *The Negro and the Nation* (1917), which is largely a collection of his editorials, reflects his despair at white radicals ever
solving the Negro problem. He is, however, regarded as the father
of Harlem radicalism. The Hubert Harrison Memorial Church,
established after his death in 1927, stands as a testimony of his continued influence.

RADICAL PRESS

Meanwhile a strong radical press, concentrating on injustices to
the black man, sprang up in Harlem. Even the older and more
conservative periodicals spoke more boldly. The public temper was
suggested by the names of some of these publications: the *Challenge,* the *Crusader,* the *Emancipator,* the *Messenger,* the *Voice,*
and the *Negro World.* Their vitriolic utterances drew the notice
of the Government and caused agents of the Department of Justice

---

[9] Powell, *Against the Tide* 70-71.
[10] Marcus Garvey, in an interview with J. A. Rogers, at Beaumont Crescent, Kens-
ington, London, England, May 1937.

to take steps to suppress them. Under the caption, "Radicalism and Sedition among the Negroes as Reflected in Their Publications" (Exhibit No 10), these organs were cited in the Department of Justice report made by Attorney General A. Mitchell Palmer in 1919. The report of the Lusk Committee in New York State, an investigation of a similar nature, devoted forty-four pages to Negro radicalism.

"Among the more salient points to be noted in the present attitude of the Negro leaders," wrote Attorney General Palmer, "are, first, the ill-governed reaction toward race rioting; second, the threat of retaliatory measures in connection with lynching; third, the more openly expressed demand for social equality, in which the sex problem is not infrequently included; fourth, the identification of the Negro with such radical organizations as the I.W.W. and an outspoken advocacy of the Bolsheviki or Soviet doctrines; fifth, the political stand assumed toward the present Federal administration, the South in general, and incidentally toward the peace treaty and the League of Nations." Revealing disgust with attempts "to cast discredit upon the late Booker T. Washington and the policies he stood for," Palmer warned that these expressions were not "the ignorant vaporing of untrained minds." He said these publications were edited by more than fifty men of education, who wrote in "fine, pure English, with a background of scholarship" and were "defiantly assertive of . . . [the Negro's] equality":

> The number of restrained and conservative publications is relatively negligible, and even some of these . . . have indulged in most intemperate utterance, though it would be unfair not to state that certain papers—I can think of no magazine— maintain an attitude of well-balanced sanity.

The group that edited these publications was by no means a small one and was made up of such new names as A. Philip Randolph, Chandler Owen, Rev George Frazier Miller, J.A. Rogers, W.A. Domingo, Edgar M. Grey, Hubert Harrison, William H. Ferris, William Bridges, Richard B. Moore, Cyril V. Briggs and Claude McKay. Most of them had a forceful, trenchant style and a remarkable command of inflammatory English. But they were not one in their social philosophy, for their radicalism ranged from left center to extreme left; all were, however, to the "left" of any previous position that Negro leaders had taken. Perhaps the fact that many of these men were West Indian born was why Kelly Miller, dean of Howard University, characterized a Negro radical as "an over-educated West Indian without a job."

In the meantime, the Federal Government was leaving no stone unturned in its campaign to ferret out agitators of whatever shade of radicalism. Even the N.A.A.C.P. came under its scrutiny when Department of Justice agents made a surprise visit to the association's headquarters. James Weldon Johnson reported that in reply to the query "Just what is this organization fighting for?," Dr DuBois had blandly said, "We are fighting for the enforcement of the Constitution of the United States." This compression of the association's program was received suspiciously, but the agents retired. They did, however, hound the editors of the influential *Messenger*, who preached socialism and social revolution, and also the editors of the *Challenge*, who passionately pleaded for Negro unity. The *Challenge* made no appeal for Negro and white unity, as did the *Messenger*, but directed its appeals to the emotions of Negroes. It attacked, not the class-line, but the color line. William Bridges, its editor, a master of impassioned prose, fought to bring the West Indian and American Negroes into a united front:

> There is no West Indian slave, no American slave; you are all slaves, base, ignoble slaves. . . . It's your color upon which white men pass judgement, not your merits, nor the geographical line between you . . . West Indians, the only things you are wanted and permitted to do that white men do is worship the king and sing 'Britannia Rules the Waves,' no matter if Britannia rules you more sternly than she ever does the waves. . . . Americans, the only thing that you are wanted and permitted to do that white men do is to be loyal and sing 'The Star Spangled Banner,' no matter how many Southern hillsides are spangled with the blood of many another innocent Negro. . . . Negroes of the West Indies and America, Unite!

MESSENGER MAGAZINE

The most widely circulated of the radical publications was the *Messenger*, edited by A. Philip Randolph and Chandler Owen, lecturers at the Rand School of Social Science. Randolph was later to become organizer and president of the Brotherhood of Sleeping Car Porters. The Lusk Committee declared the *Messenger* to be "by far the most dangerous of all the Negro publications." It was, according to its prospectus of 1917, "the only Magazine of Scientific Radicalism in the world published by Negroes," in which its editors aimed "to lift their pens above the cringing demagogy of the times and above the cheap peanut politics of the old, reactionary Negro leaders."

The publication started as the mouthpiece of the Headwaiters and Sidewaiters Society of Greater New York, being then known as the *Hotel Messenger*. But its shift to a radical position and its attack on the "grafting" of headwaiters, who exacted tribute from waiters, caused the headwaiters to withdraw their support. Dedicating themselves to a platform that would take "a courageous and sound position without regard to race, creed, color, sex, or political party," the editors declared that the time was ripe for a great mass movement. As they outlined it, it was to operate in four ways: (a) through labor unions; (b) farmers' protective unions; (c) cooperative business enterprises; (d) and Socialist party organizations for political action. An estimate of its appeal to New York Negroes may be formed from the fact that the *Messenger* rallied twenty-five per cent of the Negro vote in the 1918 elections in support of the Socialist Party's Negro candidate for Congress, the Rev George Frazier Miller.[11] The attitude of this magazine may best be summed up from an editorial, "The Cause of and Remedy for Race Riots":

> Revolution must come. By that we mean a complete change in the organization of society. Just as absence of industrial democracy is productive of riots and race clashes, so the introduction of industrial democracy will be the longest step toward removing that cause. When no profits are to be made from race friction, no one will longer be interested in stirring up race prejudice. The quickest way to stop a thing or to destroy an institution is to destroy the profitableness of that institution. The capitalist system must go and its going must be hastened by the workers themselves.

---

[11] Interview with Richard B. Moore, July 13, 1939.

The demand for a new Negro leadership was one of the burning issues of the *Messenger*. The reiteration of this demand found voice in every issue. It denounced those leaders who, while holding lucrative jobs during the war, indulged in rhetoric and bombast "which lulled the Negroes into a false sense of security." Chandler Owen, in an article, "The Failure of the Negro Leaders" (January 1918), said that race pride revolts against leaders like W.E.B. DuBois, James Weldon Johnson, Kelly Miller, and Robert R. Moton. The indictment was on grounds of "ignorance of the laws of society" and "ignorance of the methods by which to achieve the ends aimed at." The *Messenger* particularly criticized DuBois, who, in their view, fought lynching but failed to grasp the causes underlying it; who opposed Jim Crow but supported Jim Crow camps for the Negro soldiers; who spoke for interracial harmony but encouraged scabbing by Negroes against white strikers. "In criminal ignorance of the trend of the modern working world," said Owen, "the Negro leaders were supporting Negro strike breakers and preaching the gospel of hate against labor unionism, when they should be explaining to the Negroes the necessity of allying themselves with the workers' motive power and weapon—the Labor Union and the Strike." The Negro leaders were scornfully labeled "mental mannikins" and "intellectual Lilliputians."

The *Messenger* did not confine its attacks to Negro leaders who did not encourage Negroes to join trade unions; it also denounced white labor leaders like Samuel Gompers, who with the aid of Negro "compromisers" were "selling out both white and Negro labor's interests." The unity of the white and black rank and file was frankly urged, as "capitalism knows no color line."

NO MORE THUNDER

The *Messenger* had a change of heart on social questions after 1922. Its change in policy dovetailed with the split in the radical ranks, when the socialists divided into right and left, the left becoming the Communist Party. Some of the associates of Randolph and Owen, among them Richard B. Moore and Cyril Briggs, resigned from the magazine and joined the communists. The philosophy of the "New Negro" was then presented to Negro America, which, according to Randolph's explanation, was "A Formula of

Practical Righteous Idealism." Up to this time, the *Messenger,* if not openly hostile, was certainly indifferent to Negro business. It had held that Negro workers must organize and protect themselves against Negro exploitation as well as white, contending that a few successful Negro businessmen would bring no change to the status of the Negro masses. But in 1923 the *Messenger* published a "Negro Business Achievement Number," with discussions of the mutual interests of Negro capital and labor. By 1924 it had become the "World's Greatest Negro Monthly" and proudly published biographies of successful business people. Very little was said in this issue of the radical movement, the Socialist Party, or the struggles of the working class. The *Messenger* had lost its voice of thunder and greeted January 1928 with "Hail! A Prosperous and Happy New Year." This issue was decidedly racial in tone and again inspiring pieces by Negro business people appeared in its columns. The next year it passed quietly into oblivion, along with the other Negro radical publications of its day.

CHAPTER XV

THE BLACK BOURGEOISIE

BLACK METROPOLIS, 1925-1929.—The Negro as a freeman arrived tardily on the scene of capitalistic plunder and adventure. The Negro never owned or controlled the instruments and machines of production and thus he has been more of a consumer than a producer in industrial and manufacturing areas. There were, of course, a few men active in business before the Civil War, but they were mostly in the catering and barbering fields, and were patronized largely by whites.

Social upheavals have buffeted Negro business about to an irreparable degree. The influx of millions of Europeans literally swept control of a number of personal services from the Negro. The Draft Riots and the post-Civil War race riots caused a tremendous loss of Negro properties in New York, and the loss of much white patronage to the Negro businessman. Eventually, the Negro and his business were driven into strict segregation. His existence as a businessman now depends almost entirely upon Negro patronage in competition with white business.

An organized attempt to encourage Negro business activity was made in 1900, when Booker T. Washington founded the National Negro Business League in a convention held at Boston. Four hundred delegates representing thirty-four states were present. Washington was elected president and T. Thomas Fortune, then editor and publisher of the New York *Age,* was chosen chairman of the executive committee. The organization grew to more than forty thousand members and held yearly meetings until 1933. The league did not convene again until 1939.

An index to the number of Negro enterprises in New York City in the early part of this century was revealed by a paper read at the National Negro Business League, when it met in this city in 1908, which placed the figure at 565. In a study covering the period 1909-1910, Dr. George E. Haynes found that the number offered at the League's meeting included one hundred dressmakers and fourteen stenographers, and he estimated that the more probable figure was 475. Of these 309 were small barber shops, grocery stores, restaurants, poolrooms, and tailoring and dressmaking shops.[1] This was the first real survey and apparently the last thorough study of the Negro as a businessman in New York.

The Negro businessman attempted to capture the only patronage left to him by organizing the merchant and the consumer for the establishment of a local economy.[2] Despite many years of street-corner agitation and highly intellectualized propaganda from press and pulpit, the Negro merchant enjoys no discernible degree of trade monopoly. The chief reasons are the substandard incomes together with a chronic condition of unemployment, which have forced Negroes to ignore pleas to "race loyalty" and purchase from the white chain stores where they generally get more value for their money. The Negro businessman argues that Negroes should patronize him because he provides white-collar jobs for Negroes while white employers do not. In the fight for jobs in capacities hitherto denied them, Negro labor leaders (some of them of questionable repute) have raised the slogan in recent years: "Don't Buy Where You Can't Work." In many cases this has resulted in intensifying racial hatred, particularly against the Jewish and Italian merchants. This activity, with or without collusion with local agitators, has provided Negro business with an opportunity to turn an aroused racial sentiment into cash.

The provincial life of the community has placed Negro business on a somewhat non-business basis. The businessman and his customer both belong either to the same church, the same fraternal lodge, or the same club. This fraternal spirit extends into the store

---

[1] George Edmund Haynes, *The Negro at Work in New York City; A Study in Economic Progress,* Studies in History, Economics and Public Law, XLIX No. 3 (New York, Columbia University 1912) 98-99.

[2] North Harlem Community Council (1918), Harlem Stock Exchange (1920); Association of Trade and Commerce (1921), Harlem Economic Association (1924), Harlem Businessmen's Club (1927), Housewives' League (1930), African Patriotic League (1932), Business and Professional Men's Forum (1936), and Stuyvesant Business Association, Brooklyn (1936).

and very often becomes a cloak for obtaining credit, which is more than often a boomerang. This fraternal hue also has given rise to a general complaint of less courtesy on the part of Negro businessmen than is displayed by white clerks in the white-owned chain stores. The Negro businessman on his side complains that his customers feel they are doing him a "race favor" by patronizing him in preference to white stores.

The people of Harlem spend an estimated thirty-five million dollars a year in retail purchases.[3] This sum maintained twelve thousand retail stores in 1930, of which 391 were owned by Negroes, and of these 172 were groceries. That year Albon L. Holsey, secretary of the National Negro Business League, organized more than 100 Negro-owned stores into the Colored Merchants' Association, a group known as the CMA stores. This was an attempt to buy merchandise cooperatively and sell it at a price that would enable the Negro merchants to compete successfully with the large grocery chains. James A. Jackson, a Negro business specialist, conducted a training course for grocers which covered a period of three months. More than 138 Spanish- and English-speaking Negroes availed themselves of the instructions in modern management. "As only two per cent of the grocers in Harlem were colored," observed the *Journal of Commerce* (April 19, 1930), "and there had been no cooperation among these, it was hoped that now scientific management, cooperative buying, extension of credit, superior service and the establishment of a definite business policy would be the result of the CMA stores."

An attempt was also made to harness Harlem's buying power by the organization of the Housewives' League, but two years later both the League and the CMA stores were wiped out by the Depression. Soon afterwards the National Negro Business League asked white capitalists like Rosenwald and Rockefeller, who in the past had been the chief supporters of philanthropy to Negroes, to underwrite a system of Negro chain stores.[4]

---

[3] Interview with James A. Jackson, former business specialist of the U.S. Department of Commerce, November 30, 1939.

[4] "Supporters of an independent black economy sometimes view Negro business as taking its place alongside Negro schools, churches, hospitals, and interracial committees, as another charity." In Abraham L. Harris, *The Negro as Capitalist* (Philadelphia, American Academy of Political and Social Science 1936) XII, 205 p. This quotation could not be found.—Ed.

The greatest handicap of the Negro businessman is that he operates with inadequate capital and is unable to obtain adequate credit from the large finance corporations and banks owned by whites, for none of the main arteries of commerce and industry are controlled by Negroes. Attempts have been made to form Negro banks in this city, but all have been unsuccessful. That Negro business is doomed to remain small appears inevitable.

THE BLACK SWAN

When Harry H. Pace and his Black Swan Phonograph Company demonstrated that not only the Negroes but whites as well wanted the best musicianship—vocal and instrumental artists, regardless of race or color—Victor, Columbia and other phonograph companies hastened to enter the scramble for the new business developed by the Black Swan Company. From the small joints and one night stands scattered throughout the country, "scufflers" or itinerant "pluggers" who caught the tossed pennies from the customers for a livelihood beat their way to the Metropolitan area to record for one or the other of the competing companies. And for the first time the Negro musician seemd to be stepping into his own. The story of the Black Swan Phonograph Company is almost a career pattern both of Negro business and the manner in which Negroes have fared in the field of popular music. Here is Pace's version:

The organization was the outgrowth of my observation as President of the Pace and Handy Music Company located at 1545 Broadway, New York, New York, that phonograph companies were not recording the voices of Negro singers and musicians. It was my job as President of the Company to contact all phonograph companies so that our own numbers might be recorded from time to time. I ran up against a color line that was very severe. The only colored voice that had been recorded was that of Bert Williams on Columbia, and soon after Mamie Smith on O.K. Victor Company would not entertain any thought of recording a colored musician or colored voice, and I therefore determined to form my own company and make such recordings as I believed would sell.

It took me a long time to find a place where records could be pressed. All of the bigger companies refused to press records for outsiders and I finally learned of the New York Recording Labora-

*tory located at Port Washington, Wisconsin, who was willing to
press the records for me if I would have them recorded and furnish
them a complete master.*

*I organized Pace Phonograph Corporation Incorporated under
the laws of New York sometime in March 1921 with a capital
stock of $30,000. Associated with me as directors were Dr W.E.B.
Du Bois, Mr John E. Nail, Dr Matthew V. Boutte, and Mrs Viola
Bibb. I opened offices in my basement at 257 West 138th Street,
New York, where I did all of the preliminary work and correspondence necessary to locate recording laboratories, pressing laboratories, singers, musicians, and folks who would supply me with
incidentals like wrapping paper and corrugated boards.*

*The first record which I made was by Carol Clark of "Dear
Little Boy of Mine," and Revella Hughes of "Thank God for a
Garden," Katie Crippen in "Blind Man Blues." Shortly thereafter
while in Atlantic City in connection with some development of
the work, I went to a cabaret on the West Side at the invitation
of a mutual friend who stated that there was a girl there singing
with a peculiar voice that he thought I might use. I went into the
cabaret and heard this girl and I invited her over to my table to
talk about coming to New York to make a recording. She very
brusquely refused but at the same time I saw that she was interested and I told her that I would send her a ticket to New York
and return on the next Wednesday. I did send such a ticket and
she came to New York and made two records, "Down Home
Blues" and "Oh Daddy." This girl was Ethel Waters and the records were enormously successful. I sold 500,000 of these records
within six months. The next month I had her make two other
records and thereafter for a long time she made a record a month.
But none of them ever measured up to the "Down Home Blues"
record.*

*I then began to invite other well known singers and performers
and within a year I was issuing about 12 records a month and
selling them in every state in the United States, and in a good
many foreign countries.*

*The original office force consisted of Daniel L. Haynes and
Miss A. H. Bibb. Before we had been in business six months we
had completely outgrown my basement and I bought a house at*

2289 Seventh Avenue, New York, into which we moved. The two upper floors we used as offices and the street floor was used as a shipping room, of which Mr R. T. Washington was a foreman in charge of two or three men who did nothing but wrap and fill orders all day long. The office increased and C. Udell Turpin was appointed Sales Manager; J. P. Quander, Jr, was elected Secretary of the Company and took over the accounting and secretarial work. There came into the organization then William Grant Still who was Musical Director, and who arranged the material necessary to be recorded and took charge of the recordings at the laboratory. We had found a place in Long Island City with a recording room, plating outfit, and pressing room to whom we were giving our extra orders because we could not wait for them to come from Fort Washington, Wisconsin.

The pressure of arranging and recording became so great that I hired Fletcher Henderson who became Recording Manager and worked under Mr Still, so that Still would only arrange while Henderson played in the orchestra and handled recordings at the factory. There was added to our staff in the office Fredi Washington as stenographer and her sister Isabelle Washington, now the wife of Rev A. C. Powell, who served as messenger between the main office and the factory.

Business became so great that we bought a plant in Long Island City that we were using as a recording laboratory and a pressing laboratory, and shortly afterwards transferred all shipping over to the plant. We were selling around 7,000 records a day and had only three presses in the factory which could make 6,000 records daily, so that we were running behind. We ordered three additional presses in 1923 made especially for us with some improvements, and had them ready for installation in the factory. Before they were set up and ready for running, radio broadcasting broke and this spelled doom for us. Immediately dealers began to cancel orders that they had placed, records were returned unaccepted, many record stores became radio stores, and we found ourselves making and selling only about 3,000 records daily and then it came down to 1,000, and our factory was closed for two weeks at a time, and finally the factory was sold at a sheriff's sale and bought by a Chicago firm who made records for Sears & Roebuck

Company. However, this did not completely defeat us and we continued to have records made at a concern in Connecticut and sold these repeat orders for a year or so until the thing finally came to a close.

Among those who were employed in the company at various times and made records for us were Trixie Smith, Julia Moody, Creamer and Layton, The Harmony Five, of which Ivan H. Browning was a member and who later went to Europe for a long stay, Antoinette Garnes who made several operatic records, Florence Cole Tolbert who made several operatic records, and numerous others including Ethel Waters, Carol Clark, Revella Hughes. Most of the people employed by the company including William Grant Still and Fletcher Henderson became nationally known in subsequent years.

During the first two years of operation of the company, I sent out a company of singers and players, including Ethel Waters and an orchestra headed by Fletcher Henderson, who travelled all over the country and who came back to New York having advertised our records in every portion of the country as far west as Oklahoma and Texas. Lester A. Walton was manager of the troupe and he prepared and wrote several letters for the New York World *that landed him his job as reporter for the* World.

I shall try to find you a catalogue and insert it in this letter showing the number of records issued, and the names of the persons who recorded them, but of which I am not sure but will find it if possible.

The firm continued for several years owning property at 2289 Seventh Avenue, New York, and retained its masters for a number of years hoping that there would be a revival of the business. Its property was finally foreclosed and it went out of business through dissolution of its charter.[5]

The only business left to the Negro are those of primping himself and burying himself, businesses which continue to be his only because of race prejudice; and even these are increasingly coming under the control of whites through the foreclosures of mortgages on equipment.

---

[5] Correspondence with Harry H. Pace, November 17, 1939.
It is not among the writers' papers in the Schomburg Collection.—Ed.

LUSH DAYS

During the decade 1900-1910, the Negro turned his eyes toward real estate speculation and the sudden growth of Harlem actually made many Negroes wealthy. Besides Philip A. Payton, who was a pioneer in Harlem's real estate development, the name of John E. Nail, once his employee, is today most prominently known in the field. His father, John B. Nail, who was active in business from 1863 until 1909, had a hotel at 450 Sixth Avenue and dabbled in the buying and selling of property. The younger Nail, who has been in business for more than thirty years, was in the vanguard of those who made money during boom years. With Henry C. Parker he established the real estate firm of Nail and Parker in 1907, which negotiated a half million-dollar deal, involving the purchase of a block of houses for the St Philip's Protestant Episcopal Church. Late in the 1920s the partnership was dissolved, but Nail has continued in business and is regarded as a specialist in Harlem real estate.

Some Negro real estate operators, like many whites, built up considerable holdings. John M. Ryall, Watt Terry, and Augustine A. Austin were names synonymous with large deals. With the Depression and the decline in Harlem property values, most of the men active in the field passed out. The career of Watt Terry, who rose from a janitor to a millionaire and lost all his holdings during the Depression, provides an unhappy blueprint of the period. His Watt Terry Holding Company, which turned a five-million dollar real estate deal in 1918 and received a terrific trouncing in 1929, is no longer among the community's successful enterprises. The Antillean Holding Company, with assets placed at a million dollars in 1936, directed by A. A. Austin, remains perhaps the most stable of the Negro real estate enterprises.

The actual number of Harlem businesses of any stature might be boiled down to but a few. The most prominent are the Belstrat Laundry, founded in 1921 by David Doles, capitalized at $150,000, and employing 69 persons; and the Victory Mutual Life Insurance Company, organized in 1926, capitalized at $200,000, and directed by Drs C. B. Powell and P. M. H. Savory. These two men have become a force in Negro business life because they are active directors in businesses with aggregate assets exceeding a million dollars, and because, more importantly, they influence public opinion through the *Amsterdam News*. Less than a few hundred Negro businessmen limped through the Depression, but the seventy-five undertakers and the two thousand beauticians remained active, though their incomes were greatly reduced.

"TWO DOLLARS AND A DREAM"

In 1913 a matronly and alert-eyed forty-four-year-old black woman set Harlem agog when she bought three lots (108-110) on West 136th Street, tore down the old brownstone buildings then standing and built a ninety-thousand dollar "castle" of Indiana limestone. This was the first inkling the community had of the wealth of the newly arrived, be-diamonded Madame C. J. Walker. She had been a St Louis laundress who, she liked to recount, wearily left her washtubs late one summer afternoon to sink down upon a rude wooden bench and "rest a spell." Instead she had stolen a nap and had "dreamed a dream" that showed her a method of banishing the stubborn, lustreless crinkle from Negro hair, transforming it into shining smoothness. In nine industrious years, with "two dollars and a dream," she built a manufacturing plant for hairdressing products which grew into a concern that did excellent business among Negroes in the United States and in twenty-nine foreign countries. The name of the laundress became a household word in Negro homes throughout the land.

The hairdresser's products had their first success in Denver, where she started a house-to-house marketing of her wares. In each home Madame Walker sold her pomade and treated her customer's hair and it became straight. In a short time Madame Walker had more customers than she could handle. She was obliged to set up a shop and train other women to assist her in giving the hair treatments, and soon a school was organized for this purpose. The graduates received diplomas which permitted them to operate their own shops using the "Walker System," with the admonition not to use the phrase "hair straightener." They were crisply told that they were "hair culturists" and "scalp specialists." All the necessary metal implements and ointments were supplied by the Walker firm. So profitable was the sale of equipment and the return from tuitions that by 1917 the Walker concerns yearly pay roll had mounted to more than two hundred thousand dollars and its founder had become a millionairess.

Whenever a white employer inquisitively asked her radiant slick-haired Negro maid what she had done to yesterday's thatch of kinky locks to make it so gleaming and straight, the maid non-chalantly answered that she had "used Madame Walker's." Actually, the "dekinking" process that the washerwoman had so successfully introduced was intricate and tedious. Her experience as a laundress had suggested that if a hot iron would remove wrinkles from rough-dried clothes, it should be able to do the same for human hair. She made a pomade to soften the freshly washed hair and then carefully flattened out each snuggly curled strand with a headed iron comb. Briefly, the "Walker System" was a method of laundering hair.

Madame Walker was born two years after the close of the Civil War in the little village of Delta, Louisiana. Married at fourteen and widowed at nineteen, with a small daughter to support, she had had little time for schooling, but with her dazzling entrance into Negro society, she engaged a tutor and learned to speak well. She took great pleasure in display, and her houses were famous for their luxurious trappings. She entertained leading persons of her race lavishly, drawing social lines as closely as any white society leader ever essayed to do. She gave dinners, musicales, balls, and entertainments which were attended by well-to-do and influential Negroes from all over America. Booker T. Washington was frequently among her guests.

In 1916 Madame Walker attempted to purchase a property in the better residential section of Flushing, L.I., known as the "Bishop Court," but the white neighbors objected. She reasoned, she afterwards said, that if moving into a white neighborhood would create such a stir, she may as well choose the most select locality she could find. She abandoned her plans for building a country house on the Flushing site, and purchased a strip of land at exclusive Irvington-on-the-Hudson. Here in 1917 she built an elaborate cream-colored "Georgian" stucco mansion designed by the Negro architect, Vertner W. Tandy. But she enjoyed the country place only a short time for she died May 24, 1919, at the age of fifty, within two years after its completion. The bulk of her two-million dollar estate was bequeathed to her only daughter, Mrs A'Leilia Walker Robinson, but she left large sums to Negro charities and educational institutions. Among these was an academy for African girls which she had founded in West Africa and to which she left one hundred thousand dollars.

"WHITE FOLKS, TOO"

Dressing the hair of Negro women became so lucrative a business that many women were encouraged to follow Madame Walker's example and invent their own methods. Today Harlem knows the rival systems, Apex and Poro, besides many less popular ones. The Apex System, founded by Sara Spencer Washington, is much the same as Walker's; so is the Poro System, founded by Annie M. Turnbo Malone. Treatments which cost $2.50 in the 1920s may be had for one dollar today.

Early in the 1920s, the Negro systems found vogue with white women with crinkly hair, and they, too, like their darker sisters, frequented Harlem beauty parlors to straighten out stubborn locks. In the past few years the Negro shops have been thrown into competition with the most expensive beauty salons. Today Saks Fifth Avenue straightens hair in its Antoine Salon. The system used by the white operators is on the same Harlem principle of laundering. The before-and-after advertisement of an expensive Fifth Avenue specialty shop is revealing:

> STRAIGHTEN TOO CURLY HAIR . . .
>
> Have it done the way others have theirs permanently waved. . . . Transform the most stubborn locks from difficult snarls and curls to sleek, smooth or slightly wavy hair. Our new improved method of performing this miracle is painless and practical. The treatment lasts until the hair grows out. Consultation without charge.[6]

LA BOURGEOISIE NOIRE

A business means more than economic salvation to the Negro; indeed, it is a way to escape the white man's kitchen and dining room and to become a member of the Negro upper class. This group, described by E. Franklin Frazier as "La Bourgeoisie Noire,"

[6] New York *Times*, September 13, 1939.

is, in fact, lower middle-class and comprises families of professional men (doctors, lawyers, and ministers) with a salting of judges, actors, "race leaders," politicians, educators, and moneyed prize fighters. The presence of Joe Louis, the pugilist, and Walter White, the "race leader," at the same affair is a triumph for any Harlem hostess. The foundation of this social world is the businessman, property owner, and civil employee, particularly postal worker and teacher. The importance of white collar employment may be measured by the fact that prominent among the social leaders is a woman whose position in society rests upon the fact that she was the first Negro woman to be appointed to a civil service clerical job. The annual income of this group averages between two and three thousand dollars. As a group these people dress better, it is said, than any other group of people dependent upon similar incomes. The women's clothes often bear the labels of fashionable Fifth Avenue specialty shops. For the most part they are college trained and attend the Methodist or Episcopalian churches.

The furnishings of the homes of these people follow an established pattern, embracing disciplined taste, guarded orderliness, and in some cases more than a hint of luxury. Usually they are in the vicinity's better-kept areas and newer apartment houses. Best known in this category is a line of dwellings along prim, tree-dotted "Strivers Row." Although many of these houses have been altered to accommodate lodgers, who augment the family income, they are still the homes of Negroes of recognized social importance. Household routines are conducted in a manner quite like that of upper class white people. The steady increase in Harlem's population led to an overflowing of this class into the Washington Heights section, known to Negroes as "Sugar Hill." The most imposing residential dwellings are the twelve-storied Colonial Apartments and the Roger Morris Apartments with their uniformed elevator operators, doormen, and penthouses with a view of the Harlem River.

Members of Harlem's top social group maintain summer homes, country clubs, motor boats, and high-priced motor-cars. They have made successful inroads into neighborhoods where Negroes are usually barred and many stories are told of the different ways in which they manage to enter new localities. When a fashionable

Negro club sought to enter exclusive Westchester, it selected a committee of "very white looking" Negroes to conduct all negotiations relative to the purchase of a country club from its white owners. The committee did not introduce the question of color and so bought the property without resistance. In several nearby centers, northern New Jersey, upper New York state, and on Long Island, New York Negroes have set up summer colonies. They enjoy a gracious rural community life and live in spacious and attractive country homes in Asbury Park, Greenwood Lake, and Westhampton. The socialites who remain in town have their choice of tennis matches, yachting parties, and moonlight sails on the Hudson River. Besides these, the West Indian group have cricket matches as a diversion.

Negro New York has more than seven hundred social clubs who sponsor activities which range from noisy "chitterlin' suppers" and "barrel house" parties to stilted *soirees,* symposiums, and musicales. Somewhat baffling is the fact that there has been no appreciable slackening of social pace in this community where the doleful post-1929 refrain of "hard times" has had its loudest echo. While Harlem's domestics and porters frugally plan and look eagerly forward to their weekly Thursday and Saturday night sessions of "rug cuttin'" gaiety at the Savoy Ballroom, that small, exclusive unit known as Negro society moves smoothly and complacently within its own orbit.

Typical of the social affairs that fall within the formal winter season, Thanksgiving eve to the beginning of Lent, is the ball of the fashionable Alpha Bowling Club, a charity organization. Its guest list includes Harlem's school teachers, undertakers, nurses, post office employees, physicians, dentists, lawyers, business people, and a small group of dignified domestics who have long been employed by New York's white aristocracy. The ball is usually held in Harlem and lacks completely the so-called "Negro abandon," the dancers staidly refusing to "truck" or "boogie woogie" or "lindy hop." Rarely is admission charged to these formal dances, though an organization's membership may be taxed as high as twenty-five dollars a person to help defray the expenses of an affair.

The four Negro Greek-letter fraternities and six sororities are a short cut to social recognition, as they enroll only college trained

Negroes. The fraternities are national groups with local chapters in most of the country's university centers. All have chapters in New York. They give substantial help to racial endeavors, grant scholarships for special studies, and lend their support to the Negro social agencies. At the same time they sponsor a full social program and strive earnestly for correctness in the conduct of their affairs and in the manner of their dress. One fraternity warned its brothers in advance of its annual convention in New York as follows:

> Clothing for the formal affairs—Late August is likely to be moderately warm in New York City. The type of formal wear is left optional with the Brothers. They can wear either tuxedos or the various types of summer formal apparel. However, in all cases FORMAL APPAREL must be worn—NO WHITE LINEN SUITS are considered formal attire.[7]

Though not as prevalent in New York as in other communities where a Negro society has evolved, there does exist an attempt to maintain a caste based on color. As a rule admittance into Negro New York society has been a matter of money, schooling, and occupation. However, there are a scattering of Negro clubs whose membership consists entirely of fair-skinned or mulatto types, and where the black-ball is rigorously employed against the application of any potential member whose coloring is not "high-yaller." These color distinctions do not usually extend to the men, for their eligibility is based solely on the extent of their formal training, their vocations and their incomes.

As a rule debutantes make their entrance into society in much the same way as they do in white society. In an account of a coming-out party published in the New York *Post,* June 12, 1939, a debutante's mother, the socially prominent wife of a Harlem physician, is reported as saying:

> The daughters in our family have for generations been introduced to society at a gathering of this sort. However, I do suppose that this is the first time that an affair of this size has been given for one of them. Usually they have been smaller affairs and held in the home.

---

[7] *Sphinx Magazine,* XXVII No. 3 (Memphis, Tenn., Alpha Phi Alpha Fraternity August 1939) 6.

The coming-out party alluded to was held in one of Harlem's dance casinos, usually engaged by the larger social clubs for formal balls. The papers reported the party as being comparable with similar parties given to the daughters of New York's white socialites.

PENGUIN CLUB

So sharp are the racial and social lines drawn in Harlem that few whites, that is, the "po' white folks," are able to crash the doors of the ultrasocial. Occasionally whites of the intelligentsia and of the upper middle class gain access to these circles, but generally Negroes prefer not to have white persons present at their gatherings. Thus, not a ripple was caused in Harlem when a local newspaper appeared in the winter of 1936 with the headlines "Mixed Couples Charge Ban by Both Races; Form Club" and again with, "Inter-Married Couples Open Fight to End All Barriers." [8]

This was a group known as the Penguin Club, made up of more than one hundred interracial couples who had banded together to fight social ostracism in the community. Its members were selected after a character investigation; membership was also open to children of interracial marriages. Declaring itself to be without sectarianism or political aims, the organization decided upon a campaign to win a place in the community. In a formal statement to the press, they demanded that "all barriers in both races which now ban interracial couples" should end and that "whites in Harlem should be accepted into civic and community organizations on the same basis as Negroes." In spite of the "liberality" of New York, they contended, there is a sharp line of division which has always separated such couples from both Negro and white society. It was further held that a fight against this social exclusion, an exposure of its unconstitutional nature as well as its cruel social features, would represent the beginning of the end of this situation. [9]

---

[8] New York *Amsterdam News*, XXVII No. 11 (Feb. 22, 1936) 11.

[9] A precedent for such a group existed in the "Manasseh Societies," initiated in the Mid-West years ago in an attempt to "stabilize" the position of Negro and white couples.

THE NEGRO RENAISSANCE [2]

HARLEM, 1925-1929.—A new phase in the development of New York Negroes took place in the early 1920s, when black men began to emerge from the "ghetto of a segregated life," and to appear actively in the world of music, art, theater, and literature. The thing that happened did not appear at first glance as a development; it seemed rather like a sudden awakening, an instantaneous change which caused many people to refer to it as the "Negro Renaissance." This development was national in its sweep, but its most conspicuous stage was Harlem.

Many generations of New York Negroes had been more or less active in the cultural fields, but, except for the theatre, these activities had been mostly confined to a Negro world. Nevertheless, the Negro's music, speech, and folklore had slipped into the national life unnoticed and had become an integral part of the social pattern. Today its threads may be traced in the cultural fabric of the city and nation. Much that has been characterized as racial is now wholly national. This development was largely accomplished by white support. For, while the Negro business-man tussled with economic realities and boasted of the fact that he was independent of white support, the Negro artist, writer, and actor was seeking it.

Not every Negro writer went overboard with the movement. Some viewed it with cynical self-interest. In debunking the "Negro Renaissance," the Negro writer, Wallace Thurman, spoke of

---

[1] This is Chapter XVII in the Ms but it has been renumbered here because the original Chapter XVI (entitled *Black Metropolis*) has been omitted. Most of the omitted chapter was repeated in this chapter word-for-word (from the section *Innocents Abroad* to the end of *House-Rent Parties*). The remaining sections of the omitted chapter have been inserted in the appropriate places in the present chapter: *The Barefoot Prophet, Father Divine,* and *The Mahogany Millionairess* (except for its last paragraph, which was repeated in the opening of the section *Dark Tower* in this chapter).—Ed.

[2] *The Cultural Mecca* was the chapter title in the earlier draft.—Ed.

the artists and writers who exploited the white people who supported it as the "Niggeratti." "Being a Negro writer in these days," in the words of one of his minor characters, "is a racket and I'm going to make the most of it while it lasts. I find queer places for whites to go to in Harlem . . . out-of-the-way primitive churches, side-street speakeasies, and they fall for it. About twice a year I manage to sell a story. It is acclaimed. I am a genius in the making. Thank God for this Negro Literary Renaissance! Long may it flourish!" [3]

"INNOCENTS ABROAD"

Attracted by the "exotic and primitive" in Harlem, jaded white folk wearily descended upon the community and the Negro intelligentsia served as guides. Carl Van Vechten became unofficial publicity agent of the "New Negro" and described Harlem in a novel as "Nigger Heaven." Ballyhooed, exploited commercially and socially, it was inevitable that the community would assume the proportions of a colorful "Black Metropolis." That section of the Negro community which Van Vechten knew was, after all, no more than a brown-skinned edition of "bohemian" Greenwich Village.

The prosperity of the white community had caused some shekels to trickle through to the Negro population. So money appeared to flow in and out of everyone's pockets as easily as laughter from their lips. Everywhere there seemed to be gaiety, good feeling, and the impromptu sound of jazz bands. The community's heart beat to the thump of drums and echoed to the clink of glasses. Hundreds of honky-tonks prospered. Dull red or blue lights glowed from the windows of countless apartments, where silhouetted figures rocked and rolled to mellow music.

Negroes also discovered the white folk. They found them ever ready to spend money on flim-flam and Harlem speakeasies did a land-office business, but these people also spent money on Negro writers and artists, and financed plays. The community had become the stomping grounds for not only white folk, but also for all the fabulous and flamboyant characters produced in Negro America, and their tribe increased as the money continued to flow.

[3] Wallace Thurman, *Infants of the Spring* (New York, Macaulay 1932) 230.

These were, indeed, the lush days, and though Negroes did not feast on the golden calf, many of them were high up on the hog.

With all shadings of life crowded into two square miles, a section of Harlem became a vivid and glorified night spot. White sightseers who visited Harlem joints in the 1920s were alternately delighted and frightened out of their wits. But these places also provided a meeting place where Negroes came to talk over politics, religion, sex, and the "race problem." Here, too, Negroes entertained their white friends and "sponsors." So in a measure white visitors to Harlem were as much a part of the picture as Negroes themselves. It was only natural then that much of the entertainment was geared to suit their taste and at times it was rather on the bizarre side.

SUGAR CANE CLUB

One of the popular meeting places in this era was Ed Small's now-forgotten Sugar Cane Club at 135th Street and Fifth Avenue. It was Harlem's main "jump joint" and typical of the many clubs of the day. Down a steep flight of stairs and smack! you were in a damp, dimly lit cellar, with two dozen or more tables surrounding a tiny dance floor. On one side of this basement was a band, a five-piece aggregation which beat out rhythms without benefit of sheet music. None of the musicians could read music nor did there seem any need for such superfluous knowledge. During evenings when business was lively, the lights would be extinguished, a spotlight focused on a rotating mirrored chandelier which cast its million semi-bright reflections over the dance floor, as the band just played. Perhaps the clarinet would voice some unexpected phrasing, and pleased with its sound would repeat it with variations. The saxaphone would softly join in as the drums provided a muffled obbligato. The bass fiddle would pluck out a monotonous harmony, counterpointed by improvisations from the piano. This was "swing" music before it received noisy popularity. In those days it was called "gut-bucket." The music always drew the patrons to the dance floor. There they would stand and just shuffle their feet. "Dancing on a dime," it was aptly called. Out of these movements grew such dances as "The Bump" and the "Mess Around," names descriptive of themselves.

Ed Small's place, in the best tradition of hot spots off the beaten path, was particularly known for its dancing-singing waiters, who threaded their incredible way through packed houses. Twirling trays high above the heads of the customers and balancing them precariously on one or two fingers, they danced between dancing couples where paper could hardly have been passed. Their journey ended, they contrived a special flourish of the tray, an intricate flurry of dance steps, and deposited a pitcher of raw gin on a customer's table.

The featured entertainer would usually sing some good ol' down-home blues; a no-good, two-timin', back-bitin' man had done her wrong. Aloofly, yet personally, she would give a *double entendre* version. Moving from table to table, patting a cheek here, squeezing a hand there, she would dispense her largesse of personality. The house rocked with applause—this was so, so good.

THE ARISTOCRAT OF HARLEM

Many of the Harlem night clubs which catered to an exclusively white trade barred Negroes. But the people who visited such places were not the ones who associated with members of the Negro intelligentsia. A typical place was the Cotton Club, which used the trade mark, "The Aristocrat of Harlem." It was then situated on Lenox Avenue at 143rd Street and attracted principally the carriage trade. So rigidly was the color line drawn there that only light-complexioned Negroes could steal into this palace of plutocrats. A great doorman stood at its entrance to keep even this tabulation in the lower brackets. The club was famous for its "high yaller" chorus. It was so famous in fact and so lucrative a source of income that white girls were often inspired to "pass" as light-complexioned Negroes to become members of its ranks.[4]

On one occasion a famous Negro composer, in company with a white publisher and his wife, was barred. The explanation given at the time was that the Cotton Club never admitted "mixed parties." The one concession made to Harlem, characterized by the local press as a "chiseling bargain," was the benefaction of food baskets at Christmas time. But this never assuaged Harlem's wound-

---

[4] The other version of this chapter adds: "The Duke Ellington and Cab Calloway bands played a large part in drawing patrons to the club."—Ed.

ed feelings, and while few were wealthy enough to pay its exorbitant prices, Negroes still protested against its barriers.

Most of the more prosperous clubs, which catered to the "ofay" (white) sightseers, were located on 133rd Street between Lenox and Seventh Avenues, a neighborhood known as "Beale Street," a name made famous by W. C. Handy. In the days of prohibition new dives with self-descriptive names sprang up, always one jump ahead of the prohibition agents. Sliding peepholes, passwords, and "membership cards" were the order of the night. There was Gladys Bentley's clamhouse, where this exuberant lady presided over affairs in male attire without detracting in the least from the business of her next door neighbors, the Catagonia, Mexico's, the Nest, the Madhouse, and Pod's and Jerry's.

HOUSE-RENT PARTIES

Though these places attracted a free-spending trade, most of Harlem's enjoyment seekers were banished to house-rent parties, so-called because they were a means by which money was raised to pay rent. The house-rent party, a distinctly Harlem entertainment, blossomed in the 1920s. Mostly employed as "pot rasslers," "kitchen mechanics," "sud busters," and "ham heavers," Negroes found their small salaries inadequate for Cotton Clubs or the rounds of Harlem cabarets, so they sought these lower-priced entertainment places. Usually the admission was twenty-five cents, besides what you spent inside. A small bare room, with a dull red glow for light, was the ballroom. The only furniture was a piano at which a "box-beater" extracted weird and dissonant harmonies. In the kitchen a pot of chitterlings and pigs' feet were steamingly ready for the hungry dancers. A jug of corn liquor was a staple for such affairs and was sold in the kitchen or at a makeshift bar in the hallway. There would be revelry until daybreak and rent for the landlord the next day. Saturday night was the big night. Thursday night was also a favorite since it was then that "sleep-in" domestic workers usually had their day off and were free to "pitch" and "carry on."

The popularity of the Saturday night party attracted racketeers after a time. Many small-time "pimps" and "madames" who had operated undercover "buffet flats" came out into the open with the rent-party vogue as a "blind" for illegitimate activities. They catered primarily to the innocents, travelling salesmen, Pullman porters, interstate-truck drivers, and other transients. Additional business was promoted from that large army described in welfare circles as "single and unattached" males and females, who crowded the streets at night in search of adventure in preference to remaining in small, dingy, ill-ventilated rooms. These people would be greeted volubly by the hostess, introduced around, and eventually steered to the kitchen where refreshments were on sale. Often little business cards were distributed to advertise these get-togethers. The "madames" were careful to give these cards only to the "right people." [5]

The response was gratifying. At the arrival of the first few guests, the hostess would roll back the living-room carpet, dim the lights, seat the musicians (usually a drummer, pianist, and saxaphone player), and the "rug-cuttin'" would get under way. Then she would disappear into the kitchen to give a final last-minute inspection to the refreshment counter. The musicians, fortified with a drink or two of "King Kong" (home-made corn whiskey), would begin beating out their rhythm.

During prohibition the police were more diligent about raiding these apartments than they were about known "gin mills" that flourished on almost every street corner. With the repeal of prohibition, the popularity of the rent party passed,[6] and with its passing went a fertile soil for folk contributions.

---

[5] The omitted chapter included the following "samples":
    There'll be brown skin mammas
    High Yallers too
    And if you ain't got nothin to do
    Come on up to

                    ROY and SADIE'S

    228 West 126 St.

                    Sat. Night, May 12th.

    There'll be plenty of pig feet
    And lots of gin
    Jus ring the bell
    And come on in.

                    —Ed.

[6] The omitted chapter ended this sentence with "only to be revived with the advent of the Depression" in place of "and with its passing . . . . folk contributions" as above.—Ed.

THE BAREFOOT PROPHET

One of the frequent house-rent party visitors was the Barefoot Prophet, so-called because winter or summer he literally strode the streets of Harlem in his bare feet. A towering man, with his luxuriant mane of gray hair, flowing beard and a long heavenly robe from which peeked gigantic feet, he was an eternal beacon along Harlem's highways.

The Barefoot Prophet, formally known as Elder Clayhorn Martin, was a beloved figure in the community. In good weather as well as bad, this giant carried the "Word" to Harlem's corners and crevices. Patrons of gin-mills, cabarets, taverns and buffet flats were seldom surprised to see the Prophet stride in, quote a few passages of Scripture, take up a small collection, and vanish into the night.

Legends grow about a character like this, and the Prophet was wealthy in these, and in these alone. He never had a church, he never preached on street corners, but for more than fifty years he wended his way through the hearts of people from Virginia to New York. The Prophet was born in Henry County, Virginia, in 1851. At an early age he had a vision. "Take off your shoes, for this is Holy Ground. Go preach My Gospel," a voice told him and he obeyed.

Prophet Martin died prosaically in Harlem Hospital in July 1937, at the age of eighty-six. The Prophet in death as in life needed contributions to carry on. Hundreds heeded his last message, which was pinned to a box resting on his chest, as he lay in state. The appeal written in his own shaking hand, as he lay dying, read:

"Help Bury the Prophet."

FATHER DIVINE

Religion in Harlem has many curious manifestations and strange facets, and these come to the fore in a number of cults. Perhaps nowhere in America, with the possible exception of Los Angeles, is religion so extensively and so variously expressed. Cults of every description abound. Closed picture houses, dance halls, empty stores, and lodge halls are converted into places of worship, with announcements that are cheap but alluring calling the citizenry to pray. Charlatans give a swing to their collars and over night they are "ministers." Harlem calls them "jackleg preachers." They are found in "churches" that appear and disappear almost overnight. There is an imposing list of unorthodox religions which apparently maintain a prosperous existence. They receive a neat profit from the sale of dream books, love potions, number books, and incense to destroy evil spirits. A recent survey, made by the New York City Writers' project, showed nearly two hundred places operating as "spiritualist churches."

In the forty years of Harlem's existence as a Negro community, there has been a stream of cult leaders. Harlem has known Rev. Becton, of the "consecrated dime," who was murdered by kidnapping gangsters; the university-educated Prophet Costonie, who organized a boycott of public utilities and sold incense; Elder Martin Claybourne, the "Barefoot Prophet"; the "Bishop" Sufi Abdul Hamid; and Mother Horn and her "Pray For Me Church of the Air," known in more formal moments as the Mount Calvary Assembly Hall of the Pentecostal Faith. But these people, augmented by a number of herb-doctors and clairvoyants, have only transient careers in the community. They frequently receive notice all out of proportion to their influence, if any, in Harlem.

The most grandiloquent of the contemporary cults is that headed by Father Divine and known as the Righteous Government. It had its New York beginning in 1915. There have been, in recent years as in earlier periods of human history, persons whose followers claimed they were the new Messiah. While Divine has never made any statement to this effect, his followers speak of him as "God." Well-informed individuals residing in Harlem place his actual local following as not exceeding four thousand persons, with little influence in the community. Divine's own claim is twenty thousand or more. His followers are drawn largely from the very wealthy and the very poor and illiterate.

Father Divine, a diminutive and slightly bald middle-aged man with extremely keen eyes, was born, according to the best available sources, fifty or sixty years ago on a rice plantation on Hutchinson's Island in the Savannah River. In 1906, Divine, né George Baker, first turned up in the city of Baltimore; he was then a tiny underfed poverty-stricken man who maintained a measly existence mowing lawns, cutting hedges, and doing other odd jobs. A spark of ambition burned in his breast and in a short time he was teaching Sunday School. Gathering about him six men and six women, he made a southern tour and met with evangelistic success. The little band then set out for New York in 1915.

He took a place at Prince Street in Brooklyn and installed his "Communal System," and assumed the more dignified title of Major Morgan J. Divine. In 1919 he took his flock of a dozen souls to Sayville, Long Island, where he had purchased an eight-room house. There he obtained a license to conduct an employment agency to secure jobs for the domestic workers in the neighborhood.

His Sayville retreat soon became known for its sumptuous banquets, free of charge. The newspapers discovered him and blew him up into the proportions of a "mystic" who healed the sick and performed "miracles." Bus companies, with sound eyes for business, began running regular trips from Harlem to Sayville for a $1.50 round-trip, and advertising the blue-plate luncheons that Father Divine served. The publicity soon caused the townfolk to become alarmed as Divine's "angels" started to overrun the area. The property owners feared a sharp decline in real estate values. The fact that Negroes and whites mingled freely was also found irksome. In May 1932 Divine was convicted by the Nassau County Supreme Court for maintaining a public nuisance and was sentenced to one year in jail. Judge Lewis J. Smith, who sentenced him, spoke of him as a "menace to society." Father Divine said: "Pity the Judge, he can't live long now. He's offended Almighty God." The following month Judge Smith died suddenly, a victim of heart disease. Divine was heard to say from his cell: "I hated to do it."

He was released from jail by the Appellate Division of the Supreme Court in Brooklyn when it reversed the conviction and ordered a new trial. Thereupon he took his followers to Harlem. Banquets were held at local dance halls and the movement swelled in numbers. His followers then began to assume other-worldly names like Beauty Smiles, Norah Endurance, Holy Shinelight, Pearly Gates, and Rose Memory. Divine bought a number of Peace Missions, known as "heavens," throughout the Harlem area and "Peace, it's truly wonderful!" became the password. In 1936 the Peace Mission Movement had expanded into the International

Righteous Government with the platform: "One for all and all for one but not for one who is not for all." The movement then spread into the suburban areas, in a Utopian dream of a "Promised Land."

THE MAHOGANY MILLIONAIRESS

At Irvington-on-the-Hudson, austerely looking out across the river, stands the classic white Georgian mansion, now a convalescent home for white people, but built originally as the fabulous palace of a one-time Negro laundress, Sarah Jane Walker. It was called the Villa Lewaro, a name which legend says Enrico Caruso created by using the first two letters in each of the names of the rich woman's daughter, A'Leilia Walker Robinson. Madame Walker had it built at a cost of $250,000 and invested it with three hundred thousand dollars' worth of furnishings. For ten years following the manufacturer's death, the daughter was mistress of this estate.

In the fall of 1930, the house was offered for sale and A'Leilia Walker employed the same auctioneer who had sold out the old Waldorf-Astoria furnishings. Those who thronged the place and wandered in and out during the auction were received by a haughty Negro majordomo, regal in doublet and hose. They gasped at the unusual splendour of a twenty-four carat gold piano and a phonograph to match, at a clock almost as tall as a telegraph pole, at wide marble stairways, and at a Japanese prayer tree for which the pomade manufacturer had paid more than ten thousand dollars. Only a few had any interest in buying, so that the tapestries, the Heppelwhite furniture, the enormous oil paintings, the sixty thousand dollar pipe organ, the silver satyrs and cherubs, the magnificent deep-piled Persian rugs, were sold at a great loss.

A stocky, broad-shouldered, cocoa-colored woman, A'Leilia Walker Robinson was famous for her unique and extravagant clothes, her love of display, and her enjoyment of the crowds of people with whom she filled her house. In 1923, she startled the whole of Negro America with what she described as a "Million Dollar Wedding." The ceremony was conducted at fashionable St Philip's Protestant Episcopal Church, at a reputed cost of $62,000. Nine thousand persons milled about the church's doors, and Harlem traffic was blocked for hours while gaping crowds stood excitedly awaiting a glimpse of the bride, the granddaughter of a Negro laundress who had founded America's first black plutocratic dynasty.

THE "NEW NEGRO"

Before the close of the period much of the folk life of an urban community was recorded and interpreted by such Negro writers as Wallace Thurman, Langston Hughes, Claude McKay, and Rudolph Fisher. Indeed, much of what they wrote was a reflection of their own lives, for they were spare-time writers—proletarians. Most of them had been dishwashers, waiters, Pullman porters, redcaps and stokers, or worked at the various forms of rough and casual menial labor open to Negroes. A characteristic line from Langston Hughes' work is illustrative:

> The steam in hotel kitchens
> And the smoke in hotel lobbies
> And the slime in hotel spitoons
> Part of my life

Much of the material written in this period was concerned with the problems of the Negro bourgeoisie. Walter White and Jesse Fauset were among those who wrote of the Negro smart sets and of light Negroes who "passed" for white, and of the beauty and the sophistication, and, indeed, the snobbery of Colored Society. This material was, in fact, merely a restatement of what DuBois had already said in *Souls of Black Folks*. Whatever their literary merit, they had documentary importance in revealing what was on the minds of a large portion of Negroes. The work of these writers caused Alain Locke to happily accept the era as approaching a "spiritual emancipation." He confidently titled his volume on the activities of the period *The New Negro*. This was a self-respecting set who shunned the "romantic" and turned their eyes towards "realism" in their work. Carried along on the wave of post-war radicalism and the Garvey movement with its "race" idealism, they held that Negroes were no longer to be caricatured. Sterling Brown has observed that work of the period had five major concerns:

1. A discovery of Africa as a source for race pride.

2. A use of Negro heroes and heroic episodes from American history.

3. Propaganda of protest.

4. A treatment of the Negro masses (frequently of the folk, less often of the workers) with more understanding and less apology.

5. Franker and deeper self-revelation.[7]

The Negro magazines of the period were a considerable force in the cultural development, particularly the *Messenger,* the *Crisis,* and the *Opportunity.* There was also aid from sympathetic whites, who helped the writers to secure new channels for expression. The writings of the period were accurate reflections of the times and conditions, and whatever their literary form and value, they usually revealed a note of social protest. Appalled at the epidemic of lynchings in the South, Claude McKay was moved to write of crowds where men were jostled by steely-eyed women and of "little lads, lynchers that were to be." Langston Hughes, one of the more widely read poets, wrote dramatically of city workers—elevator boys and porters "climbing up a great big mountain of yes, sirs!" Though Hughes celebrated a "jazz-mad" Harlem in the 1920s in *Weary Blues,* today he is definitely interested in the Negro masses and his work sounds a decided note for social justice. His play, *Mulatto,* which appeared on Broadway during the 1930s, was a bitter criticism of the fruit of race mixture. James Weldon Johnson's poetry was concerned with recording folk idioms, and Countee Cullen, whom Brown describes as the most precocious of the contemporary Negro poets, was concerned with the polished lyric and spoke of "the winter of sure defeat."

The fiction of the period showed an increase in volume as compared with previous years, From 1914 to 1924 not a single Negro novel was written;[8] yet during the next ten years ending with 1934, twenty were produced by a new crop of authors who, with few exceptions, up to that time had produced nothing. It is still more

---

[7] Sterling A. Brown, *Negro Poetry and Drama* (Washington, D.C., Associates in Negro Folk Education 1937) 61.

[8] The writer presumably means that none was *published.*—Ed.

striking to discover that fifteen of these twenty were written between 1928 and 1933—a period of five years.[9] In recent years Zora Neale Hurston has written four novels. Richard Wright's four novellas under the title *Uncle Tom's Children* won a $500 prize offered by *Story Magazine* for the best manuscript submitted by a writer connected with the Works Progress Administration. He was granted a Guggenheim Fellowship in 1939. But it is evident that the publishers sought material about a "hot" Harlem, for few of the writers escaped writing such work.[10]

DARK TOWER

A reckless expenditure of money was the fashion of the day and A'Leilia Walker kept pace with the times. At her town house at 108 West 136th Street, the elaborate establishment built by her mother, Madame Walker, in 1914, she was hostess to socially ambitious Negroes and that fringe of intellectual and sometimes wealthy whites who had been led to Harlem by their curiosity about the "New Negro." In 1928 the mahogany millionairess decided to become a patron of the Negro cultural movement. It was also fashionable to help people who "did things." It was not enough that she have them to her house and feed them; she saw a real need for a place, a sufficiently sympathetic place in which they could meet and discuss their plans and arts, to which they could bring their friends, and at which they could eat for a price within their very limited means.

In 1928 she dedicated a floor of her Harlem mansion to the enterprise of being "patron saint" to Harlem's artists and writers. It was named "Dark Tower" for a column in the *Opportunity Magazine* conducted by Countee Cullen, one of her Negro poet friends. It was to be elaborately furnished and decorated with murals and paintings by the artists in whom she was interested. But

---

[9] The most active fiction writers were Langston Hughes, Jean Toomer, Claude McKay, Wallace Thurman, Jesse Fauset, Rudoph Fisher, George Schuyler, W.E.B. DuBois, Walter White, Arna Bontemps, and Countee Cullen, all residents of New York.

[10] There was a medley of books on this subject: Countee Cullen's on the gay abandon of lovely brown girls of Harlem; Helene Johnson's *Sonnet to a Negro in Harlem;* Rudolph Fisher's *Conjure Man* and *Walls of Jericho;* Claude McKay's *Home to Harlem;* James Weldon Johnson's *Black Manhattan;* and Wallace Thurman's *Blacker the Berry* and a play, *Harlem.*

the plans never jelled, because A'Leilia was always too busy with parties to find time to give approval, or the artists could not be found because of similarly important distractions. Whenever the little group of consultants did meet at A'Leilia's ("and this time we *really must* get something done . . . ."), there would be endless discussion, with the prominent artist Aaron Douglas contributing the soundest decorative schemes. On one thing they did agree: it was to be quite Utopian. It was to have enough quiet dignity to provide atmosphere for the poetry evenings, and there were to be hung, without ballyhoo, the pictures, the etchings, et al, of the struggling artists.

Finally the artists (and every one else) received notice of Dark Tower's "grand opening." This came as a surprise to the planning committee, who had thought that the details, great and small, were still ephemeral and negative, but they attended. The engraved invitations were a portent of what was to follow. The large house was lighted brilliantly, and an air of formality pervaded which almost intimidated them. Bravely they mounted the stairs and were greeted by the hostess and the hired man who checked their hats for a (15c) fee. This was not the only shock. The great room and hall were a seething picture of well-dressed white people, resembling a Café Society crowd of today. The artists, decidedly seedy by comparison, pushed bewilderedly through the crush looking for the refuge of friends; but colored faces were at a premium. The laughing, chattering downtown folk, resplendent in evening clothes, had come expecting that this was a new and hot night club.

When A'Leilia's protégés finally gathered their wits, they looked about them and saw, there on the cool cream-colored walls, poems by Langston Hughes and Countee Cullen painted in precise lettering. Alas, the work had been done by a sign painter! Scattered about the room were small vermilion-colored tables and chairs. Sari Price-Patton, a Harlem Elsa Maxwell, presided over the tea-room (for such it really was), simulating a stiff dignity that quite forbade the loose comfort for which the place was to have been dedicated. Nevertheless, there one went to meet and chat with Countee Cullen, Langston Hughes, Aaron Douglas, Richard Nugent, and a number of less-eminent figures who made up the coterie of the New Negro.

A'Leilia Walker gave several *soirees* to which she asked all of white social New York, visiting royalty and Rothschilds, and at which Carl Van Vechten danced attendance on her. Through these activities, she aided, quite unwittingly, in publicizing Negroes who wrote and painted. At her "salon" the Negro Intelligentsia met influential white people, particularly publishers, critics, and potential "sponsors."

Less than two years after Dark Tower's gala opening, A'Leilia Walker, in a rash of disgust, closed it. Soon afterwards she leased the house to the city for use as a health center, and carried her parties and her great following to 80 Edgecombe Avenue. In August of 1931 she died suddenly at the age of forty-six at Asbury Park, New Jersey. It is estimated that A'Leilia Walker enjoyed the spending of nearly two million dollars during her lifetime which had carried her through an impoverished Kansas City girlhood into a womanhood which rivaled in sheer luxury the existence of any queen.

ARTHUR SCHOMBURG

The literary output of New York Negroes has had a continuous flow since the colonial days of Jupiter Hammon, the first American Negro poet. Negroes chiefly began to write during the period of anti-slavery agitation, however. Much of what they wrote was autobiographical and much of the rest was in the form of pamphlets. "There is interest in the work of these obscure authors," observes Vernon Loggins in his *Negro Author*, "for if any American Negro of the early nineteenth century wrote at all, he was an unusual person with something out of the ordinary to say." Toward the close of the nineteenth century, the work of Paul Laurence Dunbar began to appear. Though he had only casual contacts with New York he is included in the local group. His contemporary, T. Thomas Fortune, though primarily a journalist, was the author of several books of poems. The largest literary figure at the turn of the century was DuBois, whose influence upon contemporary writers has been profound.

Possibly the greatest single force that has aided the Negro writer interested in historical and sociological work in recent days is the Schomburg Collection, which is a part of the Negro division of the 135th Street library. Arthur Schomburg, an immigrant Negro after whom the collection was named, came to New York in 1891 at the age of seventeen and began collecting Negro books for his own development. His early collection dealt largely with the West Indies, but soon what had begun as a hobby turned into a passion to which he eventually dedicated his life. His collection of rare books, prints, autographs, and manuscripts has been in the New York Library since 1926. Through the efforts of the New York Urban League it was purchased for the sum of ten thousand dollars, and Schomburg became curator of the Negro division. From time to time it has been augmented by purchases of books by the public library system and by gifts from persons interested in the welfare of the Negro. There are now more than ten thousand volumes in the Schomburg Collection and Negro division. Dr Lawrence D. Reddick became curator after Schomburg's death in 1939.

A "LILY-WHITE" CRAFT

The development of the Negro writer is hindered by lack of a market for his work. Also, jobs as professional writers, editorial assistants, publishers' readers, and the like are almost non-existent. The leading lecture bureaus do not handle Negro speakers. Thousands of women's clubs and forums have never had a Negro speaker. Until very recently, Negro books were considered by editors and publishers as "exotic." Negro material, as Negro writers have discovered, is placed like Chinese or Bali or East Indian works. Magazine editors say, "We can use but so many Negro stories a year." Book publishers say, "We already have one Negro novel on our list this fall."

Langston Hughes, appearing before the American Writers' Congress in 1939, attempted to throw some light on this problem. "The market for Negro writers," he observed, "is definitely limited as long as we write about ourselves. And the more truthfully we write about ourselves, the more limited our market becomes. Those novels about Negroes that sell best, by Negroes or whites, those novels that make the best-seller lists and receive the leading prizes, are almost always books that touch very lightly upon the facts of Negro life, books that make our black ghettos in the big cities seem very happy places, indeed, and our plantations in the Deep South idyllic in their pastoral loveliness. In such books there is no hunger and no segregation, no lynchings and no fears, no intimidations and no Jim Crow. The exotic is the quaint and the happy—the pathetic or melodramatic, perhaps, but not the tragic. We are considered exotic. When we cease to be exotic, we do not sell well."

"I know, of course," said Hughes, "that very few writers of any race make a living directly from their writing. You must be very lucky and very famous to do that. But a great many American writers—who are not Negroes—may make a living in fields more or less connected with writing. They may thus be professional writers living on or from their literary reputations and able, from their earnings, to afford some leisure time for personal creation. Whether their books are good or bad, they may work in editorial offices, on publishers staffs, in publicity firms, in radio, or in motion pictures. Practically never is such employment granted to a Negro writer though he be as famous as the late James Weldon Johnson or as excellent a craftsman as the living Richard Wright. Perhaps an occasional prize or a fellowship may come a Negro writer's way— but not a job. It is very hard for a Negro to become a professional writer. Magazine offices, daily newspapers, publishers' offices are tightly closed to us in America."[11]

NEGRO NEWSPAPERS

The only established place of employment for the Negro journalist in New York are Harlem's two Negro weeklies, the New York *Age* and the *Amsterdam News*. These papers, owned and operated by Negroes, print news of particular interest to Negroes and employ together a total of ten full-time editorial workers. The New York *Age* was founded by T. Thomas Fortune in 1880 and was sold to Fred R. Moore, its present publisher, in 1907. Its present staff has been recruited largely from his family, leaving the *Amsterdam News* as the only paper to which the section's remaining Negro newspapermen may turn for employment.

The meagre operating capital of both these papers precludes their subscription to the services of the United Press and to the Associated Press. Their chief revenue comes from the sale of the

---

[11] From the text of a speech made by Langston Hughes at the Public Session of the Third American Writers' Congress held at Carnegie Hall, June 2, 1939.

papers, for there is little profitable advertising. The editorial staff of the *Amsterdam News* is comprised of college-trained journalists, all members of the American Newspaper Guild. Their salaries strike an average of $30 weekly for full time work and $4 weekly for part time. Thus in the City of New York there are but a handful of writing jobs open to several hundred Negro writers.

ARTISTS

What has been said about the Negro writers' lack of employment opportunities is largely true of the artists. Few newspapers or magazines employ Negro artists. The *Amsterdam News* employs one full-time artist and one part-time. Only Richmond Barthé and Augusta Savage, among the sculptors, have received monetary support for their efforts. Savage was awarded a Carnegie grant and was assigned work by the New York World's Fair (1939). Barthé, after completion of his studies at the Art Institute of Chicago and the Art Students' League of New York, has exhibited widely and his work has been bought both here and abroad. Among the artists, E. Simms Campbell has made the most important strides economically. A member of the staff of *Esquire Magazine,* Campbell is the exception in Negro empoyment.

Many Negroes are, however, engaged in sculpturing and painting in New York; of this group, Aaron Douglas has probably made the greatest impression. After attending the University of Nebraska and teaching drawing in Kansas City high school, he came to this city where he is now active. Chief among his works are many book illustrations and murals at Fisk University and at the Sherman Hotel in Chicago. The younger artists, like Charles H. Alston and Perry Watkins, are seeking thorough grounding in their craft. They have had exhibitions, received prize moneys, fellowships, and other awards for their work.

Up to 1920, except for a few isolated artists who worked as individuals, there was no active group of Negro artists. That year the 135th Street Public Library held an exhibition. In 1925 a white philanthropist, William E. Harmon, established the foundation which bears his name, with the announced object of promoting human welfare through recognition of meritorious achievement. The Negro had attracted attention at this time as suffering from neglect and disinterest, and it was decided to concentrate on him. Nine fields were selected for this work, of which art was a principal one. The foundation's first exhibit of work by Negro artists was held in New York in 1928. Only nineteen artists submitted work. Since then nearly every important Negro artist in the United States has exhibited with the foundation, which is now in touch with more than four hundred Negro artists.

When Negroes took up brush and palette just before the Civil War, it was said that Negroes had no artistic capacity. However, Edmonia Lewis, who was born in New York in 1845, exhibited a bust of the abolitionist, Robert Gould Shaw, in Boston in 1865. She went to Rome where she spent the rest of her life to escape American color prejudice. There are only sporadic efforts by Negroes until the 1920s.

In 1935 the Harlem Art Workshop was inaugurated in the 135th Street Public Library and James Lesene Wells, now a professor of art at Howard University, was appointed director. Classes in arts and crafts, sculpturing, modeling, painting, soap carving, photography, and woodwork were offered. During the year a distinguished exhibition of primitive African sculpture and carving was held in New York; the younger artists had a showing at the Arthur U. Newton Galleries in an exhibition that was held at the local Y.W.C.A., sponsored by the Harlem Art Committee, a group of more than one hundred leading citizens of the community, whose expressed purpose was a city-sponsored art center for Harlem. The work of sixty-five artists and their pupils was shown. "This exhibit," declared the committee, "is Harlem's response to the question, 'Does New York Need a City Art Center?'"

GOVERNMENT SUBSIDY

When white philanthropists deserted the Negro artists and writers, government subsidy took their place in the role of the Works Progress Administration. The plans for art were more ambitious than those for writing. After its inception the WPA rented a large loft building at the corner of 125th Street and Lenox Avenue and established the Harlem Community Art Center. The project received the supplementary sponsorship of a committee of leading local citizens. Children and adults soon registered for its classes in lithography, photography, painting and drawing, and composition, sculpture, metal craft, textile design, and weaving. Under WPA sponsorship, a group of Negro professionals completed murals for Harlem hospitals. The New York City Writers' Project has employed an average of twenty Negro writers and research workers up to 1940.

CHAPTER XVII[1]

THE DEPRESSION

BLACK HARLEM, 1929-1935.—Hand-to-mouth living had been the rule in Harlem for many years. Though some had tasted of the fatted calf during lush days, more than two thousand Negro families were destitute at the height of prosperity.[2] Before the full effects of the Depression were felt, the average weekly income of a Negro workingman had been eighteen dollars. Sixty per cent of the married women worked, a figure four times higher than that of the native-born white Americans.[3] In twenty-five years Harlem's population had increased more than six hundred per cent to more than 350,000 (equal to the total population of Rochester, N.Y.), with an average density of 233 persons per acre compared with 133 for the rest of Manhattan. The community had become a vast swarming hive in which families were doubled and trebled in apartments meant for one family.[4] But with the financial collapse in October 1929, a large mass of Negroes were faced with the reality of starvation and they turned sadly to the public relief. When the few chanted optimistically, "Jesus will Lead Me and the Welfare will Feed Me," the many said it was a knowing delusion, for the Home Relief Bureau allowed only eight cents a meal for food; meanwhile men, women, and children combed the streets and searched in garbage cans, many foraging with dogs and cats.

---

[1] Chapter XVIII in the Ms.—Ed.

[2] The New York Charity Organization Society reported 592 Harlem Negro families under their care from 1927 to 1928, and these comprised only 24.7 per cent of all Negro families receiving charity.

[3] Beverly Smith, New York *Herald Tribune,* February 10, 1930.

[4] State of New York, *Report of the New York State Temporary Commission on the Condition of the Urban Colored Population to the Legislature of the State of New York* (Albany, J. B. Lyon 1938) 44-56.

TENEMENT DWELLINGS

The crashing drop of wages drove Negroes back to the already crowded hovels east of Lenox Avenue. In many blocks one toilet served a floor of four apartments. Most of the apartments had no private bathrooms or even the luxury of a public bath. Wherever a tub was found it usually had been installed in the kitchen. Without exception these tenements were filthy and vermin-ridden. Along Fifth Avenue, between 135th and 138th Streets, were flats with old-fashioned toilets which rarely flushed and, when they were, they often overflowed on the floors below. In the winter the gaping holes in the skylights allowed cold air to sweep down the staircase, sometimes freezing the flush for weeks. Coal grates provided the only heat. The dwellers scoured the neighborhood for fuel, and harassed janitors in the surrounding districts were compelled to stand guard over coal deliveries until they were safely stored in the cellars. Landlords in this section hired a janitor for nothing more than a basement to exist in, for which he had to clean six floors, take care of sidewalk and backyard, haul garbage, make minor repairs, and where a house had a hot-water furnace he had to stoke it.[5]

10,000 in Dungeons

Many families had been reduced to living below street level. It was estimated that more than ten thousand Negroes lived in cellars and basements which had been converted into makeshift flats. Packed in damp, rat-ridden dungeons, they existed in squalor approaching that of the Arkansas sharecroppers. Floors were of cracked concrete and the walls were whitewashed rock, water-drenched and rust-streaked. There were only slits for windows. A tin can in a corner covered by a sheet of newspaper was the only toilet. There was no running water in some, and no partitions to separate the adults from the curious eyes of the young. Packing boxes were used as beds, tables, and chairs. In winter rags and

---

[5] More than 85 per cent of these buildings were old-law tenements.

This information—and much of this chapter—is derived from the report of The Mayor's Commission on Conditions in Harlem, "The Negro in Harlem: A Report on Social and Economic Conditions Responsible for the Outbreak of March 19, 1935" (La Guardia Papers). Although the report was not published at the time, the *Amsterdam News* (July 18, 1936) later printed a summary, and some of the commission's findings were also reported in E. Franklin Frazier, "Negro Harlem: An Ecological Study," *The American Journal of Sociology* XLIII (July 1937) 72-88.—Ed.

newspapers were stuffed into the numerous cracks to keep out the wind.

> *I wish the rent*
> *Was Heaven sent*
> —Langston Hughes

Shunted off into these run-down sections, Negroes were forced to pay exorbitant rents while landlords relaxed supervision and flagrantly violated the city building and sanitary codes. Compared with twenty to twenty-five per cent of their income generally paid by white families for rent, Negro tenants paid from forty to fifty per cent.[6] More than half of the Negro families were forced to take in lodgers to augment the family income. Frequently whole families slept in one room. Envied was the family who had a night worker as a lodger. He would occupy a bed in the day that would be rented out at night—same room, same bed, same sheets, and same bedbugs. This was described as the "hot bed." If the family had a bathtub, it, too, after being covered with boards, would be rented out.

The artificial scarcity of dwellings was accentuated by white property owners who in making a Negro district had heightened the housing problem of Negroes and thus were able to maintain high rents. A prominent member of the New York City Realty Board is quoted as saying:

> I believe a logical section for Negro expansion in Manhattan is East Harlem. At present this district has reached such a point of deterioration that its ultimate residential pattern is most puzzling. Many blocks have a substantial section of their buildings boarded up or demolished and a goodly percentage of those remaining are in disrepair and in violation of law . . . An influx of Negroes into East Harlem would not work a hardship on the present population of the area, because its present residents could move to any other section of New York without the attendant racial discrimination which the Negro would encounter if he endeavored to locate in other districts.[7]

---

[6] Mayor's Commission Report. (See preceding note.—Ed.)
[7] *Report of the New York State Temporary Commission* 49

"LAST HIRED, FIRST FIRED"

Discrimination against employment of Negroes had practically closed the doors to any and all types of occupations. Generally, the poorer half of the colored population lived on an income which was only forty-six per cent of that of the poorer half of the white population.[8]

The people of Harlem regarded the public utilities and trade unions as the chief agencies of discrimination. Particularly were these barriers extended to white-collar employment. During the period 1930-1935 the Consolidated Gas Company employed 213 Negroes as porters among its ten thousand employees; the New York Edison Company, with the same number of employees, had only sixty-five Negroes, all of whom were porters, cleaners, and hall men. The New York Telephone Company had a similar situation. The Interborough Rapid Transit Company had 580 Negroes employed as messengers, porters, and cleaners, out of ten thousand employees. The Western Union Telegraph Company had two clerks and two operators and a few messengers employed in Harlem. Except for this office, Negroes employed by this corporation occupied the same menial positions as colored employees had in the other public utilities. The Fifth Avenue Coach Company's policy of excluding Negroes had assumed the aspects of a caste system.

These companies had already placed themselves on record. In January 1927, the *Messenger* published a reply to an inquiry made by the magazine concerning the employment of Negroes in the Consolidated Gas Company. The letter signed by the company's vice-president, H.M. Bundage, said:

> Replying to your favor of November 23rd, have to advise that Negroes employed by us render common labor, maid service and the like. We do not assign Negroes as stenographers, clerks or inspectors.

The New York Telephone Company in response to this same inquiry wrote:

---

[8] Including relief and employed families of all classes together, one-half of all native white families of New York City had incomes of less than $1,814 yearly, but one-half of all Negro families had incomes of less than $837.

As to the question of employment by the company of persons of known Negro descent, we might say that we do employ such persons having some on our payroll at the present time assisting us in the conduct of our restaurant and lounge facilities.

The trade unions, particularly the craft unions, were active in keeping the large employment fields barred to Negroes. In 1936 Charles L. Franklin, in his book the *Negro Labor Unionist of New York,* listed twenty-four international unions which excluded Negroes by initiation rituals. Out of the sixteen of these unions, covering a membership of 609,789 workers, who answered Franklin's inquiries concerning racial discriminations, thirteen said their restrictions remained. One answered that its constitution had been changed to include Negroes. Another reported that the word "white" had been removed from the constitution, but that this was meaningless since there were no colored telegraphers. Still another declared it had changed its policy and admitted colored lodges but would not have colored representation at its conventions.

SLAVE MARKET

After 1930 wage standards all but disappeared. This was particularly true of domestic work, which absorbed the vast majority of Negro women workers who, with the almost complete unemployment of Negro men, were becoming the sole support of the family. Unable to find positions through regular employment agencies or newspaper advertisements, many of them traveled to the Bronx in search of a day's work.[9] Frequent complaints of exploitation caused two young Negro women, Ella Baker and Marvel Cooke, to visit the area and describe their experiences in a magazine article. Here, they said, was "a street corner market where Negro women are 'rented' at unbelievably low rates for housework. The heaviest traffic is at 167th Street and Jerome Avenue where, on benches surrounding a green square, the victims wait grateful at

---

[9] "The practice of hiring for housework Negro women who congregate on street corners in the Bronx, known as 'domestic slave markets,' was severely condemned by the Bronx Citizens' Committee for the Improvement of Domestic Employees meeting. . . . It was proposed that centers of special agencies be established in the sections where they congregate in order to shelter them in severe weather and also see that prospective employers pay them fair wages."—New York *Times,* December 1, 1939.

least for some place to sit. At Simpson Street and Westchester Avenue they pose wearily against buildings and lampposts or scuttle about in an attempt to retrieve discarded boxes upon which to sit. Not only is human labor bartered and sold for the slave wage, but human love is also a marketable commodity. Whether it is labor or love, the women arrive as early as eight a.m. and remain as late as one p.m. or until they are hired. In rain or shine, hot or cold, they wait to work for ten, fifteen, and twenty cents per hour. They wash floors, clothes, windows and etc. Some had been maids and domestics in wealthy homes. Some were former marginal workers." [10]

Unemployed, the last refuge of these people was the relief offices, but here, they complained, they were often met with red tape and prejudice. At this time it was estimated that more than fifty thousand Negroes were neither working nor receiving relief.

> *I went to see my investigator*
> *She smile and say*
> *Come back later, come back later.*
>
> —Abe Hill

Negro sharecroppers of the South who had lost their land drifted into the big cities and thousands found their way to Harlem, swelling the total of destitutes. Before the relief system was instituted, Negroes had tried every device from "Hoover block parties" [11] to "house rent parties" to tide over the bleak times. Negro churches took an active part in the feeding of many of the people, for private welfare agencies were flooded with pleas for aid. There was bitter waiting and more bitter street fighting.

In the first month in 1933 the Home Relief Bureau opened its doors and was immediately deluged with thousands of demands for food, clothing, and employment; some even asked for transportation to the South and the West Indies. Nine months later more than twenty-five thousand Negro families were receiving un-

---

[10] Ella Baker and Marvel Cooke, "The Bronx Slave Market" *Crisis Magazine* XLII No. 11 (Nov. 1935) 330.

[11] President Hoover called for neighborhood endeavor to raise relief funds for the unemployed. This resulted in numerous "street" or "block" parties at which money was raised.

employment relief from the city, almost fifty per cent of all the families in Harlem. By 1936 the figure had become twenty-one percent of the city's entire relief rolls. But Negroes had only nine per cent of the work relief jobs allotted by the Home Relief Bureau.[12] At the same time, the Welfare Department allowed $4.15 for food for two weeks to a male over sixteen years old, an increase over $3.30 in 1934 and $3.55 in 1935.[13]

Negroes made considerable complaint against the manner and the amount of relief distributed. But discrimination is a wisp which cannot be nailed down, and investigations of it were never very fruitful, though standardized relief under Mayor La Guardia's administration (1934-40) reduced the number of complaints. When Negroes received work relief they were assigned chiefly to menial jobs and were given an inferior status despite their previous training and experience.[14]

THE "LUNG BLOCK"

Unemployment, congestion, and substandard dwellings took their toll of Negro health. In 1934 a survey of twenty thousand residents of Negro Harlem, chiefly on the relief rolls, revealed three per cent suffering from pulmonary tuberculosis, comprising five per cent of the city's deaths from this disease. One block, especially, was known as the "lung block," where more than three thousand persons resided. The death rate there was twice that of white Manhattan.

"Tuberculosis," wrote Dr Louis T. Wright, a Negro, Fellow of the American College of Surgeons and surgical director of Harlem Hospital, "we all know, is a disease that is rampant among the poverty stricken of all races. Colored people, therefore, show high morbidity and mortality rates from this condition alone, due to bad housing, inability to purchase food in adequate amounts, having to do laborious work while ill, little or no funds for medical care and treatment." But most hospitals treating T.B. refused to admit Negro patients or limited the type of ward service available, except Sea View Hospital in Staten Island.

---

[12] Mayor's Commission Report.

[13] The city's relief allowance for a male adult was raised to $6.25 by 1939.

[14] Mayor's Commission Report.

The story was the same with social diseases. For the five-year average from 1929-33 there were more than three thousand venereal cases among Negroes per hundred thousand, twice that among whites.[15] "It is not due to lack of morals," said Dr Wright, "but more directly to the lack of money, since with adequate funds these diseases could have been easily controlled." The real dread of Harlem was and still is pneumonia, in which the death rate was double that among whites. More dreadful was infant mortality, which took a toll of one in ten, twice that of the city as a whole. Twice as many Negro women died in childbirth as white women. A vital commentary on Harlem's health was the Central Harlem Health Center's report that it had filled approximately twenty thousand cavities in children's teeth in a six-month period.

THE MORGUE

Only one hospital in the city was and is concerned with the health of Negroes—Harlem Hospital, a public institution which has been a sore aggravating the life of the community for many years. Situated in the heart of the Harlem area, it attempted to care for more than 350,000 Negroes and all Puerto Ricans, Italians, and Jews living in East Harlem. Harlem Hospital contained 273 beds and 52 bassinets in 1932. Investigators for the Mayor's Commission discovered that "patients were forced to sleep on the floor, on mattresses and on benches, even in the maternity wards. Patients recently operated upon slept on benches or on chairs." Besides being the only city hospital in the community, Harlem Hospital also received Negro patients routed from other institutions in the city.

In 1932 proportionately twice as many people died at Harlem Hospital as at Bellevue Hospital.[16] It was for this reason that Negroes feared going to Harlem Hospital and referred to it fiercely as the "morgue" or "butcher shop." Many cases were refused admittance because of overcrowding; sometimes there were as many as fifteen patients waiting for attention in the emergency clinics. Only three ambulances were available for calls in Harlem in 1932. Most of the other hospitals refused to admit Negroes, and the few

---

[15] New York Department of Health, Vital Statistics, December 1938.
[16] Harlem Hospital reported a 11.2 mortality, Bellevue 5.7, and Coney Island Hospital 5 per cent in 1932.

that did allow them to enter practiced segregation. In March 1937, the wife of W.C. Handy, composer of St Louis Blues, lay critically ill in an ambulance more than an hour before the doors of Knickerbocker Hospital while the hospital officials debated whether or not a Negro should be admitted.

The city lacked also sufficient facilities for the training of Negro physicians and nurses. Negro internes were admitted in only three hospitals and Negro staff members only in hospitals "where there was a predominance of Negro patients." The medical staff of Harlem Hospital, Negro newspapers charged, pursued a policy of preventing Negro doctors and nurses from serving. In 1929 there were fifty-seven white doctors and only seven Negroes on the staff, though there were almost three hundred Negro physicians from whom to draw. The problem was identical for Negro nurses; they were admitted to only two training schools in the city—Lincoln Hospital and Harlem Hospital—and these had no white students. Even certain specialized sources were frequently not opened to them.[17]

BITTER BLOSSOM[18]

Crime was the bitter blossom of poverty. The evil effects of bad housing and the lack of recreational facilities caused an alarming increase of juvenile crime. There were more Negro children in New York City than in any other city in the world.[19] In 1919, the first year that the Courts of Domestic Relations kept special records of children, a little more than four per cent of the cases arraigned were Negroes. The ratio of Negro children arraigned in the Children's Court increased from 4.2 per cent in 1919 to 11.7 per cent in 1930. By 1938 almost twenty-five per cent of the cases were Negroes. This occurred while the total white children arraigned decreased 38.3 per cent.

The overwhelming bulk of Negroes are Protestant, and since the provisions of the New York State law insist upon neglected

---

[17] *Report of the New York State Temporary Commission* 31.

[18] Note on 2nd Draft : "Call it *Crime* (less flowery but better)."—Ed.

[19] The U.S. Census of 1930 reports 75,123 Negro children under fifteen years of age in this city, 46,580 in Manhattan. Under twenty there were 60,402 in Manhattan and 96,243 in the five boroughs. Owen R. Lovejoy, *The Negro Children of New York* (New York, The Children's Aid Society 1932) 5.

children being fostered only within their own religion, this left most of them without care. Only six out of thirty-four Protestant agencies cared for Negro children, though Roman Catholic care was found to be more adequate. During the five-year period 1931-1935, the Children's Court adjudged more than three thousand Negro children to be neglected and assigned most of them to a state institution to solve the problem of food and shelter. More than a third of the boys arrested were charged with offenses involving property, though most of them were arrested for hitching on trolleys, stealing subway rides, selling newspapers after 7:00 p.m., and shining shoes on the streets.[20]

Negro adults were chiefly arrested for their participation in the "policy racket"; a little less than eight per cent were women. Almost fifty per cent of the women arrested in the city during the period 1930-1935 were Negro and eighty per cent of these were charged with prostitution. The widespread operations of the "policy racket," which extracted so much money from the community for the benefit of racketeers, were due to a large extent to the desperate economic conditions of the people who had hoped to gain through luck what had been denied them through labor. A percentage of Negro arrests was the result of "the unconscious or deliberate discrimination on the part of the police force against Negro people."[21]

... WHILE ROME BURNS

Unemployment mounted to staggering totals as the country sank deeper in the mire of Depression. The Federal, State and City administrations failed to act in the unemployment crisis at a time when the New York *Times* was acknowledging that bread lines were feeding thousands of people a day. Regarded as only a temporary situation, the relief financing began with popular contribution, for private charity had been overtaxed. When the Depression still did not pass, the city assumed partial support of the unemployed on a pay-as-you-go basis. A day did not pass without demonstrations in front of Harlem's Home Relief offices because of this unhappy plan.

---

[20] Mayor's Commission Report.
[21] Mayor's Commission Report.

Meanwhile, the affairs of the city had gone from bad to worse. The Seabury investigation began its hearings and turned up evidence which made it apparent that Mayor Walker was in a highly vulnerable position. Particularly was Harlem stirred when Seabury uncovered a vice ring which framed innocent women, a fact which Negro women knew only too well. There were many Negroes with friends who had been so victimized.

After Mayor Walker's resignation in 1932, the new city administration was faced with a relief problem that clamored for attention. It first threatened to tax the Stock Exchange and then borrowed money for relief. The point had been reached where the richest city in the richest country in the world could barely meet the needs of the emergency. Two vital things then happened: Roosevelt was elected President in 1932, and with his support La Guardia became Mayor in 1934. But an impenetrable wall of discrimination and segregation, of despair and unhappiness, had sprung up around Harlem. The appalling specter of sickness, poverty, and death grimly faced the Negro.

PROTEST

The long-expected explosion came on March 19, 1935, when ten thousand Negroes swept through Harlem destroying the property of white merchants. At the time, the outburst was labeled incorrectly a "race riot." White New York was almost panic-stricken as a nightmare of Negro revolt appeared to be a reality. In the very citadel of America's New Negro, "crowds went crazy like the remnants of a defeated, abandoned, hungry army." So formidable did the demonstration become that the Harlem Merchants' Association, a group of white shopkeepers, demanded unsuccessfully that Governor Lehman send troops to patrol the district.

An absurdly trivial incident furnished the spark. On the afternoon of March 19, a Puerto Rican lad was caught stealing a ten-cent penknife from the counter of a 5-and-10c store at West 135th Street. In resisting his captors, the boy hit them. Incensed at what appeared to be a retaliatory display of brutality by the store's white male employees, the Negro shoppers attacked them. Others spread the alarm that a Negro boy was being beaten. A general alarm brought police reserves. Rumor then followed that the boy had been beaten to death, and Negroes rushed to the scene intent upon "avenging" the "murder."

The police estimated that by 5:30 p.m. more than three thousand persons had gathered. Several step-ladder speakers addressed the crowds, charging the police with brutality and the white merchants with discrimination in employment. They were pulled down by the police and arrested. Two hours later protest leaflets were hurled through the neighborhood by members of the Young Communist League.

Large detachments of uniformed police, plainclothes men, and mounted police charged the crowds. Radio cars were driven on the sidewalks to disperse the people. Instead of withdrawing, the crowds grew in numbers and in hostility. Stirred to traditional anger against the police, they surged through the streets smashing store windows, hurling bricks, stones, and other missiles at the police. The mob broke into bands of three and four hundred and looted stores owned by whites. An anecdote is told of a Chinese laundryman who rushed out on the street and in self-defence hurriedly posted a sign on his store window which read: "Me colored too." On Lenox Avenue, the scene of most of the disorder, laden rioters emerged from shattered shop windows, while women stood on the fringe of crowds and shouted their choice of articles. A more humorous side of this was the case of a ragged youth who entered a wrecked tailor shop, outfitted himself with a new spring coat, complaining bitterly that he would be unable to return for alterations.

Sporadic outbursts continued until the early hours of the morning. Five hundred uniformed policemen, two hundred plainclothes men and mounted police, and fifty radio cars were active in quelling the outburst. At least two hundred stores owned by white merchants were smashed and their goods carried away. The total damage was estimated at more than two million dollars. Three deaths—all Negroes—were reported. Thirty-odd people were hospitalized for bullet wounds, knife lacerations, and fractured skulls, and more than two hundred persons received minor injuries, cuts and abrasions. Some one hundred persons, the majority of them Negroes, were arrested on charges of inciting to violence, unlawful assemblage, and looting. The boy, in the meantime, had actually been released, after the manager had refused to press charges.

". . . FOAM ON TOP THE BOILING WATER"

Many reasons were offered for the uprising. The daily papers were particularly alarming in their reports, characterizing it as Harlem's worst riot in twenty-five years. The *Daily News* said that "Young Liberator orators whipped the fast-gathering crowds into a frenzy of hysteria . . . apparently to seize the opportunity to raise the issue against the store which had been picketed (by Negroes) for its refusal to hire colored clerks." The *Evening Journal,* manifestly incensed, traced its cause directly to "Communistic agitators circulating lying pamphlets." The *Post* said editorially that it would have been impossible to inflame Harlem's residents "if there had not been discrimination in employment and on relief, and justifiable complaints of high rents." The New York *Sun* derided the district attorney's (Dodge's) attempt to find Red propaganda behind the disturbance. "Actually," said the *Sun,* "Communists are more likely to have been passengers on the ebullience of a volatile population than authors of its effervescence."

Harlem's Negro leaders said that "seeing Red" was an official privilege and divergence, for the disorder had deep social, economic, and political roots. The Rev William Lloyd Imes, pastor of St James' Protestant Episcopal Church, felt that the white merchants were "reaping a harvest that they had sown," because of their refusal to employ Negroes. Channing Tobias, Negro field secretary of the Y.M.C.A., summed up the situation in this manner:

> It is erroneous and superficial to rush to the easy conclusion of District Attorney Dodge and the Hearst newspapers that the whole thing was a Communist plot. It is true there were Communists in the picture. But what gave them their opportunity? The fact that there were and still are thousands of Negroes standing in enforced idleness on the street corners of Harlem with no prospect of employment while their more favored Negro neighbors are compelled to spend their money with business houses directed by white absentee owners who employ white workers imported from every other part of New York City.

The views of the Negro leaders followed almost a uniform pattern. For example, George W. Harris, publisher of Harlem's *News* said: "They [the rioters] were inspired because the colored people have been denied a decent economic opportunity. Private business, public utilities and the city government have oppressed a despondent Negro population and the result is a magazine of dynamite which it is only too easy to set off. The City of New York has consistently denied positions to colored boys and girls. . . . The riots were born of impatience at segregation, dominations of underworld leaders, who have found a fertile field for their activities among the credulous Negroes of the neighborhood." Roy Wilkins, editor of the *Crisis,* felt that it was a great mistake to dismiss the riot as the demonstration of a few agitators and attributed it to "a demonstration induced by discrimination against the Negroes in economics, employment and justice, and living conditions." In a series of articles for the New York *Post,* Rev Adam C. Powell, Jr, pastor of the Abyssinian Baptist Church, sought to prove that the outburst was essentially a social protest.

PEOPLE'S COURT

Mayor La Guardia immediately named an investigating committee composed of prominent citizens, of which seven were Negro and five whites.[22] It was known as the Mayor's Commission on Conditions in Harlem, and its report was prepared by E. Franklin Frazier, a professor of sociology at Howard University. The public, anxious to air its grievances, appeared at the public hearings which were conducted by the commission at the Harlem Heights Court. Officials of large firms and utilities were placed on the stand and interrogated by the public and the commissioners alike. The witnesses who appeared also represented welfare and civil employee groups and labor unions. Anyone who had a complaint was welcomed to take the stand. This privilege often caused heated demonstrations by Negroes.[23]

---

[22] Its members included Dr. Charles H. Roberts, Oswald Garrison Villard, Mrs. Eunice Hunton Carter, Hubert T. Delany, Countee Cullen, A. Philip Randolph, Judge Charles E. Toney, William Jay Schieffelin, Morris Ernst, Arthur Garfield Hays, Col. John G. Grimley, Rev. John W. Robinson, and Rev. William McCann.
    Seven Negroes and five whites make twelve. There are 13 names here. Presumably the final draft would have corrected this arithmetic.—Ed.
[23] Interview with Arthur Garfield Hays, Nov. 22, 1939.

On Saturday afternoons the Mayor's Commission held its public hearings. Hundreds of Negroes would crowd into the small municipal courtroom at West 151st Street, and before a member of the commission who presided as chairman, the people presented their case. Often emotional and incoherent, some timid and reticent, some noisy and inarticulate, but all with a burning resentment, they registered their complaints against the discriminations, the Jim-Crowism, and all the forms of oppression to which they had been subjected.

The testimony carried, despite its tragic character, an undertone of humor when expressed in the Negro idiom. In the relating of a story of the killing of a Negro youth by a white policeman, several Negroes who had been eyewitnesses to the incident were called to the stand. The first witness was a man who approached the stand reluctantly and in a lowered, muffled voice, as though he feared too open a discussion of the shooting or too blatant a knowledge of it might involve him unpleasantly with the police authorities, recounted what he had seen. His impatient audience punctuated his testimony with encouraging shouts of "Aw, man, talk up, you ain't down South!" This co-operation failed to help and the man completed his mutterings and sat down. A clean cut, aggressive, sharp-tongued youth succeeded him. In clear, resonant tones he measured out his answers. When the chairman asked, "Did you see any one throw any milk bottles at the police?," the boy answered, "Man, you know ain't nobody gonna throw no milk bottles at a cop who's got a forty-four [gun] staring him in the face . . . people ain't crazy!" Suddenly remembering the difficulty that the audience had had in hearing the testimony of his mouselike predecessor, he good-naturedly bellowed out, "Am I talkin' loud enough?," and the courtroom displayed its approval with a howl of laughter.

The city's commission turned over its report to Mayor La Guardia in March 1936, one year later. The 35,000-word document was published by the *Amsterdam News,* July 18, 1936. Whereas columns and columns of material appeared in the daily press during the riot, the same papers published only sedate accounts of the report. The *Amsterdam News'* "scoop" went practically unnoticed, except for the *Daily Worker.*[24]

---

[24] This paragraph followed the next one in the Ms, but obviously belongs here.—Ed.

During the 1937 session of the legislature, a commission was named to submit a report on the condition of the urban colored population in New York State before March 1938.[25] The commission submitted its first report in March 1938 and had its tenure extended in order to submit a second report in February 1939. Lester B. Granger, Industrial Secretary of the National Urban League, who served as executive director of the commission, was assigned the task of preparing the first report. Many private agencies launched investigations on various phases affecting Negro life.

DEEP SOCIAL ROOTS

Both investigations concluded on one note: a Harlem riot in 1935, at the height of modern times, in the great city of New York, must have had deep roots. The conditions confronting Negroes were found to spring from several distinct and closely related causes. As a population of low income, it suffered from conditions that affected low-income groups of all races, but the causes that kept Negroes in this class did not apply with the same force to whites. These conditions were underscored by discrimination against Negroes in all walks of life. The rumor of the death of a boy which spread throughout the community had "awakened the deep-seated sense of wrongs and denials and even memories of injustices in the South." The Mayor's Commission reported as the riot's cause "the smouldering resentments of the people of Harlem against racial discrimination and poverty in the midst of plenty." Together with the diminished wage scale, the relief standards had further lowered the already degraded position of these people. Poverty, it was claimed, had taken its toll in the Negroes' health, morale, and general living conditions. The riot was, in the New York State Temporary Commission's view, "a spontaneous and an incoherent protest by Harlem's population against a studied neglect of its critical problems."

---

[25] The commission was composed of Harold P. Herman, chairman, William T. Andrews, Rev. Michael Mulvoy, John J. Howard, Leon A. Fischel, Walter J. Mahoney, Robert W. Justice, Henry Root Stern, Francis B. Rivers, Mrs. Elizabeth Ross Haynes, Rev. John H. Johnson, and Henri W. Shields.

CHAPTER XVIII [1]

"I, TOO, SING AMERICA"

HARLEM, 1935-1940.—In the swiftly moving events of the period, accelerated by the Depression, Negroes broke away from their traditional attitudes and thinking. The Harlem vote shifted from the Republican party to the Democratic party. New racial solidarity was stimulated by the Italo-Ethiopian War, for Negroes viewed that struggle as an assault upon the last Black Nation. Soap-box oratory again flourished. Easter parades of finery gave way to the trade union marches of dungarees. The church again took its historic place in the stern affairs of the Negro. Where, in the decades up to 1935, Negroes had suffered because of neglect and indifference, the white community now began to recognize them as an integral part of the social family, and they began to assume their places in the civil, political, and economic life of New York.

JOB CAMPAIGN

The sharp change in the Negro's position from that of a labor reserve to a settled element in industry during the period 1914-1930 brought the Negro face to face with the problems of working conditions. By 1934 he had recognized both his political and labor importance. Excluded from the official American labor movement, Negroes, nevertheless, attempted to organize separately and secure gains for themselves within their limited orbits. The passage of the National Recovery Act in 1933 gave militancy to the workers and added drive to this movement.

In the summer of 1933, the Citizens' League for Fair Play was organized. Included among its members were Rev John H. John-

---

[1] Chapter XIX in the Ms.—Ed.

son, pastor of St. Martin's Protestant Episcopal Church, and Fred R. Moore, editor and publisher of the New York *Age*. Its purpose was to persuade white merchants in the community to employ Negroes. The league argued that they received the bulk of their trade from Negroes and therefore they should have Negro help. After some months of unsuccessful negotiations, the league threw pickets around the stores in the 125th Street shopping area. The boycott of the stores began with the slogan "Don't buy where you can't work." As a lure to Negro trade, stores hung out such signs as: "This place owned and operated by Negroes." A store that employed no Negro help was labeled "Lily White." In time some gains were made, and a number of Negroes were placed in jobs as clerks and sales people. But whenever the organization relaxed its vigilance, the Negroes lost their jobs. When the Harlem Labor Union was organized by Ira Kemp and Arthur Reid, with essentially the same objectives, the drive for jobs became a "crusade against Jewish merchants."

THE BLACK HITLER

Professing aims similar to the Citizens' League, the Negro Industrial Clerical Alliance was formed by a bizarre character who, resplendent in turban and green blouse, strode the picket line. A former "herb doctor" and clairvoyant, he preached anti-semitism and fostered hatred between the white and black races. He was referred to as the "Black Hitler." There were many clashes between his group and the league. When the Citizens' League won its fight against a large department store, he had his men picket the store because "only light colored Negroes were employed." Soon afterwards he was hailed into court on October 9, 1934, on the charge of disorderly conduct by Edgar H. Burman, commander of the Jewish "Minute Men," who accused him of anti-semitic acts and violence, and freed after a three-day trial.[2] Sufi Abdul Hamid's end as a "labor leader" came soon after the March 19, 1935, incident. Later, he secured thirty thousand dollars from unknown sources and formed the Universal Holy Temple of Tranquility, with himself as "bishop." On July 31, 1938, he was killed in an airplane accident.

[2] New York *Herald Tribune*, January 20, 1935.

BLACK JEWS

The anti-semitic propaganda, which had begun with the street fulminations of Sufi Abdul Hamid, did not end with his demise. The Harlem Labor Union now became the chief source. Traces of anti-semitic sentiment among Negroes did not stem from a racial or religious conflict. This is made clear by Harlem's attitude toward the Black Jews, a sect of Hebrew-speaking orthodox Jewish Negroes who congregate in their own Synagogue of Bayis Taefelo, at 87 West 128th Street, under the spiritual leadership of Rabbi Wentworth Arthur Matthews. The denomination was incorporated in 1920 under the name of The Commandment Keepers, and enjoys the freedom which is traditionally accorded to every religious group in Harlem. Not the slightest feeling is manifested against the group by Negroes.

There is no centrally organized anti-semitic movement in Harlem, though propaganda is definitely carried on by groups which serve to articulate and channelize the material grievances of Negro people against an imaginary racial foe. In the Negro's view the people with whom he has direct dealings are his chief exploiters and his rental collectors, employers, merchants and money lenders are Jewish. However, the treatment of Jews in Germany late in 1938 brought a full discussion of Negro-Jewish relations into the Negro press of this country. A characteristic expression came from Elmer Carter, editor of *Opportunity Magazine,* who called upon the "Negro press and Negro organizations" to "utilize every first resource at their command" to stop anti-semitism from spreading among the Negro masses.

THE "AMSTERDAM NEWS" STRIKE

During the local fight for jobs, the *Amsterdam News* had supported editorially the Citizens' League for Fair Play. In fact, throughout the thirty years of its existence, the paper had strongly supported Negro workers in their fight against discrimination within the trade unions, public utilities, and civil service. Paradoxically, when its editorial staff applied for membership in the American Newspaper Guild in November 1933, the publishers frowned. In August 1935, when the *Amsterdam News* unit of the

Guild began negotiations with the management of the paper for union recognition, the first open dispute between organized Negro workers and Negro employers began. This was unique in the history of the American Labor movement and threw into discard the tradition that Negroes would not act against Negro employers.

These efforts caused the lockout of the entire editorial department. Immediately the Guild set up strike headquarters for the *Amsterdam News* unit. The financing of the strike included the payment of partial salaries to the locked-out employees. Scores of the Guild's white members did picket duty for the eleven weeks' duration of the strike. The presence of white members, including Heywood Broun, President of the American Newspaper Guild and columnist for the New York *World Telegram,* dramatized the role of the trade union movement in Negro life. Picket duty was also done by outstanding Negro citizens—among them ministers, doctors, and lawyers—and the representatives of Negro and white civic, social, and trade union organizations. It was well-nigh impossible for a Negro leader to remain neutral toward the strike, and the position that he took toward it became a fundamental test. Large support came from the Harlem Labor Center and the Negro Labor Committee, which were organized late in the summer of 1933, and which had organized almost forty thousand Negro workers by 1935.[3]

The management of the paper refused to negotiate with the strikers, and editorially characterized the American Newspaper Guild as an "outlaw dues collecting organization." It declared that its discharged employees were "misled by Communists."[4] Heywood Broun was criticized because, as the *Amsterdam News* said, his associations with the Negro were limited to the Negro intellectuals, and therefore he could not be expected to understand all of the angles of a situation involving the Negro people. "We submit," said the paper, "that it would be cheaper for the Guild to obtain jobs for these men and women now walking the streets than it is going to be for the Guild to support them in their attempt to wreck a Negro Business."

[3] Charles Lionel Franklin, *The Negro Labor Unionist of New York,* Studies in History, Economics and Public Law No. 420 (New York, Columbia University Press 1936) 211-214.

[4] *Amsterdam News,* Oct. 19, 1935.

Mayor La Guardia took a hand in the situation and attempted to bring the publishers and the workers together to end the strike. On October 14, Mrs Sadie Warren Davis and her daughter, together the major stockholders, failed to appear at a scheduled conference at the office of Mrs Elinore Herrick, chairman of the Regional Labor Board, a meeting which had been agreed upon by the publishers and the Guild. Mrs Herrick, acting as the representative of Mayor La Guardia, listened to the Guild's side of the story. The last paragraph of Mrs Herrick's report to the Mayor said in part:

> It seems very clear to me that these workers were fired because of their organizational activities and their membership in the Guild . . . The real issue of this case was a determination on the part of the employers to defeat unionization. The repeated refusals to confer or to bargain collectively with their employees since August 20th are borne out in the failure of the principals to appear last night.

During the time of the lockout the Central Trades and Labor Council of Greater New York endorsed the Guild's fight. The Guild was successful in its campaign to influence the paper's advertisers to cancel advertisements, and financial troubles finally downed the paper. The Powell-Savory Corporation purchased the paper at auction and took active control on December 24, 1935. A union contract was finally signed with the new publishers early in 1936. This contract called for a forty-hour week, salary increases and severance pay. A short time afterwards friction between the management and the employees caused the dismissal of several strike leaders. In 1940 only three of the original strikers were employed by that newspaper.

PULLMAN PORTERS

Meanwhile the passage of the NRA with an Emergency Railroad Transportation Act was approved by the NRA Board. The Brotherhood of Sleeping Car Porters and Maids, like all the other labor organizations, immediately seized upon Section 7 of the NRA code to force through amendments to the labor codes. The Brotherhood was especially concerned with the ERTA code which essentially provided for the conditions of labor and labor practices to be employed by the railroads, and demanded the inclusion of the Pullman porter as a railroad employee. Heretofore, the Pullman porter had lacked status because of his employment by the Pullman Coach Company, rather than the railroad upon which the Pullman car was operated. The winning by the Brotherhood of an amendment placing the porter under favorable railroad labor conditions brought in new members and new hopes for the eventual betterment of porter working conditions.

Talk of organizing Pullman porters was heard as early as 1913. But no serious attempts were made until 1925 when A. Philip Randolph turned his attention to the organization of the Pullman porters. At this time the railroads had come under Federal control. The Railway Men's International Benevolent and Industrial Association once took a fling at it, but after securing a wage increase its activities ended. One of the difficulties in organizing porters was that as a class they had fairly secure work. Besides, their aspirations were typically middle-class. The porter had all the familiar middle-class prejudices of the white-collar worker and the higher-salaried servant. His doings assumed added importance, for thousands of white people had their only personal contact with the race through the Pullman porter.[5]

The men had real grievances, for their wages were low. In 1925 their salary was $67 a month. To augment this salary they had to depend on tips from the passengers. With this as an issue, a mass meeting was held in Harlem, August 25, 1925, at which the Brotherhood of Sleeping Car Porters and Maids was organized. Randolph's magazine, the *Messenger,* furnished the movement with an organ already well known in Negro and white labor circles. By 1927 more than fifty per cent of the 3,500 eligible workers in New York carried union cards.

An abortive attempt at a strike shook the confidence of the porters in January 1929. The Depression further discouraged the Brotherhood's leaders. The ardor of the early days of organizational work had cooled among many of the porters as they faced the frozen front of one of America's greatest corporation set-ups. Membership fell off. Dues dribbled in at so slow a pace that the telephone had to be disconnected and the lights discontinued at the

---

[5] Spero and Harris, *The Black Worker* 430 ff.

Brotherhood headquarters. People began to look upon A. Philip Randolph as a defeated man, a tragic figure clinging desperately to the dead body of a lost hope. The *Messenger* suspended publication and several organizers were dropped. After 1930 the Brotherhood's membership did not exceed two thousand.

The NRA stimulated anew the Brotherhood's activities. By 1935 the Brotherhood, with a membership of 5,982 as against the company union's Protective Association's 1,422, was able to force the Pullman Company to recognize it as a bargaining agent. But it was not until October 1, 1937, that the Brotherhood and the Pullman Company officials agreed upon the rates of pay, rules, and working conditions for Pullman porters. The agreement as concluded provided for an increase in the rate of pay. The most important concession won was that of the establishment of a Bureau of Claims and Adjustments to handle the Brotherhood's grievances.

NEGRO CHAMPION

The task of organizing an oppressed minority demanded monumental courage and patience. To unionize Negro porters and compel the Pullman Company to recognize the organization was a feat of no small proportions. And to force the A.F. of L. Executive Council to grant the Brotherhood of Sleeping Car Porters an international charter—the first awarded to an all-Negro union in the forty-seven years of A.F. of L. history—seemed almost like accomplishing the impossible.

A. Philip Randolph and a small determined group who worked with him managed finally to surge ahead in his endeavor. A veteran of the radical movement, Randolph had devoted his life to the struggle against racial discrimination. Frequently rebuffed, Randolph actively pressed forward. Many times he was a lone but commanding figure at the A.F. of L. conventions, meeting resistance of prejudice and indifference.

Earning a living was always a pressing problem to Randolph. He was born April 15, 1889, at Crescent City, Florida. His father, a poor Methodist minister, had to augment his family income by operating a small cleaning and dyeing establishment in the Negro district. Young Asa was forced to go to work as an errand boy for a grocer, a job which was followed by work as section hand on a railroad, driver of a delivery wagon, and newsboy. After completing his high school studies at Cookman Institute in Jacksonville, Philip traveled North and entered the City College of New York where he studied political science, economics and philosophy. To finance his education he took a job one summer as a waiter on the Fall River Line. After organizing a protest against the living quarters assigned to the Negro workers on board ship, Randolph was fired. He did, however, work for more than five years as a porter for the Consolidated Edison Company of New York City.

Though he was firmly convinced that education was of major importance to the Negro, he discovered that the handicap of Jim Crow and discrimination could not be overcome by intellectual attainment. Impatient with the views of the contemporary Negro leaders, Randolph joined the Socialist party. In 1915 he became co-editor and publisher with Chandler Owen of the *Messenger Magazine*. A few days after Eugene Debs' arrest, Randolph's occured because of his stand against this country's participation in the War. But unlike Debs, he was released a few days later, when it was discovered that it would be extremely difficult to prove a case against an American Negro under the Espionage Act. The drive was primarily against alien radicals. After his release, he began his fight for the Negro's entrance into trade unions. In subsequent years he ran for the Assembly and Congress as a Socialist candidate. It was not until 1925, however, that Randolph rose to full stature as a labor leader. The Brotherhood of Sleeping Car Porters stands today as a monument to racial progress and as a testimony to the intelligence of Negro leadership.

The movement for jobs soon burst the confines of Harlem and extended to white-collar jobs throughout the city. To this end the Greater New York Coordinating Committee for the Employment of Negroes was founded in March 1937 by A. Philip Randolph, Rev A.C. Powell, Jr, Arnold J. Johnson, and Rev Lloyd Imes. In the spring of 1938, the organization adopted a black-out boycott. Every Tuesday night, in its battle against the Consolidated Edison Electric and Gas Company to force them to hire Negroes, electric lights gave way to two-cent candles. From many apartments these lights flickered stubbornly. This act was climaxed by a Bill-Payers' Parade before the offices of the utility at 32 West 125th Street. Hundreds of bill-payers converged on the Harlem office and paid their bills in coins of nickels and pennies. Simultaneous action against other public utilities took place. Negotiations produced few gains. The organization then geared itself for more militant action. At a mass meeting attended at Rockland Palace, April 25, 1938, at which more than three thousand Harlemites were present, Rev Adam C. Powell, Jr, sounded the key-note: "Harlem is sick and tired of promises. The hour has struck to march!" In flaying discrimination against Negroes, Rev Lorenzo King, pastor of St Mark's Protestant Episcopal Church, afterwards declared, "We're tired of religion that puts us to sleep. We've got to put religion to work—for us!"

The Coordinating Committee has steadily grown in prestige and influence. It has received ever wider attention from broad sections of white labor and from civic leaders. Mayor La Guardia characterized the Harlem Chamber of Commerce Agreement, which the committee finally negotiated in 1939, as "a tribute to common sense and justice." Today the Coordinating Committee numbers over 205 affiliated organizations with a combined membership in excess of two hundred thousand. While fair play in the employment of Negroes is the Central plank of the organization's platform, other related economic issues are given active support by the committee.

> Young man, young man,
> Your arm's too short to box with God.
> —James Weldon Johnson

For a number of years following the World War, the press rivaled the church as a medium for racial self-expression. Indeed, the Negro church had become a complex organization of men's clubs, women's societies, young people's associations and a host of activities for children. Besides, it was an active political organization, voting pretty much as a bloc and dispensing political patronage. Today secular interests dominate church life under the title of "institutional work." The Harlem church has also produced outstanding leaders who exert powerful influence over the community.

Negro churches in Harlem came about with the northward movement of Negroes from downtown Manhattan to uptown Harlem, and the stranded churches were forced to pursue their migrant flocks. In 1930, the most significant commentary on this phase of

Negro life was the fact that ninety million dollars were invested in temples of worship.[6] That same year, it was estimated that close to seventy thousand Negroes, most of them women, were members of churches. It was found that Negro men did not attend church as often as Negro women, and that Negro men who attended churches presented even a lower figure than white men.[7] By and large the pattern of the Negro church has developed along the same lines as the white church.

One of the typical "institutional" churches in Harlem is the Abyssinian Baptist church, situated at 132 West 138th Street. It is believed to be the largest Protestant church in the world. Its letterhead speaks of it as "the church of the masses," and this boast is supported by a membership of fourteen thousand. This great church was organized in 1808 by a few Negro members who withdrew from the First Baptist Church, which was situated at Gold Street. For a number of years after its establishment, the church held services at Anthony Street, the present Worth Street. Dr A. Clayton Powell, father of the present pastor, became its leader in 1908 and remained until 1936. Just before the church moved to Harlem it was situated on West 40th Street. In 1916 it sold its site to the New York *Times* for $190,000. The present Gothic structure was built at a cost of $350,000 and the mortgage was publicly burned in 1928. Its membership had observed a rigorous tithing system in order to accomplish this. The cost of maintenance of the church and its manifold activities is estimated at fifty thousand dollars annually. Although the Depression made severe inroads into the living standards of Negroes, the budget of this church has remained on an even keel.

At the beginning of the Depression, Negro churches fed hundreds of unemployed persons until the city launched its public relief program. Most all of the ministers are leaders in the economic matters of the community. The bulletin boards of their churches are fair indexes of this. They are usually loaded down

[6] Greater New York Federation of Churches, *The Negro Churches of Manhattan* (New York, Greater New York Federation of Churches [1930?]) 11-18.

[7] "These findings tend to explode the idea that the church has a peculiar hold upon the Negro temperament. Certainly, if interest in organized religion was primarily the result of a racial attitude of mind, this factor should influence Negro men as well as women."—C. Luther Fry, *The U.S. Looks at Its Churches* (New York, Institute of Social and Religious Research 1930) 11.

with announcements of labor mass meetings, notices for those who are on relief, calls for jobs, and a variety of social gatherings and meetings. Briefly, the church provides a clearing house for the multitude of community interests. Many Harlem churches house large WPA projects. They often hold forums at which speakers, whose views range from those of James W. Ford, the Negro Communist candidate for vice-president, to those of Margaret Sanger, the birth-control advocate, appear on their platforms. The Negro church is the foundation of most mass movements among Negroes.

> "The path of progress... has always been a siz-zag course amid justice and injustice. . . . ."
>
> —Kelly Miller

An explosive celebration, delirious in its expression, took place June 22, 1937. A Negro, Joe Louis, had won the world's heavyweight boxing championship. There was wanton destruction of property and hilarity until the early hours of the morning. A Negro boy, up from an obscure farm in Alabama, had given hope to the lowliest black boy of Harlem's slums. The porter, the handyman, the unemployed man, envisioned new hope in Joe Louis' symbolic victory. It was frankly commented by Negroes who jostled on the streets of Harlem that night: "Yes, life is worth living, for who can say now what's in store for black boys and girls with the rising of tomorrow's sun." The defeatist saying, "A man born of a dark woman is bound to see dark days," was thrown into discard. Obviously moved by the celebration of Louis' victory, Richard Wright, the Negro novelist, wrote:

> The eyes of these people were bold that night. Their fear of property, of the armed police fell away. There was in their chant a hunger deeper than that for bread as they marched along. In their joy they were feeling an impulse which only the oppressed can feel to the full. They wanted to fling the heavy burden out of their hearts and embrace the world. They wanted to feel that their expanding feelings were not limited; that the earth was theirs as much as anybody else's; that they did not have to live by proscription in one corner of it; that they could go where they wanted to and do what they wanted to, eat and live where they wanted to, like others. They wanted to own things in common and do things in common. They wanted a holiday.

But the prize-ring triumphs of Joe Louis, together with the cinderpath successes of Jesse Owens, are milestones. Indeed, Marian Anderson's signal appearance on the concert stage was just another stride in the Negro's progress. The names of Paul Robeson, Dorothy Maynor, Duke Ellington, Ethel Waters, Maxine Sullivan, and Bill Robinson, have served to encourage the quest for better days. These people have been, however, the glitter of more substantial and more solid progress.

The elevation of a number of Negroes to key positions in the city and state governments has had a profound effect upon Negroes, particularly upon the youth of Harlem. For Negroes thereupon broke away, in a large measure, from their traditional roles as singers and dancers. Mayor La Guardia, recognizing segregation and discrimination as social evils, attempted to mitigate it in tangible ways. Beginning in 1934, he appointed Negroes to positions of honor and responsibility: Hubert T. Delaney was made a tax commissioner, Myles Paige a magistrate, and Jane Bolin a judge in the Domestic Relations Court. He reappointed Ferdinand Q. Moton a civil service commissioner. The New York *Times,* in applauding the Myles Paige appointment, observed that "the Negro community in New York City has every right to share in the administration of justice."

The mayor's advanced social views have been reflected by other city officials. A new awareness of Harlem's problems has been demonstrated by sweeping improvements in the various city departments. The Board of Education promoted Mrs Gertrude E. Ayer to the principalship of Public School No 24, Manhattan, in 1936, and she became the first Negro woman to advance to such a position. That same year the Department of Hospitals appointed Dr John West, formerly of the Veterans' Hospital, Tuskegee, Ala., the director of the new Central Harlem Health Center which had been built at a cost of $250,000. At the same time, the mayor reported that 435 buildings were torn down in the Harlem slum area. New schools, a housing project, a large recreational center with a swimming pool, sports fields, tennis courts, and a band concert stadium known as the Colonial Recreation Center, situated at 145th Street on Bradhurst Avenue, have been part of the city's acknowledgment of the need of the Negro people.

And so for more than three centuries, the record reveals, the Negro has struggled for integration into this community. During these years he has bequeathed song, dance, and laughter to a grim and busy new world society. His sweat has been mixed with the steel, brick, and mortar of this great city. American laws, customs, traditions, and institutions, as they are known today, have been shaped with an awareness of the Negro's presence. It is, therefore, impossible to stand on the sidelines and ignore Negro life, so inextricably is it tied up with that of the city and the nation.

Throughout his long American history, the Negro's faith has been in the ultimate triumph of democracy. At no time has this goal been as visible as it is today.

BIBLIOGRAPHY

SELECTED BIBLIOGRAPHY (193-?)

The bibliography in this third draft is not only out-of-date in that it ends at the time of writing in the late thirties but it is also incomplete. A list of contents headed *Bibliographies* shows thirteen sections, but only the first nine are in the Schomburg Collection, and even these are in a rough, unedited form. *Fourteen* sections, for example, are listed in the manuscript, whereas there are only thirteen headings; the manuscript jumps from Section IV to Section VI. *X*s were also scrawled opposite certain items, but no clue was left as to whether this indicated that the marked items were to be omitted, rewritten, or given greater prominence in the final draft. These items are shown with an [X] at the end.

The nine existing sections are: *Manuscripts; Documents, Records and Collections; Histories: General and Local; Travel; Haiti and San Domingo; Slavery and the Slave Trade; Abolition: 1. Histories of the Abolition Movement, 2. Biographies of Abolitionists, 3. Abolition Literature, Reports, Propaganda, 4. Underground Railroad, 5. Slave Insurrections; The Negro, Historically Considered: 1. Negro Histories, 2. Negro Biographies, 3. Negro Church History, 4. Special Studies* (This part is missing, but another section headed *Special Studies connected with New York* was inserted after *Histories: General and Local* above); and *Immigration*. A new section, *Colonization*, not given in the list of contents, was added at the end.

The missing sections are: *Civil War Period; The Negro in Modern Times; Periodicals and Newspapers;* and *Miscellaneous*. The earlier draft of this history also includes a very rough bibliography which is based on a different plan but has several sections—*Representative Periodicals; Theatre; Art, Music and Dance;* and *Sports* —presumably covering the same field as some of the missing sections in this draft; they have therefore been inserted at the end as indicated.—Ed.

MANUSCRIPTS

Dixon, Robert S., *The Education of the Negro in the City of New York, 1853 to 1900* (Master's Thesis, The College of the City of New York 1935)

Grim, David, Papers and Charts of David Grim, c. 1810 (New York Historical Society)

Society for Promoting the Manumission of Slaves and Protecting such of them as have been or may be Liberated, *Minutes and Reports, 1785-1849*, 12 vols (New York Historical Society) [X]

Porter, Dorothy Burnett, *Afro-American Writings, Published Before 1835* (New York, Columbia University Press 1932)

DOCUMENTS, RECORDS AND COLLECTIONS

Brown, Henry Collins, ed, *Valentine's Manual of Old New York* [Year Book of the Museum of the City of New York] (New York: Published by the Museum 1916-1929) [X]

Cadwallader Colden, *Letters and Papers of Cadwallader Colden, 1711-1775* 9 vols (New York: New York Historical Society 1918-1937)

Catterall, Helen Tunicliffe, ed, *Judicial Cases Concerning American Slavery and the Negro* 5 vols (Washington, D.C.: Carnegie Institution of Washington 1928-1935) [X]

Common Council of the City of New York, *Minutes, 1675-1776*, 8 vols (New York: Dodd, Mead and Company 1905) [X]

Donnan, Elizabeth, ed, *Documents Illustrative of the History of the Slave Trade to America* 4 vols (Washington, D.C.: Carnegie Institution of Washington 1930-1935) [X]

Fernow, Berthold, ed, *Records of New Amsterdam from 1653 to 1674* 7 vols (New York: Knickerbocker Press 1897)

Hurd, John Codman, *The Law of Freedom and Bondage in the United States* 2 vols (Boston: Little Brown and Company 1838)

Jameson, J. Franklin, ed, *Narratives of New Netherland, 1609-1664. (Original Narratives of Early American History)* (New York: Charles Scribner and Sons 1909)

Moore, Frank, *The Rebellion Record: A Diary of American Events, with Documents, Narratives, Illustrative Incidents, Poetry, etc* 11 vols (New York: G. P. Putnam 1861-1868)

————, *Diary of the American Revolution* 2 vols (New York: privately printed 1860)

New York Genealogical and Historical Society (Collections), *Records of the Reformed Dutch Church in New Amsterdam: 1 Marriages, 1639-1801* (New York: Published by the Society 1890)

O'Callaghan, Edmond Bailey, ed, *Documentary History of the State of New York* 4 vols (Albany: Weed, Parsons and Company 1850) [X]

————, ed, *Documents Relative to the Colonial History of the State of New York* 15 vols (Albany: Weed, Parsons and Company 1856)

————, ed, *New York State Calendar of Historical Manuscripts* 2 vols (Albany: Weed, Parsons and Company 1865)

Phillips, Ulrich B., ed, *A Documentary History of American Industrial Society I-II.* (Cleveland: A.H. Clark Company 1910)

Stokes, I. N. Phelps, *The Iconography of Manhattan Island* 6 vols (New York: Robert H. Dodd 1915-1928) [X]

United States Department of Commerce (Bureau of the Census), *Negro Population, 1790-1915* (Washington; Government Printing Office 1918)

Valentine, David T., comp, *Manual of the Corporation of the City of New York* (New York: Common Council of the City of New York 1841-1866) [X]

HISTORIES: GENERAL AND LOCAL

Bancroft, George, *History of the United States* (Boston: Little, Brown and Company 1874)

Beard, Charles A. and Mary R., *The Rise of American Civilization* 2 vols (New York: Macmillan Company 1933)

Belden, Ezekiel Porter, *New York-Past, Present and Future* (New York: G. P. Putnam 1849)

Bimba, Anthony, *The History of the American Working Class* (New York: International Publishers 1927)

Booth, Mary L., *The History of the City of New York* 2 vols (New York: J. R. C. Clark 1867)

Bridenbaugh, Carl, *Cities in the Wilderness* (New York: Ronald Press 1938)

Brodhead, John Romeyn, *History of the State of New York* 2 vols (New York: Harper and Brothers 1839)

Brown, Henry Collins, *The Story of Old New York* (New York: E. P. Dutton and Company 1934)

Caldwell, A. B., *History of Harlem* [A lecture] (New York: Small Talk Publishing Company 1882)

Cole, Arthur Charles, *The Irrepressible Conflict 1850-1865* [*A History of American Life VII*] (New York: Macmillan Company 1934)

Dayton, Abram G., *The Last Days of Knickerbocker Life in New York* (New York: George W. Harlan 1882)

Fish, Carl Russell, *The Rise of the Common Man* (New York: Macmillan Company 1927)

Flick, Alexander, C., ed, *The History of the State of New York* 10 vols (New York: Columbia University Press 1937) [X]

Footner, Hulbert, *New York, City of Cities* (Philadelphia, New York and London: J. B. Lippincott Company 1933)

Foster, George G., *New York by Gas-light; with here and there a Streak of Sunshine* (New York: R. M. De Witt 1850)

Furman, Gabriel, *Antiquities of Long Island* (New York: J. W. Bouton 1875)

Goodwin, Maud, *Historic New York* (New York: G. P. Putnam's Sons 1898)

Greeley, Horace, *The American Conflict* 2 vols (Hartford: O. D. Case and Company 1866)

Irving, Washington, *A History of New York, from the Beginning of the World to the End of the Dutch Dynasty* (Philadelphia: Inskeep and Bradford 1809)

Lamb, Martha, *History of the City of New York; Its Origin, Rise and Progress* 2 vols (New York: A. S. Barnes and Company 1877)

Lincoln, Charles Z., *The Constitutional History of New York* 5 vols (Rochester: New York Lawyers' Co-operative Publishing Company 1906)

O'Callaghan, Edmond Bailey, ed, *History of New Netherland; or New York under the Dutch* 2 vols (New York: D. Appleton and Company 1848)

Pomerantz, Sidney Irving, *New York, An American City, 1783-1803 (A Study of Urban Life)* (New York: Columbia University Press 1938)

Rhodes, James Ford, *History of the United States from the Compromise of 1850* 7 vols (New York: Macmillan Company 1892-1907)

Riker, James, *Revised History of Harlem and Early Annals* (New York: New Harlem Publishing Company 1904)

Roosevelt, Theodore, *New York* (New York and London: Longmans Green, and Company 1891)

Schuyler, George W., *Colonial New York* 2 vols (New York: Charles Scribner's Sons 1885)

Ulmann, Albert, *A Landmark History of New York* (New York: D. Appleton-Century Company 1939)

Van Pelt, Daniel, *Leslie's History of Greater New York* 3 vols. (New York: Arkell Publishing Company 1898)

Van Rensselaer, Mrs Schuyler, *History of the City of New York in the Seventeenth Century* 2 vols (New York: Macmillan Company 1909) [X]

Watson, John E., *Annals and Occurrences of New York City* (Philadelphia: H. F. Anners 1846) [X]

Wilson, James Grant, *Memorial History of the City of New York* 4 vols (New York: New York History Company 1892-1893)

SPECIAL STUDIES CONNECTED WITH NEW YORK

Bayles, W. Harrison, *Old Taverns of New York* (New York: Frank Allaben Geneological Company 1915)

Bourne, William Oland, *History of the Public School Society of the City of New York* (New York: G. P. Putnam and Sons 1873)

De Voe, Thomas Farrington, *The Market Book, a History of the Public Markets in the City of New York from its First Settlement to the Present Time* (New York: Published by the Author 1862) [X]

Earle, Alice Morse, *Colonial Days in the Old New York* (New York: Scribners' Sons 1909)

Fox, Dixon Ryan, *The Decline of Aristocracy in the Politics of New York* (New York: Columbia University Press 1918)

Ladies of the Mission, *The Old Brewery, and the New Mission House at the Five Points* (New York: Stringer and Townsend 1854)

Scoville, Joseph A. (Walter Barrett, pseud), *Old Merchants of New York City* 4 vols (New York: Carleton 1863-1866)

Singleton, Esther, *Social New York Under the Georges, 1714-1776* (New York: D. Appleton and Company 1902)

TRAVEL

Abdy, Edward Strutt, *Journal of a Residence and Tour in the United States of North America, from April, 1833 to October, 1834* 3 vols (London: John Murray 1835)

Boardman, James, *America and the Americans* (London: Longman, Rees, Orme, Brown, Green and Longman 1833)

Buckingham, James Silk, *America, Historical, Statistic, and Descriptive* 3 vols (London: Fisher, Son and Company 1841)

Burn, James D., *Three Years Among the Working Classes in the United States During the War* (London: Smith, Elder and Company 1865)

Burnley, James, *Two Sides of the Atlantic* (London: Simpkin, Marshall and Company 1880)

Campbell, Sir George, *White and Black; the Outcome of a Visit to the United States* (New York: R. Worthington 1879)

Candler, Isaac, *A Summary View of America* (London: T. Cadell 1824)

Dickens, Charles, *American Notes for General Circulation* (Boston: Tickner and Fields 1867)

Duncan, Mary Lundie, *America as I Found It* (New York: Robert Carter and Brothers 1852)

Finch, I., *Travels in the United States of America and Canada* (London: Longman, Rees, Orme, Brown, Green and Longman 1833)

Fisch, Georges, *Nine Months in the United States During the Crisis* (London: James Nisbet and Company 1863)

Hole, Samuel Reynolds, *A Little Tour in America* (London and New York: Edward Arnold 1895)

Janson, Charles William, *The Stranger in America* (London: James Cundee Albin Press 1807; reprinted, New York: The Press of the Pioneers 1935)

Knight, Madam Sarah, *The Private Journal of a Journey from Boston to New York* (Albany: Frank H. Little 1865)

Playfair, Robert, *Recollections of a Visit to the United States in the Years 1847-48-49* (Edinburgh: Thomas Constable and Company 1856)

Porteous, Archibald, *A Scamper Through Some Cities of America* (Glasgow: David Bryce and Son 1890)

Power, Tyrone, *Impressions of America During the Years 1833, 1834 and 1835* 2 vols (London: R. Bentley 1836)

Pulszky, Francis and Theresa, *White, Red, Black* 2 vols (New York: Redfield 1853)

Rose, George, *The Great Country; or, Impressions of America* (London: Tinsley Brothers 1868)

Russell, Charles, Lord, *Diary of a Visit to the United States of America in the Year 1883* (New York: The United States Catholic Historical Society 1910)

Russell, William Howard, *My Diary North and South* (Boston: T. O. H. P. Burnham 1863)

Shirreff, Patrick, *A Tour Through North America* (Edinburgh: Oliver and Boyd 1835)

HAITI AND SAN DOMINGO

Chazzotte, Pierre Etienne, *The Black Rebellion in Haiti* (Philadelphia: privately printed 1927)

Davis, Harvey P., *Black Democracy* (New York: The Dial Press 1929)

Edwards, Bryan, *The History of the Island of St. Domingo* (Edinburgh: T. Brown and W. Lang 1802)

Holly, James Theodore, *A Vindication of the Capacity of the Negro Race for Self-Government and Civilized Progress as Demonstrated by Historical Events of the Haytian Revolution* (New Haven: T. P. Anthony 1857)

Herskovitz, Melville J., *Life in a Haitian Valley* (New York: Alfred A. Knopf, 1937)

James, C. L. L., *Black Jacobins* (New York: The Dial Press 1938)

Perkins, Samuel G., *Reminiscences of the Insurrection in St. Domingo* (Boston: Massachusetts Historical Society 1886)

Rainsford, Marcus, *The Black Empire of Haiti* (London: B. R. Scott 1805)

Smith, James McCune, *A Lecture on the Haitian Revolution* (New York: D. Fanshaw 1841)

Saunders, Prince, *Haitian Papers* (London: W. Reed 1816)

Stephens, James, *The Crisis in the Sugar Colonies: Insurrections* (London: J. Hatchard 1802)

——————, *The Opportunity; or, Reasons for an Immediate Alliance with St. Domingo* (London: J. Hatchard 1804)

SLAVERY AND THE SLAVE TRADE

Albion, Robert G., *The Rise of the Port of New York* (New York: Charles Scribner's Sons 1939)

Clarkson, Thomas, *History of the Rise, Progress and Accomplishment of the African Slave Trade by the British Parliament* (London: John W. Parker 1839)

Cairnes, J. E., *The Slave Power: Its Character, Career, and Probable Designs* (New York: George W. Carleton 1862)

Carey, H. C., *The Slave Trade, Domestic and Foreign* (London: Sampson Low, Son and Company 1853)

Dow, George F., *Slave Ships and Slaving* (Salem, Mass.: Marine Research Society 1927)

DuBois, W.E.B., *The Suppression of the African Slave Trade to the United States of America* [Harvard Historical Studies I] (New York: Longmans, Green and Company 1896) [X]

Ellms, Charles, comp,*The Pirates' Own Book* (Portland, Me.: Francis Blake 1855)

Jenkins, William Sumner, *Pro-Slavery Thought in the Old South* (Chapel Hill: University of North Carolina Press 1935)

King, George S., *The Last Slaver* (New York: G. P. Putnam's Sons 1933)

McKee, Samuel, *Labor in Colonial New York 1664-1776* (New York: Columbia University Press 1936) [X]

Moore, George H., *Notes on the History of Slavery in Massachusetts* (New York: D. Appleton and Company 1866)

Morgan, Edwin Vernon, *Slavery in New York* [Half-Moon Series II] (New York: G. P. Putnam's Sons 1898) [X]

Northrup, Ansell Judd, *Slavery in New York* [New York State Library Bulletin: History No. 4] (Albany: University of the State of New York 1900) [X]

O'Callaghan, Edmond Bailey, ed, *Voyages of the Slavers St John and Arms of Amsterdam 1659, 1663; with Additional Papers Illustrative of the Slave Trade under the Dutch* (Albany: J. Munsell 1867) [X]

Spears, John R., *The American Slave Trade* (New York: Charles Scribner's Sons 1907)

Phillips, Ulrich B., *American Negro Slavery* (New York: D. Appleton Company 1918)

ABOLITION

1. Histories of the Abolition Movement

Adams, Alice Dana, *The Neglected Period of Anti-Slavery in America* (Boston: Ginn and Company 1908)

Barnes, Gilbert H., *The Anti-Slavery Impulse* (New York: D. Appleton-Century Company Inc 1933) [X]

Goodell, William, *Slavery and Anti-Slavery, a History of the great struggles in both Hemispheres; with a view of the slavery question in the United States* (New York: William Goodell 1853)

Hart, Albert Bushanll, *Slavery and Abolition* [The American Nation XVI] (New York: Harper and Brothers 1906)

Locke, Mary Stoughton, *Anti-Slavery in America* (Boston: Ginn and Company 1901)

Macy, Jesse, *The Anti-Slavery Crusade. (The Days of the Cotton Kingdom Part 2.)* (New Haven: Yale University Press 1919)

Poole, William P., *Anti-Slavery Opinions* (New York: Robert Clark and Company 1873) [X]

Wesley, Charles H., *The Negroes of New York in the Emancipation Movement* [Journal of Negro History *XXIV* Jan 1939] (Washington D.C.: Association for the Study of Negro Life and History 1939) [X]

Wilson, Henry, *History of the Rise and the Fall of the Slave Power in America* 3 vols (Boston: James R. Osgood and Company 1873) [X]

2. Biographies and Memoirs of Abolitionists

Anon, *The Rev J. W. Loguen, as a Slave and as a Freeman* (Syracuse, N.Y.: J.G.K. Truair and Company 1859)

Birney, William, *James G. Birney and His Times* (New York: D. Appleton, and Company 1890)

Child, Lydia Maria, *Isaac T. Hopper: A True Life* (Boston: John P. Jewett and Company 1853)

Douglass, Frederick, *My Bondage and Freedom* (New York and Auburn: Miller, Orton and Mulligan 1855) [X]

——, *Narrative of the Life of Frederick Douglass, an American Slave. Written by Himself* (Boston: The Anti-Slavery Office 1845) [X]

Garrison, Wendell Phillips and Francis Jackson, *William Lloyd Garrison: Story of His Life Told by His Children* 4 vols (Houghton, Mifflin and Company 1894) [X]

Grimke, Archibald H., *William Lloyd Garrison* (New York: Funk and Wagnalls 1891)

May, Samuel Joseph, *Some Recollections of Our Anti-Slavery Conflict* (Boston: Fields, Osgood and Company 1869)

Northup, Solomon, *Twelve Years a Slave: Narrative of Solomon Northup, a Citizen of New York* (Auburn: Derby and Miller, 1853)

Pennington, James W. C., *The Fugitive Blacksmith* (London: C. Gilpin 1849)

Russell, Charles Edward, *Blaine of Maine, his Life and Times* (New York: Cosmopolitan Book Corporation 1931)

Steward, Austin, *Twenty-two Years a Slave and Forty Years a Freeman* (Rochester, N.Y.: William Alling 1857)

Tappan, Lewis, *The Life of Arthur Tappan* (New York: Hurd and Houghton 1870)

Ward, Samuel Ringgold, *Autobiography of a Fugitive Negro* (London: John Snow 1855)

Wood, A. Sand Mott, *Narratives of Colored Americans* (New York: Bowne and Company 1882)

Haynes, Elizabeth Ross, *Unsung Heroes* (New York: DuBois and Dill Company 1921)

Lovell, Malcolm R., *Two Quaker Sisters, Elizabeth Buffum Chace and Lucy Buffum Lovell* (New York: Liveright Publishing Corporation 1937)

3. Abolition Literature, Reports and Propaganda

American Convention for Promoting the Abolition of Slavery and Improving the Condition of the African Race, (Title variations.) *Minutes* (Philadelphia, 1794-1828) [X]

American Anti-Slavery Society, *Annual Reports* (New York: 1834-1841, 1855-1861) [No reports published between 1841 and 1855] [X]

American and Foreign Anti-Slavery Society, *Reports*

New York City Anti-Slavery Society, *Reports*

British and Foreign Anti-Slavery Society, *Proceedings of the General Anti-Slavery Convention...Held in London from Friday, June 12th, to Tuesday, June 23rd, 1840* (London: 1841)

Weld, Thedore, *American Slavery as It Is: Testimony of a Thousand Witnesses* (New York: American Anti-Slavery Society 1839)

Garnet, Henry Highland, *An Address to the Slaves of the United States* [Report of the National Convention of Colored Citizens, Held at Buffalo, New York, 1843] [X]

American Anti-Slavery Society, *The Fugitive Slave Law and Its Victims* (New York: A.A.S.S. 1861)

4. Underground Railroad

Still, William, *The Underground Railroad* (Philadelphia: Porter and Coates 1872) [X]

Siebert, Wilbur H., *The Underground Railroad from Slavery to Freedom* (New York: Macmillan Company 1898) [X]

Mitchell, William M., *The Underground Railroad* (London: William Tweedie 1860)

Bradford, Sarah Hopkins, *Harriet, the Moses of her People* (New York: G. R. Lockwood and Son 1886)

Ray Family, The, *Life of Charles Bennet Ray* (New York: J. J. Little and Company 1887)

Sperry, Earl E., *The Jerry Rescue Case* (Syracuse, New York: Onandaga Historical Association 1924)

Siebert, Wilbur H., *The Underground Railroad in Massachusetts* (Worcester, Mass.: The American Antiquarian Society 1935)

————, *The Vermont Anti-Slavery and Underground Railroad Record* (Columbus, O.: The Spahr and Glenn Company 1937)

McDougal, Marion, *Fugitive Slaves, 1619-1865* (Boston: Ginn and Company 1891)

New York Committee of Vigilance, *First Annual Report, for the year 1837, Together with Important Facts Relative to their Proceedings* (New York: Piercy and Reed 1837) [X]

5. Slave Insurrections

Drewry, William Sidney, *Slave Insurrections in Virginia* (Washington, D.C. Neale Company 1900)

James, G. P. R., *The Old Dominion; or the Southampton Massacre* (New York: Harper and Brothers 1856)

Carroll, Joseph C., *Slave Insurrections in the United States 1800-1860* (Boston: Chapman and Grimes Inc. 1938)

Aptheker, Herbert, *Negro Slave Revolts in the United States. 1526-1860* (New York: International Publishers 1939)

Horsmanden, Daniel, *A Journal of the Proceedings in the Detection of the Conspiracy Formed by some White People in Conjunction with Negro and other Slaves, for Burning the City of New York in America and Murdering the Inhabitants. By the Recorder of the City of New York* (New York 1741)

Victor, Orville J., *History of American Conspiracies* (New York: James D. Torrey 1863)

Higginson, Thomas Wentworth, *Travellers and Outlaws* (New York: C. T. Dillingham 1889)

James, C. L. R., *History of Negro Slave Revolt* (London: Fact 1938)

Coffin, Joshua, *An Account of Some of the Principal Slave Insurrections, and others, which have occurred or been attempted, in the United States and elsewhere, during the last centuries, with various remarks* (New York: American Anti-Slavery Society 1860)

THE NEGRO, HISTORICALLY CONSIDERED

1. Negro Histories

Brawley, Benjamin, *A Social History of the American Negro* (New York: Macmillan Company 1921) [X]

Brown, William Wells, *The Black Man, His Antecedents, His Genius, and His Achievements* (New York: Thomas Hamilton 1863)

Brown, Ina Corinne, *The Story of the American Negro* (New York: Friendship Press 1936)

Cromwell, John W., *The Negro in American History* (Washington, D.C.: American Negro Academy 1914)

Dowd, Jerome, *The Negro in American Life* (New York: The Century Company 1926)

DuBois, W.E.B., *The Negro* (New York: Henry Holt and Company 1915)

Johnson, James Weldon, *Black Manhattan* (New York: Alfred A. Knopf 1930) [X]

Livermore, George, *Negroes as Slaves, Citizens and Soldiers* (Boston: J. Wilson and Son 1862)

Nell, W. C. *Colored Patriots of the American Revolution* (Boston: R. F. Wallcutt 1855).

Washington, Booker T., *The Story of the Negro* (New York: Doubleday Page and Company 1909)

Williams, George W., *History of the Negro Race in America* 2 vols (New York: G. P. Putnam's Sons 1883) [X]

Wilson, Joseph T., *The Black Phalanx* [Hartford, Conn.: American Publishing Company 1888]

Woodson, Carter Godwin, *The Negro in Our History* (Washington, D.C.: Associated Publishers Inc 1922)

2. Negro Biographies

Brawley, Benjamin, *Negro Builders and Heroes* (Chapel Hill: University of North Carolina Press 1937)

Crummell, Alexander, *Eulogy on the Life of Henry Highland Garnet* (Washington, D.C.)

Douglass, Frederick, *The Life and Times of Frederick Douglass* (Hartford, Conn.: Park Publishing Company 1882)

Fauset, Arthur Huff, *Sojourner Truth—God's Faithful Pilgrim* (Chapel Hill: University of North Carolina Press 1938)

Gregory, James Monroe, *Frederick Douglass, the Orator* (Springfield, Mass.: Wiley Company 1893)

Holland, Frederick May, *Frederick Douglass, the Colored Orator* (New York: Funk and Wagnalls Company 1891)

Lee, Hannah, F. S., *Memoir of Pierre Toussaint, Born a Slave in San Domingo* (Boston: Crosby, Nichols and Company 1854)

Simmons, William J., *Men of Mark* (Cleveland: G. M. Rewell and Company 1887)

Smith, James McCune, *Biography of Henry Highland Garnet* [Introduction to *A Memorial Discourse,* by Henry Highland Garnet.] [Philadelphia: Joseph M. Wilson 1865]

Thatcher, B. B., *Memoir of Phillis Wheatley* (Boston: Lyceum Press 1834)

Titus, Frances W., *Narrative of Sojourner Truth* (Battle Creek, Mich: Herald and Review Office 1884)

3. Negro Church History

De Costa, B. F., *The Story of St. Philips' Church* (New York)

DuBois, W.E.B., *The Negro Church* (Atlanta: Atlanta University Press 1903)

Greenleaf, Jonathan, *A History of the Churches in New York City* (New York: E. French 1846)

Hood, Bishop J. W., *One Hundred Years of the American Methodist Episcopal Zion Church* (New York: A. M. E. Z. Book Concern 1895)

Rush, Christopher, *A Short Account of the Rise and Progress of the African Methodist Episcopal Church in America* (New York)

Wakely, Joseph Beaumont, *Lost Chapters Recovered from the Early History of American Methodism* (New York: Nelson and Phillips 1858) [X]

Woodson, Carter Godwin, *The History of the Negro Church* (Washington, D.C.: Associated Publishers 1921)

IMMIGRATION

Bagenal, P. H., *The American Irish and their Influence on Irish Politics* (Boston: Roberts Brothers 1882)

Condon, Edward, *The Irish Race in America* (New York: A. E. And R. E. Ford 1887)

Cox, Ernest Sevier, *White America* (Richmond: White America Society 1923)

Crimmins, J. D., *Irish American Historical Miscellany* (New York: Published by the Author 1905)

Douglass, Frederick, *Three Addresses on the Relations Subsisting between White and Colored People of the United States* (Washington, D.C.: Gibson Brothers 1886)

Eaton, Allen H., *Immigrant Gifts to American Life* (New York: Russell Sage Foundation 1932)

Fairchild, Henry Pratt; and others, *Immigrant Backgrounds* (New York: J. Wiler and Sons Inc 1927)

Higgins, Patrick and Connolly, F. V., *The Irish in America* (London: J. Onsley Ltd 1909)

Maguire, John Francis, *The Irish in America* (London: Longmans, Green and Company 1868)

Peters, Robert, *Immigrant Races in North America* (London: Y. M. C. A. 1912)

COLONIZATION

Cornish, Samuel E., and Wright, Theodore S., *The Colonization Scheme Considered in its Rejection by the Colored People* (Newark: 1840) [X]

Fox, E. L., *The American Colonization Society 1817-1840* [Baltimore: John Hopkins Press 1919]

Garrison, William Lloyd, *Thoughts on African Colonization: or An Impartial Exhibition of the Doctrines, Principles, and Purposes of the American Colonization Society, together with the Resolutions, Addresses, and Remonstrances of the Free People of Color* (Boston: Garrison and Knapp 1832)

[The following four sections are from the *Selected Bibliography* in the earlier draft.—Ed.]

REPRESENTATIVE PERIODICALS

Crisis, The. Ed by Roy Wilkins (New York: National Association for the Advancement of Colored People)

Interracial Review. Published monthly (New York: Catholic Interracial Council)

Journal of Negro Education (Washington D.C.: Department of Education, Howard University)

Journal of Negro History. Ed by Carter G. Woodson (Washington D.C.: The Association for the Study of Negro Life and History)

Negro Digest. A mirror of Negro life, thought and achievement (New York)

Opportunity. Journal of Negro life, ed by E. A. Carter (New York: National Urban League)

West Indian Review. Ed by Ester Hyman (Jamaica, B.W.I.)

THEATRE

De Voe, Thomas Farrington, *The Market Book* (New York: Author 1862)

Kendal, Margaret Shafto Robertson, *Dramatic Opinions* (Little Brown and Co 1890)

Moses, Montrose J., *Representative Plays by American Dramatists* (New York: Dutton and Co 1930)

Odell, Geo. C., *Annals of the New York Stage* (New York: Columbia University Press 1927-1939)

Pemberton, Thomas Edgar, *The Kendals* (New York: Dodd, Mead and Co 1900)

ART, MUSIC AND DANCE

Locke, Alain, *The New Negro* (New York: Albert and Charles Boni 1925)

SPORTS

Babcock, *Boxiana* (London: Sherwood Jones and Co 1828)

Egan, Pierce, *Every Gentleman's Manual* (London: Sherwood and Boyer 1845)

Fleischer, Nathaniel S. *Black Dynamite* (New York: C. J. O'Brien Inc 1938)

Smith, Harry Worcester, *A Sporting Family of the old South* (Albany, N.Y.: J. B. Lyon Co 1936)

INDEX

INDEX

A

Abdy, E. S., 63, 65

Abolitionists, 83-84, 87, 103, 105, 106; negro, 85, 87, 99; white, 87, 97, 100-102; *See also* American Anti-Slavery Society; Anti-slavery movement; New York Anti-Slavery Society

Abolition societies, 59, 100-103

Abyssian Baptist Church, 55, 197, 278, 290

"Act to prevent the Importation of Negroes and Indians", 24

Adams, John Quincy, 69

Africa, 68, 69, 90, 91, 211, 213

African Communities' League, Inc., of the World, 212, 220

African Free Schools, 63-64, 87-88, 100

African Grove, 72-73, 158

African Methodist Episcopal Zion Church, 55, 99

African Slavery, 83

African Society for Mutual Relief, 60-61

Afro-American, 168

Afro-American Council, 165

Afro-American Realty Company, 184, 185

Albany Argus and City Gazette, 74

Aldridge, Ira Frederick, 73, 88

Alexander, Cato, 61f., 180-181

Allen, Richard, 89

Alston, Charles H., 262

American Anti-Slavery Society, 88, 89, 100, 102, 103, 105, 123; *See also* Abolitionists; Anti-slavery movement; New York Anti-Slavery Society

American Colonization Society, 68-72, 88-89, 90, 93, 94, 95, 102, 217

American Federation of Labor, 138-140, 287

American Newspaper Guild, 262, 283, 284, 285

American Notes, 77

American Revolution, 31, 35-38, 39-40, 43, 44, 54, 55, 70

American Writers' Congress, 260

Amsterdam News, 237, 261-262, 279; strike against, 283-285

"An Act Preventing the Conspiracy of Slaves", 22

Anderson, Hank, 131

Anderson, Marian, 292

Anderson, Osborn P., 108

A New York Tempest, 79

Anglo-African magazine, 90

Anglo-Saxon clubs, 216

Anson, Adrian C. (Pop), 149f.

Antillean Holding Co., 236

Anti-semitic propaganda, 282, 283

Anti-slavery movement, 34, 44, 45, 90, 97, 105; effect of Civil War on, 110-113; leaders of, 98-102; *Manifesto*, 100; pressures against, 102-103. *See also* Abolitionists; American Anti-Slavery Society; New York Anti-Slavery Society

Antony, Domingo, 12

315

Library, 135th St. Public 260, 262, 263

Little, Arthur W., 202f.

Lincoln, President Abraham, 109, 112, 122, 123, 124, 172; and support of colonization scheme, 113-114; and view on slavery and union, 111

Lispenard Meadows, 41

Livingstone College, 165

Locke, Alain, 255

Loggins, Vernon, 259

London, Jack, 152

London *Journal,* 73

London Saturday Review, 160

Louis, Joe, 240, 291, 292

L'Ouverture, Tousiaint, 51-52, 213

Lovejoy, Elijah P., 103

Lucas, Sam, 159, 160f.

Ludlow, Israel, 167

Lusk Committee (NY), 224, 226

M

MacKenzie, Charles, 53

Mack, Judge Julian, 218

Madison, President James, 45

Maiden Lane Insurrection (1712), 22-24

Malone, Annie M. Turnbo, 239

Manumission Society, The, 45, 59, 62, 63-64, 100

Marshall, Louis, 175

Martin, Reverend Charles, 199f.

Martin, Elder Clayton, *See* Barefoot Prophet

Massachusetts Anti-Slavery Society, 98

Matzeliger, Jan E., 142

Maynor, Dorothy, 292

Mayor's Commission on Conditions in Harlem, The, 266f., 267f., 271, 272, 274f., 278-279, 280

McCoy, Elijah, 142

McDougald, Cornelius W., 218

McGovern, John J., 119

McGraw, John J., 148-149

McGuire, Archbishop George Alexander, 213

McKay, Claude, 224, 255, 256, 257f.

McKinney, Susan, 133

Megapolensis, Dominie Johannes, 4

Merchants' Committee for the Relief of Colored People Suffering from the Riots, 120-121

Merilees, Thomas A., 219

Messenger, magazine, 214, 217, 218f., 256, 268, 286, 287, 288; and role in development of radical press, 223, 225-228

Methodist Church, 54-55, 56; split in the, 96

Miller, Reverend George Frazier, 224, 226

Miller, Kelly, 197, 225, 227, 291

Mills, Samuel J., 71

Minstrelsy, 157-161

Minuit, Peter, 1, 2

Moody, Julia, 235

Molineaux, Tom, 67-68, 150

Moore, Fred R., 175f., 197, 261, 282

Moore, Richard B., 224, 227

Moscowitz, Dr. Henry, 173

Moton, Ferdinand Q., 292

Moton, Dr. Robert R., 197, 205, 227

Mulatto, 256

Mulattoes, 216-217

Murphy, Isaac, 146

Myers, Isaac, 137

N

Nail and Parker, 185, 236

Nail, John E., 199f., 233, 236

Nail, John B., 236

National Advocate, 73

National Asociation for the Advancement of Colored People (NAACP), 172, 173-175, 199, 217, 225

National Association for Baseball Players, 148

National Association of Colored Women's Clubs, 125

322

323

New York *Herald,* 97, 109, 122, 153

New York *Indicator,* 185

New York *Journal,* 21

New York *Journal and Patriotic Register,* 49

New York *News,* 218

New York *Post,* 242, 277, 278

New York *Post Boy,* 37

New York *Royal Gazette,* 36, 40

New York State Temporary Commission on the Condition of the Urban Colored Population to the Legislature of the State of New York, Report of the, 265f., 267f., 273., 280

New York *Sun,* 133, 135f., 145f., 166, 168, 196, 277

New York *Telegram,* 41

New York Telephone Company, 268-269

New York *Times,* 167, 269f., 274, 290, 292

New York *Tribune,* 113, 120, 123

New York Urban League, 260

New York *World,* 115, 153, 184, 202, 235

New York *World Telegram,* 284

Niagara Movement, 172, 173

Nicolls, Governor, 13, 14

Ninety-Second Division (National Guard), 200

Ninety-Third Division (National Guard), 200

Noble Order of the Knights of Labor (Knights of Labor), 138

North Star, 90, 98

Nova Scotia, 39

Nugent, Richard, 258

O

Oberlin, 134

O'Connell, Daniel, 98, 104

Official Guide of Colored Baseball (1907), 149

Opportunity Magazine, 176, 189, 256, 257, 283

Overton, Aida, 156, 161, 162

Ovington, Mary White, 139f., 172, 173, 182f., 183

Owen, Chandler, 214, 224, 225, 227, 288

Owens, Jesse, 292

P

Pace, Harry L., 232-235

Pace Phonograph Corporation Incorporated, 232-235

Paige, Myles, 292

Paine, Thomas, 35

Palmer, A. Mitchell, 224

Parker, Henry C., 236

Parker, Judge, 174

Parker, Theodore, 97

Patroonships, 3, 180

Payton, Philip A., 183, 185, 236

Peace Mission Movement, 253

Penguin Club, 243

Pennington, James W. C., 98

Pennington, Reverend W. C., 105

Pennsylvania, Assembly of, 23-24

Pershing, General John, 204

Peterson, John, 64, 121

Philadelphia Giants, 149

Philippines, 190

Phillips, Wendell, 82

Physician, first negro, 12

Pickens, William, 175, 218

Pig Foot Mary, 187-188

Pillsbury, Parker, 98

Poland, 43, 46

Portugese, Anthony, 2

Powell, Jr., Reverend Adam Clayton, 278, 288, 289, 290

Powell, Sr., Reverend A. Clayton, 186, 197-198, 222-223, 234, 290

Powell, Dr. C. B., 236

Powell, John, 216

Presbyterian Church, 55

Price, J. C., 165

Price-Patton, Sari, 258

Propaganda, German, 203